American School Reform

American School Reform

What Works, What Fails, and Why

JOSEPH P. MCDONALD

WITH

JOLLEY BRUCE CHRISTMAN

THOMAS B. CORCORAN

NORM FRUCHTER

MILBREY W. MCLAUGHLIN

GORDON PRADL

GABRIEL REICH

MARK SMYLIE

JOAN TALBERT

THE UNIVERSITY OF CHICAGO PRESS   CHICAGO AND LONDON

KH

JOSEPH P. MCDONALD is professor of teaching and learning at the Steinhardt School of Culture, Education, and Human Development at New York University. He is the author or coauthor of many books, including, most recently, *Going Online with Protocols* and *Going to Scale with New School Designs*. THE CITIES AND SCHOOLS RESEARCH GROUP consists of Jolley Bruce Christman, Thomas B. Corcoran, Norm Fruchter, Milbrey W. McLaughlin, Gordon Pradl, Gabriel Reich, Mark Smylie, and Joan Talbert.

The University of Chicago Press, Chicago 60637
The University of Chicago Press, Ltd., London
© 2014 by The University of Chicago
All rights reserved. Published 2014.
Printed in the United States of America

23 22 21 20 19 18 17 16 15 14   1 2 3 4 5

ISBN-13: 978-0-226-12469-8 (cloth)
ISBN-13: 978-0-226-12472-8 (paper)
ISBN-13: 978-0-226-12486-5 (e-book)
DOI: 10.7208/chicago/9780226124865.001.0001

Library of Congress Cataloging-in-Publication Data

McDonald, Joseph P., author.
    American school reform : what works, what fails, and why / Joseph P.
  McDonald ; with Jolley Bruce Christman, Thomas B. Corcoran, Norm Fruchter,
  Milbrey W. McLaughlin, Gordon Pradl, Gabriel Reich, Mark Smylie, Joan Talbert.
      pages cm
    Includes bibliographical references and index.
    ISBN 978-0-226-12469-8 (cloth: alk. paper)
    ISBN 978-0-226-12472-8 (pbk. : alk. paper)
    ISBN 978-0-226-12486-5 (e-book)
      1. Educational change—Illinois—Chicago.   2. Educational change—New York
  (State)—New York.   3. Educational change—Pennsylvania—Philadelphia.
  4. Educational change—California—San Francisco Bay Area.   I. Title.
  LA217.2.M394   2014
  370.973—dc23

                                                          2013043365

9/8/15

THIS BOOK IS DEDICATED TO DONALD A. SCHÖN, WHO LED OUR GROUP
BEFORE HIS UNTIMELY DEATH, AND WHOSE IDEAS ABOUT THEORY OF
ACTION LIE AT THE HEART OF THE BOOK THAT LATER EMERGED

Contents

Acknowledgments

The authors acknowledge the immense contribution to this work of the Annenberg Foundation and the Spencer Foundation. They acknowledge as well the many other foundations that funded the research that informs the book. These include especially the MacArthur Foundation, the Rockefeller Foundation, the Hewlett Foundation, the Pew Charitable Trusts, the Joyce Foundation, and the Bill and Melinda Gates Foundation.

We also acknowledge the reform leaders whose work we have had the privilege to follow closely and document, and who have helped us in various ways to understand what they meant to do and why. They include especially Ted Sizer, Vartan Gregorian, Barbara Cervone, Merrill Vargo, Ken Rolling, Bill Ayers, Paul Vallas, Deborah Meier, Heather Lewis, Priscilla Ellington, Sy Fliegel, Beth Lief, Eric Zachary, Joel Klein, Eric Nadelstern, David Hornbeck, and Vicky Phillips.

Finally, we acknowledge the support of many others who have helped us sustain this work over many years through their encouragement and willingness to read and respond to drafts. These include especially Barbara Cervone, Tony Bryk, Barbara Neufeld, Ellen Lagemann, Paul Goren, Kathleen Cushman, Susan Neuman, Ethan Lowenstein, Mary Brabeck, Jeff Henig, Sherry King, Steve Goodman, John Scott, Leslie Siskin, Peter Heaney, John Deasy, and several anonymous reviewers. They also include members of New York University's fabulous salon on the high school, and doctoral students in an NYU seminar on cities and their schools, which Joe McDonald and Gordon Pradl taught a decade ago when the book project was brand new: Sharon Avni, Margaret Caspe, Nell Daniel, Michael Guinan, Darrell Hucks, Kevin Maness,

Margary Martin, Jody Polleck, Bree Picower, Eliza Ross, and Gabriel Reich, who stayed on for the long haul.

The book has also enjoyed the support—direct and indirect—of an abundant number of reform- and research-focused institutions, especially the Annenberg Institute for School Reform, the Consortium on Chicago School Research, Research for Action, the Stanford Center for Research on the Context of Teaching, the NYU Institute for Education and Social Policy, and the Consortium for Policy Research in Education. Finally, it owes much to superb reporting by numerous education journalists, especially John Merrow, and those who work at *Education Week*, the *New York Times*, the *Philadelphia Inquirer, Catalyst Chicago, GothamSchools*, and the *Philadelphia Notebook*.

CHAPTER ONE

Introduction

To answer the three questions in its title—what works in school reform, what fails, and why—this book raises other questions meant for readers. What do you think about when you think about school reform? Are you hopeful about it or skeptical? What do you think is at stake for you? And what arguments would you make—whether to educators, policymakers, funders, or others—about how to pursue positive outcomes? These questions are not meant to lead toward answers we authors have worked out in advance. This is not that kind of book. These questions simply invite readers to enter the territory we've staked out with certain perceptions heightened.

The territory has both a landscape and a timescape. It features major school reform efforts in four places—Chicago, New York, Philadelphia, and the Bay Area—over two decades. Our own studies of these efforts form the basis of our accounts, supplemented by the work of the other researchers and journalists we cite. Our learning from each other over two decades informs the accounts too. Since the mid-1990s, the authors have participated in a learning community that we call the Cities and Schools Research Group. Its purpose has been to pool our understanding of large-scale school reform and make it available for others to use. The group's name reveals an original intention, later modified. This was to add substantially to what is known about big-city school reform, as if big-city school reform were distinctly different from school reform in other places. Today, we think this difference is often overplayed. Although we continue to respect the role that context plays in school reform, we think that some reform dynamics stay constant across contexts, and we focus here on these dynamics. The inclusion of the Bay Area among our research sites—with its three big cities and numerous small ones, as well as vast suburban and rural swaths—helped us understand this. One might say that it disrupted our intention nearly from the start, and this book is partly about the ways in which disrupted intention can be plumbed for creative advantage. Moreover, we noticed over time that our other three sites influenced school reform policy nearly everywhere, not just in other cities.

Our research and writing partnership was created at the invitation of the Annenberg Foundation and the Annenberg Institute for School Reform at Brown University. It was led originally by Donald A. Schön of the Massachusetts Institute of Technology, until his death in 1997. And it remains inspired by his perspectives—for example, on the value of pooled understanding in matters of great civic importance, and on the need for grounding reform in rigorously honed theories of action. Since 1997, the group has been led by Joseph McDonald, who is also the principal author of this book, the one charged by the group with figuring out a way to pool understanding and to make the result lively and accessible. Thus the book is not a compilation of separate chapters prepared by separate authors, with an introduction and conclusion meant to tie them together. Nor is it written, as some research reports are, in a corporate voice. The book has a single distinctive voice throughout—one that is, as we suggest below, an indispensable element of its message. Still, the book draws substantially on and cites the original research, writing, and thinking of all the other authors. Thus Jolley Bruce Christman's and Tom Corcoran's research is at the heart of our Philadelphia stories, as Mark Smylie's is for Chicago. Our Bay Area account rests on Milbrey McLaughlin's and Joan Talbert's research there, and our New York accounts on that of Norm Fruchter, Gordon Pradl, and Gabriel Reich. Yet their individual contributions have been refracted by years of conversation, drafting, and rhetorical experimentation.

The Research Base

Our partnership took root when we tried to devise a cross-project evaluation of eighteen diverse school reform efforts funded by the Annenberg Foundation and collectively known as the Annenberg Challenge (Annenberg Foundation, n.d.). The Challenge was announced at the White House in late 1993 by media magnate, philanthropist, and former US ambassador to Great Britain Walter H. Annenberg and his wife Lenore in the company of President Bill Clinton. At the time, the Annenbergs' $500 million gift was the largest philanthropic investment ever in K–12 public education. The places we write about here—Chicago, New York, Philadelphia, and the Bay Area—were early beneficiaries of the gift, using the funds to launch major projects. Other cities and metropolitan areas benefited too, including Los Angeles, Detroit, Houston, South Florida, Atlanta, Chattanooga/Hamilton County, and Boston. There was also a Rural Challenge.

Our conception of a cross-project evaluation design for this massive effort included summative and formative studies of the locally designed projects, to be done using locally available evaluation experts. The summative component would employ a set of common measures keyed to what we called an impact map. The latter was the first iteration of the *theory of action space* that we sketch out in this book. The formative component involved a plan, first, to help project leaders clarify the theories of action underlying their unique projects and, second, to align these theories across multiple levels of design and action. The underlying idea is captured by the title of a monograph by Schön and McDonald, published by the Annenberg Institute in 1998: *Doing What You Mean to Do in School Reform: Theory of Action in the Annenberg Challenge.* The monograph suggests that alignment between meaning and doing is intermittent at best in projects that initiate complex change, yet crucial to the projects' development and impact; and it holds that external perspectives (such as those evaluators may supply) are invaluable aids toward continual realignment.

Both our formative and summative plans depended on the creation and persistence of a strong cross-project community of researchers and practitioners who would review each other's work in the manner of critical friends. Our hope was that the combination of common measures, a different kind of formative evaluation, and the involvement of researchers and reform practitioners across multiple contexts would sharpen the effectiveness of the Annenberg reforms, and prove influential as an evaluation design.

However, our efforts failed. In fact, no common approach to formative evaluation was implemented across all of the Challenge projects, and no common summative measures were adopted. Thus the opportunity to affect the direction of a giant natural experiment in school reform, and to track its impact, mostly vanished. Several factors account for the failure. They include the sheer complexity of the Challenge itself; the high cost of evaluating it as we proposed; the hesitation of some funders and some reform projects to undergo such thorough evaluation; the diversity of research expertise and research perspectives among the local evaluators; and the fact that, in the mid-1990s, our conception of the kind of research needed simply seemed outsize to many. As we demonstrate in this book, however, some of the Challenge projects proved nonetheless influential in terms of school reform policy. But the influence was of a kind rarely acknowledged—one associated with what we call *connection*.[1] More about this below.

With respect to evaluation design, the influence of the Annenberg Challenge has been even more indirect. Several of the Annenberg cities—as well as other places—eventually built at the local level the capacity for cross-project formative and summative evaluation of school reform that we imagined. They are using this capacity to build longitudinal tracking systems and ongoing data analysis systems with good feedback loops to districts and schools (Sparks, 2012). Most have been inspired in this regard by the success of the Consortium on Chicago School Research, one of whose earliest projects was the evaluation of the Chicago Annenberg Challenge. One purpose of our book is to encourage more cross-city conversation about such local studies. Indeed, our book exists (despite the failure of our larger plans) because the Spencer Foundation invested in *our* cross-city conversation. It sensed the value of the community of practice we had formed within the context of the Annenberg study and hoped that others might learn from it. We had visited each other's projects, had read and responded to each other's research reports, had talked together regularly about the prospects and pitfalls of contemporary school reform, and had begun to write together. Spencer provided funding to keep our community of practice going post-Annenberg—long enough to gain a better perspective on the data we had collected in a small number of Challenge sites; to share data and perspectives on similar work we did later; to refine our emerging ideas of how *meaning* and *doing* relate in the context of school reform; to construct a theory of how ambitious reform arises, proceeds, collapses, and in a sense survives; and to report on all this. This book is our report.

Theory of Action Space

Four interrelated ideas emerged from our study. They constitute what we call our theory of action space. We introduce these ideas briefly below, then explore them more thoroughly in the next chapter. Finally, we illustrate them throughout the book in stories.

Idea 1: The necessity of reframing deeply
held beliefs about school reform

In 2005, newly sworn-in US senator John Thune spoke to a *New York Times* reporter about having just met newly sworn-in US senator Barack Obama. "Barack and I have talked about exchanging visits," he said, "him coming to South Dakota to see a working ranch or an Indian reservation, and me coming to Chicago to see the inner city" (Stolberg, 2005, p. A21). We have not been able to determine whether this exchange of visits ever took place, but we think it was a good idea, and Thune's mention of it helps us illustrate what *reframing* is. In our terms, he implicitly invited his new colleague to help him reframe what he calls "the inner city"—which for him is as tangible as a ranch or an Indian reservation, though it is also in some sense elusive, requiring an interpretive guide. To our ears, Thune's phrasing conveys attraction but also fear—a familiar combination in the American context whenever race is involved. As Thune may have sensed, seeing first hand is fundamental to working out this tension. He may also have understood that seeing is not enough, that it must be followed by reflective conversation about what *is* seen, always in tension with what *might be* seen.

Over the years, several scholars have explored the difference between this *is* and this *might be*—beginning with Erving Goffman (1974), and including Lee Bolman and Terry Deal (1997), Frank Fischer (2003), George Lakoff (2002, 2004), and Donald Schön and Martin Rein (1994). The frames our minds favor in ordinary perception are rooted in class, race, age, gender, geography, and political and cultural orientation, as well as other sources of "common sense." As Schön and Rein (1994) put it, these frames rest on belief and appreciation. In other words, we ordinarily see what we expect to see and also what we like to see—a formidable combination that makes our ordinary frames inescapable without the conscious effort that Schön and Rein call frame reflection and that we call reframing.

Reframing is what Thune and Obama planned and what we think school reform requires. It is a necessary precursor to gaining the resources that support reform. In this book, we explore the reframing of certain deeply held beliefs. Some of these beliefs are positive—or, as we put it, *encouraging*—with respect to taking action. For example, there are the widespread beliefs that school reform can save the economy, and that it can also end social inequality. And there is the similarly widespread belief that business is a good source of ideas for how to conduct school reform. These three beliefs have arisen from the larger political economy in which all schools and reformers operate, and they seem compelling to many people as a spur to action, a matter of common sense. However, they may encourage too much, raising false expectations. And they may propel action at such high speed and with such unwarranted confidence that the action falls short of its mark. Reframing uncovers this downside, and leads to inventive ways to avoid it. Meanwhile, other beliefs, also widely held and deeply felt, are negative with respect to taking action. They discourage it. These also need to be reframed. For example, there is the widespread belief that many schools serving low-income communities are essentially incorrigible, and that money spent on school reform there is wasted.

Of course, reframing does not alter facts about schools—ones that include incoming reading scores and reading readiness, teacher qualifications, children's birth weights, family income and access to medical care, neighborhood violence and employment statistics, and more (Bryk, Sebring, Allensworth, Luppescu, and Easton, 2010; Neuman, 2009). Nor does it alter large social trends that include obstacles in the United States to social mobility and educational attainment (Chetty, Hendren, Kline, and Saez, July 2013; Duncan and Murnane, 2011). However, the frames people bring to facts affect whether they invest in gathering them, whether they pay attention to them, whether they want to change them, whether they think they *can* change them, and, finally, what they think change should entail.

Idea 2: The surprising impotence of school reform arguments

Arguments for school reform prescribe particular courses of action: do this or do that. They are the offspring of encouraging beliefs. The pronouncements about reform that we typically encounter are more declarations than arguments in a strict sense because they are unburdened by evidence. Thus we use the word somewhat in the manner of Lawrence Levine, who quipped that arguments are "examples of how things do not happen" (1996, p. 29). He meant that arguments do not come easily to the ground, being too rigid in their construction to accommodate actual contexts and their complications. Instead, they hover in the air, contributing a sometimes confusing, if nonetheless helpful, strategic chatter. Arguments are insistent, even strident. They seem sure of themselves. When revealed, their actual limitations can take proponents by surprise.

In chapter 2, we present and explore a list of contemporary school reform arguments, but for readers already feeling lost in abstraction, here are a few examples, drawn from a recent film called *Waiting for Superman* (Chilcott & Guggenheim, 2010). We use imperative verbs to capture their stridency: (1) fire ineffective teachers and hire better ones; (2) close the big failing neighborhood schools and open an array of small, choice-based ones; (3) surround schools with social services to overcome the effects of poverty on learning. Even when such arguments are made more concrete—use value-added assessments to identify ineffective teachers; open no-excuses charter schools; replicate Geoffrey Canada's Harlem Children's Zone—they still tend to oversell themselves. And they sometimes resist combination. The fiercest proponents of each reform imply that theirs is all that is needed, and that it is adoptable instead of merely adaptable. Their arguments become in the process alluring beyond reason, and a source of incoherence. In any given context, stakeholder groups crucial to a civic alliance for reform—parents, educational leaders, teacher unions, politicians, business roundtables, and foundations, among others—find themselves attracted to arguments, though often different and conflicting ones. Or they may be attracted to different interpretations of the same argument but lack opportunities to discover and bridge the differences. Thus arguments make the politics of reform very complex.

Still, arguments are hugely valuable, rhetorically and politically. Reform requires, among other things, that people be rallied, goals set, and plans devised. Arguments help us do these things. And they at least tell us what to try, point us in specific directions. Then, when what we try falls short, they supply something else to try. At first, movement is everything. The trick, however, is to learn soon enough that something more is needed. Learning this prods us to take command of arguments—wrestling them to the ground, bending them to the demands of context, combining them to attract and hold together coalitions of support. In the best circumstances, we also spell out our assumptions—say why we think a particular argument will work when modified as we plan. and devise means of tracking the results over time. Finally, we use the evidence gained through this tracking to modify our plans and even our goals. By these means, we channel the energy of arguments into theories of action (Argyris and Schön, 1996). All this happens within what we call action space.

Idea 3: The crucial role of action space in school reform

When policy grows really ambitious, David Cohen and Susan Moffit (2009) claim, it outstrips the capacity of practitioners to implement it— all things being equal. This is an important insight. In this book, how- ever, we focus on what happens when all things are *not* equal—that is, when especially talented people manage to assemble exceptional ca- pacity for making the real conditions of schooling *actionable*. We use the word as litigators do: giving cause for taking action; but also as pol- iticians and activists might: motivating actors, and helping them think that action can pay off. The result, we say, is *action space*, and it has the power to disturb equilibrium.

Action space is built at opportune intersections of three resources. The first is *professional capacity*—people on hand who really know their stuff as educators, leaders, and reformers. They contribute essen- tial skills and ideas, and also guide action once action becomes possi- ble. The second is *civic capacity*—people with clout and stake, from both elite and grassroots circles, who have come forward in support of reform, bearing investments of social capital: partnerships, consultations, in- kind contributions, and the like. This may serve to connect the reform to the resources of the larger community—what Robert Putnam (2000) calls bridging capital. Or it may act as bonding capital—connecting the reform to the deep local culture. Investors may be from big business or a corner store, from cultural or arts institutions of any size, from major re- ligious bodies or modest congregations. They may be from the chamber of commerce or small, community-based organizations. Their invest- ment, in any case, signals the backing of important people beyond edu- cation. It provides political cover for the educators, educational policy- makers, parents, and students who are most on the line. It encourages these primary stakeholders to take greater risks themselves, and it warns off potential opponents of reform (Comer, 2009; Henig & Rich, 2003; Hill, Campbell, & Harvey, 2000; Stone, Henig, Jones, & Pierannunzi, 2001). Finally, the third resource crucial to the formation of action space is *money*—whether from governments, foundations, intermediary part- ners, corporations, private donors, or all of the above, whether millions of dollars or thousands. This is money for more than ordinary operations. It is money that aims to boost these ordinary operations into a different orbit.

Within the action space that these three resources create, reformers exercise their reform leadership. They motivate others to take action, devise action plans, and build trust. They also push hard for change, manage turbulent politics as best they can, reflect in and on action, and change course as needed—all the while striving to keep resources flowing. In the best circumstances, they also contract with people like us to make records of their action that they and others can read and use.

For the most part in this book, we refer to action space at a citywide or metropolitan level. But it is important to note that the construct can apply at other levels too—for example, when the right catalytic leadership and sufficient capacities become available at the level of a neighborhood, a small district, or a network of schools. Moreover, as we know well from our research, and have written about elsewhere, the construct can also apply at the level of an individual school. In any case, regardless of scale and the circumstances of its formation, action space eventually collapses. Yes, good action space is engineered to expect and deal with profound stress and resistance, and it is surprisingly prevalent and frequently resilient. Still (to paraphrase Robert Frost), there is something that doesn't love an action space, something that wants to knock it down. Thus most of the action space we describe in this book is now down. We insist, however, that such collapse is not tragic. What *is* tragic is a failure to learn from past experience.

Idea 4: The redeeming power of connections

School Reform is fundamentally political work, and politics is not kind to memory, except in creating and evoking icons. Leaders often seek political advantage by denying indebtedness to recent predecessors, by claiming to be the first to imagine a plan, by seeming categorically sure of the plan, and by resisting competitor plans (at least at first). Of course, much of this is just posturing; true solipsism would be counterproductive within an enterprise that also depends on shaping collective vision and rallying collective effort. Still, reformer amnesia remains a problem, particularly when memory is most needed—namely, in devising new reform efforts. To combat amnesia in this book, we tell stories in bunches and try otherwise to pull back for a wider view of the connections that we think can feed thoughtful reinvention and generate reform energy across context, sector, actor, and time. We ask explicitly what might happen if people stopped forgetting, and deliberately built on others' expertise and past experience.

Where it occurs, making connections is a mutual undertaking of many parties. It is not enough to ask, for example, that younger reformers seek to understand what older reformers have learned and contributed. For their part, older reformers must resist the temptation to think and say that they *solved* such and such a problem before, or that such and such a strategy has little effect. Instead, they must think to themselves (bracketing in the same instant whatever skepticism seizes them), "Ah, another opportunity to make some progress, another generation to lend its energy to the tasks." In short, everyone has to think in long-haul terms. It helps in this regard if the shapers of action space create good records of what they intend to do, what they actually do, and what impact their actions have. Typically, they make such records by partnering with evaluators. A problem, however, is that prevailing conceptions of practice and of evaluation may interfere. On the one hand, as Schön and Rein (1994) put it in their critique of these conceptions, practitioners may be considered incapable of reflecting systematically and rigorously. Thus an important source of knowledge may not be cultivated. And evaluators, constrained by conceptions of rigor, may fail to meet standards of practical utility. Their findings may be too abstract, their reflections too cool, and their reports too late to have any formative impact. Conversely, they may be too complicit in the practice, or too limited in their resources or methods to generate the data necessary for a genuinely critical perspective.

Whatever the quality of the records that actors in action space leave behind, however, all the rest of us must search them for possible connections—connections between the past and the present. We must confront in general the political aversion to memory and, despite the discomfort the questions may generate, must ask again and again, "Who did this work before? What resulted? How do we know?" These questions apply whether the work involves the construction of policy, the creation of action space, the funding of reform, or the study of reform.

We know, as in the title of another book one of us coauthored, that school reform is steady work in the sense that it is highly prone to collapse (Elmore & McLaughlin, 1988). But we are interested in how reformers might get smarter as they do this steady work, how they might more consciously and deliberately pass on knowledge from one action space to the next.

A Different Voice

As we suggested above, this book is not a conventional collection of case studies. To be sure, the book is *founded* on case studies—highly elaborate ones undertaken over multiple years by researchers at the Consortium for Chicago School Research, the Institute for Education and Social Policy, the Stanford Center for Research on the Context of Teaching, Research for Action, the Consortium for Policy Research in Education, and the Annenberg Institute for School Reform. The Challenge-related material was originally published, like most educational evaluation reports, in low-circulation monographs—sixty-one in all, plus ancillary documents. But as we also suggested above, the book refracts all this, as it does other research material about other reform efforts in our four places, through the many conversations we authors have had over time, and through narrative experiments in which the coauthors have engaged.

These experiments applied two methods that Catherine Kohler Riessman describes in her 2008 book, *Narrative Methods for the Human Sciences.* The first involves what she calls thematic analysis—the application of a theory to archival material and other data sources. As typically happens in thematic analysis, the application is recursive as the archive speaks back to theory. Thus our theory evolved over time—beginning with Donald Schön's theory-of-action perspective on the dynamics of school reform, and leading to the one articulated above (Argyris & Schön, 1996; Schön & McDonald, 1998). We coauthors applied this evolving theory to the study's archive of research documents by means of successive conversations and much drafting and redrafting.

Meanwhile, McDonald, Reich, and Smylie pursued the second narrative method—what Riessman calls structural analysis. In our case, this involved a series of experiments in tone of voice. The term *tone of voice* refers to an author's attitude toward his or her topic. From the beginning of our book project, we knew that our attitude toward our topic—twenty years of school reform in four huge and complex places—could neither be skeptical (the normal tone in social science writing) nor impartial (normal

though hardly pervasive in journalism). One reason is that we are writing
here about events that are for the most part in the past. Since we know
how they turned out, at least in broad strokes, what's the point of being
either skeptical or impartial? On the other hand, these events are tied so
tightly to the present that the historian's detached tone seems inappropri-
ate too. We tried for a time what we called a *comic* tone, using the word
in the narrow classical sense that distinguishes comedy from tragedy and
aims to provoke hope rather than evoke dread. However, the very word
comic seemed to early readers disrespectful of our protagonists' efforts
and dismissive of the high stakes involved. We next experimented with a
tone that we called *ironic*. Thus we took full advantage of the dramatic
irony that comes from knowing now what neither we nor the reformers
we studied could possibly have known at the time. An ironic tone seems
generally suitable for exploring well-meaning and even well-designed reform efforts that nonetheless failed to reach ambitious targets, or failed
by various degrees to link intention, action, and impact. Irony seems suitable too for exploring reform efforts that at first succeeded but later fell
apart; it allows for admiration of ambition and achievement, even as it
acknowledges fallibility and transience. It is a tone, moreover, that can
accommodate looking squarely at failure without diminishing the possi-
bilities of learning and progress. All of these effects are germane to our
message. Yet again, however, some readers—while appreciating what we
had to say—quibbled with how we said it. We appreciate their feedback.
They find irony discouraging in the way we use that word throughout the
book—that is, discouraging with respect to taking action. Yet they think
school reform action is needed, and so do we.

Finally, we adjusted our tone one notch more, and we associate
the adjustment with a rhetorical technique made famous by the great
twentieth-century playwright Bertolt Brecht. He called it (unpronounce-
ably, for non–German speakers) *verfremdungseffekt*. In English, this is
often translated as *theatrical estrangement*. Think of Brecht's charac-
ter Mother Courage bursting into song amid the horrors of the Thirty
Years War. The technique is a staple now of theater, contemporary fic-
tion, television, and to some extent film, though it admittedly shows up
only rarely in social science writing. Essentially, it consists of any textual
element—for example, a surprising juxtaposition or an aside—that calls
attention to the fact that the whole text is an artifice, not a real experience, though one constructed to help viewers and readers think about

real experience. "This is not the real Thirty Years War," Mother Courage's songs suggest (as does her name and the sparsely designed stage), "so don't get caught up in pity and dread. Use the text instead to think about war in *your* time." The technique is sometimes used by authors who think that what they have to say may call upon their viewers or readers to engage in some unlearning. And this is how we feel. We think that readers often turn to books like ours to satisfy either their enthusiasm for reform or their skepticism of it, and we want to challenge both mindsets. We want, as we suggest above, to warn enthusiasts that reform efforts are prone to entropy and collapse, but we also want to tell skeptics that reform efforts can endure in practice even when all acknowledgment of them has vanished. Meanwhile, we want to acquaint all of our readers with a paradox—namely, that the arguments for reform that they variously embrace and debate are as impotent in one sense as they are crucial in another sense. And we also want to invite them to engage in the cognitively uncomfortable but necessary work of reframing how they think about school reform.

You will likely be pleased to know that in contrast to Brecht, we include no songs in this book, though we do other things you may find strange. For example, we slice up three of our case studies rather than tell them as continuous narratives, and we tell our stories in pairs to heighten appreciation of the theory they illuminate. Sometimes we also put special emphasis on estrangement—for example, in chapter 5, when we compare school reform in Philadelphia to a nineteenth-century Russian novel, and reform in Chicago to a made-for-TV movie.

How the Book Is Organized

This book has a thematic thread. Laid bare, it runs like this:

> What may seem the craziness of school reform has a hidden logic of great strategic utility. It has to do with the fact that reframing commonly held ideas makes room for action space, which is where civic and professional capacity meet up with money, and where arguments in the air *can* come to the ground. While action space collapses sooner or later, the collapse leaves residues of achievement and expertise on which new action space can build. Thus school reform can avoid a Sisyphean fate.

The book overall relies on the complementary power of exposition and narration. Obviously, this chapter is expository, as is chapter 2, where we lay out the theory of action space more explicitly in words and figures. Then chapters 3 through 6—the narrative chapters—illustrate the theory. Chapter 3 examines the dynamics of action space over time in Chicago and New York, and attends closely to how these dynamics are affected by shifts of argument, changes in leadership, and variations in supply of the three capacities. Chapter 4 takes a broader view—this time in reference to Philadelphia and the Bay Area—in order to examine the impact on action space of state politics, culture, and economics. Chapter 5 focuses on collapse, and chapter 6 on connection. Finally, chapter 7 mixes exposition with narration (in this sole instance, fictional narration) in order to draw out the practical implications of the theory of action space for current and prospective reform leaders.

CHAPTER TWO

The Theory of Action Space

In 1928, the sociologist George Counts published a book called *School and Society in Chicago*. There he portrays school reform as a terrain of contested arguments, each more complicated than it appears and each falling short of a perfect fit with a still more complicated context. The arguments are products of what Counts termed a welter of social forces and an inheritance of disagreements. We would say that they are products of an atmospheric clash of encouraging and discouraging beliefs. In Counts's Chicago, the beliefs had to do with the role that education might play in a still emerging industrial age, the power of efficiency, and the demands of democracy. In today's Chicago (as well as New York, Philadelphia, and the Bay Area), they have to do with the role of education in a postindustrial age, the strategic inventiveness of business, and the demands of equality. The discouraging beliefs discourage action: change is too hard, too expensive, and too likely to be ineffectual. Meanwhile, the encouraging beliefs urge action, and generate arguments about what action to take—lots of arguments.

Counts's readers, as he acknowledges in an introductory chapter, would have preferred something less messy than all of this. You might also. But those who describe school reform with fidelity to its real dynamics have to contend with social embeddedness, Counts explains. This means dealing with what he vividly calls the "smoking, teeming, vibrating, shifting, and kaleidoscopic" setting and the "hurrying, pushing, loving, hating, worshiping, playing, and battling groups" who make their home there (p. 27). "The Chicago schools," he adds wryly, "always have been and probably always will be in Chicago" (p. 28). In other words, there is no escape from the complications of context and argument. But there is a trick, Counts suggests, one that can help us avoid being swamped by the complications of context and argument. It is "to provide channels through which the living energies of society [arising from beliefs and expressed in arguments] may flow into new forms and patterns . . . to devise some means of making the school responsive to . . . more fundamental social realities, and of enabling it at the same time to maintain an even keel amid the clash and roar of the contending elements" (pp. 353–54).

Channeling the living energies of society into new forms and patterns is the role of what we call action space. It provides, as Counts suggests, an arena of control for both professional interests and all legitimate civic interests—from those of the community's elites to those of its lowliest organized voices. We would add that the space is shaped by money too. In this chapter, we explore not only the elements but the dynamics of action space, explaining in words and figures what in the next four chapters we will explore in data-laden stories.

Reframing Beliefs

When it comes to school reform, all of our cities have been driven by a set of encouraging beliefs, and have faced off more or less squarely against a set of discouraging ones. The encouraging beliefs suggest that the time for taking action is now and the likelihood of success high given the right amount of effort. The discouraging ones, by contrast, suggest that action is futile or at least that success is unlikely.

Both encouraging and discouraging beliefs feed what we call (with due respect for the limitations of the metaphor and a touch of irony) the capital market for school reform. A capital market, according to W. Warner Burke, is an "informal aggregation" of potential investors and investment advisors and their collective spin (2008, p. 15). The capital market for school reform determines at a given time whether school reform is a good investment or not, and if so, then which particular investment opportunities seem most to least promising. The capital market crowd includes legislators and legislative staff at state and federal levels; educational policy advocates of all stripes; and researchers, journalists, think tank analysts, bloggers, and others who think about, write about, and talk about education. It also includes philanthropists—an extraordinary array of them in our time—many of whom work avowedly and in a hands-on way as investors or venture capitalists (real or metaphorical). They highlight the reform strategies they favor and leverage other resources to support these. Finally, the capital market for education includes educators, particularly those in leadership positions, who continually make claims about investment worthiness—whether to attract new resources or to allocate discretionary ones already on hand.

At this moment in US educational and political history, the capital market for school reform is bullish. What this means for reformers is that they find themselves reframing encouraging beliefs more often than discouraging ones. They may not need to convince a foundation officer, mayor, or hedge-fund philanthropist (or faculty, parent groups, or civic coalitions) that investing in school reform makes sense, but they may have to challenge these potential investors' assumptions about what kind of investment is needed. The purpose of reframing is to challenge common sense—that is, to suggest that one may really want something other than what one imagines.

As we suggested in chapter 1, the following three encouraging beliefs are dominant in the United States today, and powerfully shape what we think about when we think about school reform:

- School reform can save the economy.
- School reform can bring about social equality.
- Business can show the way.

School reformers cannot choose the encouraging beliefs they work with. Nor can they afford simply to refute prevailing ones. After all, no one is likely to invest in something that seems nonsensical. On the other hand, investors appreciate a fresh perspective, a new spin. What the smart reformer does is to offer one—that is, to work the margin between expectation and novelty. To do this, he or she engages in what Donald Schön (1983) calls frame experiments. So the reformer might ask what is meant by such and such a term—*economy, equality, business*. What have the terms meant historically? What else might they mean in the future, given certain conditions that seem plausible? He or she might, for example, acknowledge the givenness of the first belief above—about the relation of school reform to the economy, but then ask, "What kind of economy do we want, given the trajectory of globalization? Where does it exist now in the world, and what do we know about schooling there?" Such reframing is an invitation to look more deeply and think more broadly, without necessarily questioning a basic inclination.

Reframing always involves probing questions and often uses other texts as leverage. So, for example, a reformer seeking to reframe the American belief in the efficacy of school reform as a strategy in the pursuit of social equality might cite a 2010 United Nations report that ranks the twenty-four member countries of the Organization for Economic Cooperation and Development (OECD)—the world's richest countries—in terms of how much inequality they tolerate in educational attainment, children's health, and children's material well-being (for example, housing conditions). The United States, it finds, ranks low not only in educational attainment (19 out of 24) but also in health (22 out of 24) and material well-being (23 out of 24)—cumulatively, in fact, it comes in dead last (UNICEF, 2010).[1] "What are we to make of this?" the reframing reformer asks, implicitly challenging the belief in the efficacy of school reform *alone* as a response to inequality. Similarly, a reframing reformer might point out a historical contradiction that underlies the first two encouraging beliefs above, as discussed by David Labaree (1997). American education has long been expected to advance both the economy and social equality, Labaree says, but at the same time it assists individual families in their efforts to preserve or advance their children's economic and social advantages relative to other children. The point of reframing is not to turn encouraging ideas into discouraging ones but to gain a fresh perspective on encouragement. What if school reform planning took more account of children's health care and housing? What if efforts to address excellence and equity took more account of the real tension between them? These are future-oriented inquiries, though reframing involves making historical connections too, as Labaree's example suggests. Indeed, all three of the beliefs listed above are long-standing ones with roots that might be usefully cited to elicit new and generative perspectives. In her extensive history of Chicago school reform, for example, Dorothy Shipps (2006) points out that the idea of using schools to ameliorate the impact of international economic competition—combined with the idea that business can show the way—propelled early twentieth-century American school reform, just as it now does twenty-first-century reform. The question then was how to educate more efficient factory workers to compete with Germany, and the answers involved the application to schooling of standardization, factory assembly, and a high tolerance for factory rejects (for example, students who failed to complete high school but learned just enough to be good factory workers). "So what is the question now?" a reframing reformer might ask, "and what are the answers?" Again, the reframing does not challenge the encouraging belief directly—indeed, it exploits the energy it produces, while channeling it in a somewhat surprising way. In the process, it may chip away at the belief's face validity, and thus prove ultimately subversive. By this means—over time—new encouraging ideas can emerge. The idea that school reform can advance American equality is likewise an old belief. A reframing reformer might point out, however—illuminating a shift in school reform energy between roughly the 1970s and the new millennium—that it is typically expressed today with a sense of economic rather than democratic urgency. "Maybe the reason," the reformer might say, "is the growing proportion of children of color in the US population (48 percent of newborns in 2009) and the persistence of an achievement gap" (Tavernise & Gebeloff, 2010).

We believe that reframing encouragement (as well as discouragement) is a necessary precursor to gaining the resources needed to open up action space. By appealing at once to common sense, but at the same time giving it a twist, reframing makes room for investments that might not otherwise be contemplated—not just investments of money but of support, expertise, and sweat equity. In turn, these investments make room for crucial invention. Meanwhile, the toll that each reframing takes on confidence in the encouraging beliefs makes room for the evolution of school reform.

School Reform Arguments Today

Encouraging beliefs give rise to arguments. Amid the ambiguity that invariably attends encouragement, each argument insists: Do this! On one level, arguments become popular only because they seem reasonable, yet it is in their nature also to be oblivious to their limitations and to the inevitability that the contexts to which they are applied will exact some adjustment. They are, in a word, brash. In listing here some of the arguments that have figured in the recent reform histories of Chicago, New York, Philadelphia, and the Bay Area, we capture that brashness with imperative verbs and other insistent rhetoric:

- Mobilize civic elites—corporations, philanthropies, cultural institutions—to demand and support better schools.
- Mobilize grassroots groups—neighborhood groups, faith-based groups, parents and students—to demand and support better schools.
- Adopt clear outcome standards for schooling—indeed, national standards—then align curriculum, teaching, and assessment to these. Hold everyone accountable for the results, especially students themselves. Reward and sanction appropriately.
- Standardize the curriculum, script the lessons, and monitor teachers' use of the scripts.
- Create new designs for schooling, adopting as benchmarks the best designs worldwide, and scale up faithful implementation of the designs.
- Identify best instructional practices through rigorous research, and focus all systems on learning them and using them. Use instructional coaches, peer learning networks, demonstration classrooms, and inspections.
- Network schools to create virtual districts for mutual support, resource development, exchange of best practices, policy leverage, and accountability.
- Neutralize the bureaucracy. Put the mayor in charge of schooling—as with public safety, sanitation, and snow removal. Hold the mayor accountable for the results at election time.
- Create twenty-first-century knowledge management systems and evidence-based practices at the district and school levels. Press for richer performance data, more collective analysis of the data, and more collective action based on the analysis. Mobilize educators into professional learning communities and data teams.
- Improve teacher quality by recruiting smarter people, screening them more effectively based on clear indicators of quality, mentoring them as early career teachers, and providing them continual job-embedded and performance-focused training. Meanwhile, fire those whose students do not make consistent gains on tests of their learning.
- Push resources down to the level of schools. Empower principals to use resources as they see fit. Develop accountability tools that track the consequences for student learning. Hold principals accountable for the results: fire them if they don't measure up.
- Diversify educational options and intensify choice. Introduce multiple curricula, multiple school designs, multiple management systems. Let parents and students choose. Regard the schools as investments in a portfolio, and winnow the portfolio regularly.
- Create small schools where students can be better known and teachers can

work together to teach them well. Give the schools themes to make them focused and attractive.

- Give poor families the kind of choice in schooling that middle-class families gain through house hunting. Award vouchers on the demand side. Create
charter schools on the supply side. Let the marketplace decide which schools
work best.

- End the public monopoly on schooling. Contract with school management
companies, curriculum designers, and teacher headhunters. Outsource everything to the best providers. Hold them all accountable.

Of course, we do not typically encounter such arguments in lists. We
meet them entangled in action plans and press announcements, or in the
writing and speeches of advocates who tell us that one or another is the
best or only real option. But listing them is useful. It pins them for examination. It helps us discern patterns that underlie as well as separate sets
of them. They are not, after all, just a grab bag. They reflect larger strategies borrowed from the zeitgeist—notions, for example, about the value
of choice and voice, about the role of markets, and about whether centralization or decentralization is a better guarantor of efficiency. In strategy and in passion (even bombast), they reflect the encouraging beliefs
we identified above.

In other words, arguments are creatures of their time, not artifacts
of progress. There is no reason to assume that arguments are getting
smarter. Yet noticing the patterns among those in the air at any moment can make *reformers* smarter, and also more adept at combining arguments. For example, why should Americans have to choose between
voice and choice, or between centralization and decentralization—examples of what Ann Berthoff (1999) calls killer binaries? Why not instead craft artful combinations of these?

Listing is useful for another reason too. Stripped of the advocacy that
usually attends it, each argument seems more vulnerable than it might
otherwise appear. Seeing it thus, a reformer may be more apt to appreciate what a generation of reform researchers has suggested, namely that
successful reform depends, in the end, not on clever arguments but on
clever reformers who bend arguments to context (Berman & McLaughlin, 1978; Datnow, Hubbard, & Mehan, 2002; Henig & Rich, 2004;
McLaughlin, 1998; Oakes, Quartz, Ryan, & Lipton, 1999; Stone, Henig,
Jones, & Pierannunzi, 2001). Recall Lawrence Levine's quip, quoted in
chapter 1, that arguments are "examples of how things do not happen"

(1996, p. 29). Coming to terms with context always exacts a transformation (Berman and McLaughlin, 1978; Flyvbjerg, 2001; McDonald, Klein, & Riordan, 2009; Olson, 2003).

Nevertheless, as we also pointed out also in chapter 1, arguments are exceedingly useful, even though they never reach practice intact. For one thing, they catalyze the allocation of resources. State or federal policy may promote an argument, and the state legislature or Congress may appropriate money to "implement" it. Arguments may stoke the ambitions of the professional community, arouse the interests of a civic coalition, or marshal the priorities of a foundation. Arguments provoke people to say, "We want to do something, we *can* do something, and here is something we can try!" Arguments are also the raw material for the construction of *theories of action*. These, as Richard Elmore puts it, connect "big ideas" to the "fine grain of practice" (1996, p. 317). They clarify concretely the reform's intentions and the expected paths of design, action, and impact within the context. We like to say that theories of action lay out what reformers mean to do and how (Argyris & Schön, 1996; Schön & McDonald, 1998; Weiss, 1998). The more explicitly they do this, we think, the more power they gain. In the face of what Seymour Sarason (1990) calls the predictable failure of school reform, theories of action enable us to learn from failure and revise systems and efforts accordingly. Of course, theories of action are not magical. Some are clever and adaptive blends of arguments, while others are awkward patchworks of them. Both kinds must contend with the transformative powers of context, and with vagaries in the supply of necessary resources.

In fashioning the theories of action that guided the cities on our watch, reformers used every argument in the list above. Some of the resulting combinations were artful, some incongruous. Most of them contained—as Hubbard, Mehan, and Stein put it (writing about school reform in San Diego)—"the seeds of many, many disagreements waiting to blossom into subversions" (2006, p. 245).

Action Space

As we pointed out in chapter 1, action space is exceptional space. Although it pops up from time to time nearly everywhere, it is not ordinary work space. It is endowed with extraordinary resources pulled together by luck and pluck. These provide the margin that makes reform conceivable. Action space disturbs the equilibrium of schooling-as-usual in a way that policy and professional education cannot manage to do. In the process, it offers inspiration to policy and professional education, and provides exemplars and cautionary tales to guide more routine and ongoing improvement efforts. To explain action space, we begin with the figure of it, then move on to how it functions and the kinds of action it demands and supports. Along the way, we examine its theoretical roots.

In an environment bombarded with arguments about what kind of school reform to undertake, three resources coalesce—not through sheer chemistry but through the efforts of social entrepreneurs who use the arguments to leverage resources. The resources that matter are money, civic capacity, and professional capacity. By *money*, we mean the amount of capital, from any sources, available to initiate and sustain reform operations. *Civic capacity*, as we define it, is the extent to which various sectors of the community understand, support, and actively contribute to reform. They range from downtown businesses and elite nonprofit organizations to grassroots community organizations, religious groups, and those people in a direct line of impact—notably parents and students. *Professional capacity* denotes the distributed intellectual, technical, and organizational know-how available to sustain a creative and accountable teaching and learning community.

These resources are, of course, variable. Although the triangle in figure 1 is equilateral, the dimensions and proportions of real action space

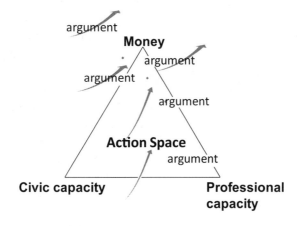

FIGURE I

change continually, the angles growing and shrinking. Taking account of this variability is important for understanding school reform. It means that there is seldom an *it*, a reform project stable enough in its three key resources to be evaluated in a simple way. The honest answers to simple questions—How did *it* succeed? What did *it* achieve?—will always be conditional: Do you mean when *it* had a lot of money or when there was hardly any left? Before or after all the downtown corporate supporters left the city? During phase 1, when *it* relied on one kind of professional capacity, or phase 2, when *it* cultivated a very different kind?

We can learn a lot by tracking the perturbations of an action space—discovering, for example, where the perturbations come from, and how they are managed or mismanaged by reform actors. Such learning may come too late, however, to save a particular action space. If any of the angles go to zero, the action space collapses. We say it flatlines. This is inevitable, our theory holds, but not disastrous because of the connections left behind.

Sources of the Theory

The model of action space presented in figure 1 originated in conversations the authors of the book had over more than a decade, discussions aimed at making sense of our collective studies of school reform. In this process, we drew not only on theories that had emerged from our individual research projects in the four cities and elsewhere, but on the theoretical and practical work of our colleagues in the organizations with which we have been associated. We also drew on the work of other researchers of school reform—especially the research of Clarence Stone, Jeffrey Henig, and their colleagues in defining and exploring civic capacity in urban school reform (Henig, Hula, Orr, & Pedescleaux, 1999; Stone et al., 2001); that of Paul Hill and his colleagues in imagining new arenas for reform and new conceptions of schooling in cities (Hill, Campbell, & Harvey, 2000; Hill & Celio, 1998; Hill & Harvey, 2004); and that of other research groups that have studied school reform in New York and the Bay Area (Bloom, Thompson, & Unterman, 2010; Bloom & Unterman, 2012; Hemphill & Nauer, 2010; Hemphill, Nauer, Zelon, & Jacobs, 2009; Loeb, Bryk, and Hanushek, 2007; O'Day, Bitter, & Gomez, 2011; Porter & Snipes, 2006).

Finally, we drew on the work of other theorists and researchers who have studied and written about organizational change in general. Among these is W. Warner Burke (2008), whose elucidation of open-system theory informs our model of action space. We draw especially on his work in what follows.

Dynamics of Action Space

Open-system theory emphasizes the dependence of all organizations on their environments. The environment for action space consists of three intertwining strata of influence. One hosts the clash of encouraging and discouraging beliefs. In our time, these include the belief that markets can solve all social problems, and also the belief that cities and their schools are incorrigible. The currents of such beliefs course through our politics and culture as jet streams move through the upper levels of our atmosphere, inflecting the weather nearer the ground. Thus the different agencies, interest groups, and stakeholder groups that inhabit and contribute to the politics and culture affecting school reform end up formulating and expressing arguments that in some sense embody encouragement and discouragement. And in a market bullish on encouragement, these political and cultural forces raise and deploy lots of resources to advance their favorite arguments.

In our figure, the political stratum incorporates the influences of multiple sources of policy authority and money—especially the relevant state education department and the US Department of Education—as well as

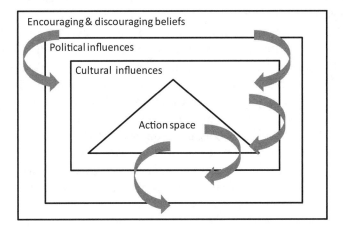

FIGURE 2

multiple local agencies and school district offices. This stratum also typically includes nongovernmental entities that may in a given place have considerable political clout (for example, a chamber of commerce, an arts council, the Urban League), as well as grassroots groups—for example, neighborhood and parent activists. It also includes numerous labor unions, representing teachers, administrators, custodians, and possibly others. Finally, the political environment often includes nongovernmental funders—the Annenberg Foundation, Hewlett Foundation, Gates Foundation, Broad Foundation, Atlantic Philanthropies, Stuart Foundation, Pew Charitable Trusts, and Joyce Foundation are among those that figure in our stories. Complicating the picture further, these funders sometimes operate through intermediary organizations. The Annenberg Challenge, for example, did not fund school districts directly. Intermediaries may be permanent—for example, the local public education fund—or temporary, tied to a particular large-scale funding initiative. The Bay Area School Reform Collaborative and the New York Networks for School Renewal, for example, were established for the sole purpose of organizing and conducting school reform in their respective places. Whether permanent or temporary, intermediaries tend to be irregular, boundary-spanning organizations, invested with resources but ambiguous in their mission and sometimes precarious in their political standing (McDonald, McLaughlin, & Corcoran, 2000). Overall, the influences of the political stratum are sometimes supportive and sometimes overbearing in their individual impact, and typically fractious in terms of the arguments they push and the clout they wield. They are therefore often experienced as incoherent.

The environment for action space also has a cultural stratum in our figure—though the simplicity of the figure belies the substantial overlap of culture and politics. Nonetheless, action space for school reform is subject to distinctly cultural forces—indeed, dazzlingly multicultural forces in the places that concern us. This stratum represents the diverse practices, values, expectations, and rituals that spread in a complex pattern within and across schools, communities, districts, and cities. These cultural elements may encourage or discourage risk taking and entrepreneurship. They may expect a certain style of leadership, favor a certain tenor for classrooms and buildings, be warm or cool toward norms of collegiality, be liberal or conservative in matters ranging from curriculum to professional dress to parent involvement to student agency and voice.

Our spatial terms and figures are, of course, metaphorical. The strata are not really strata, and the action space is not really space. Burke's (2008) theory holds that the former are really sets of transactions, and the latter a predictable but volatile cycle in which the transactions take place. The components of the cycle are *input* (for our purposes, the capacities, encouraging and discouraging beliefs, and arguments), *throughput* (the intensely relational activities "inside" the action space—more about these below), and *output* (the actual impact of the theory of action on the schools and districts). Meanwhile, output loops back as pressure on input. Based on the initial output of an action space, for example, a foundation may offer more support, or cut back; a community group may cheer or jeer; and so on. Leaders of the action space monitor this feedback selectively since they cannot read all the feedback the environment delivers. As Burke advises, however, they must especially attend to negative feedback. This is hugely difficult, however, since in the passion of all that is going on, this is the last thing the actors want to notice. Finally, leaders of the action space must store up surplus capacity however they can: putting aside some money, seeking a surfeit of civic support, larding on professional expertise—all to tide them over predictable gaps in capacity.

All the action that happens within action space can be parsed into input, throughput, and output. Building capacity, attending to negative feedback, searching for more capacity, and storing up surplus capacity all have to do with input. Such action helps stave off what we call collapse

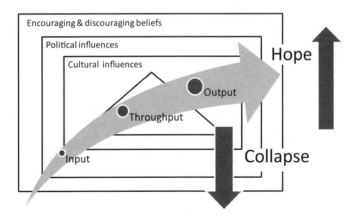

FIGURE 3

and what Burke calls entropy. Although entropy—or running down toward complete inertness—is the natural state and outcome of an open system, it is possible for the system to achieve a quasi-stationary state for relatively long periods. As Kurt Lewin (1947) claimed, however, this is merely apparent equilibrium, a kind of averaging of ups and downs. Still, average suffices: it satisfies the first demand of accountability, namely to stick around long enough to do something.

But to do what? This is where throughput comes in. It involves setting goals and aligning intentions and designs toward them. It involves wrestling some set of arguments into explicit theories of action and submitting them to the test of single-loop inquiries that may lead to adjustment, as well as double-loop inquiries that may lead to fundamental revision (Argyris & Schon, 1996). Ultimately, it requires serious encounters with political and cultural forces. Beliefs must be examined and reframed, and stakeholders must be engaged and persuaded or appeased.

Then there's output. We think of output as more than the sum total of changes to policies, institutions, behaviors, and so on. It also involves how these changes affect the polemics, politics, and cultures with which they contend, and in particular whether they tilt them toward hope. Our colleague Donald Schön, describing what we subsequently came to call action space, called it a wellspring of hope. He was speaking informally to an interviewer in his office at MIT, and the tape of the interview surfaced at his memorial service. Here is what he said:

> Under circumstances in which you have the creation of a community of reliable inquiry, capable of drawing on multiple sources of knowledge and upon multiple sources of intuition, in a context in which something is at stake, and our worry is how to take action, with a sense that we *have* to take action, and that there is a *we* here that's trying to do this. Under *those* circumstances, there's greatest grounds for hope.

Yet, as we suggested above, action space eventually collapses despite all effort. Sometimes it collapses suddenly, sometimes by slowly running down. We explore both the rise and collapse of action space in chapters 3 and 4 by means of long tracking views. We illuminate how action space coalesces, what happens after it does, and what survives it. Then in chapters 5 and 6, we examine closely and respectively the dynamics of collapse and of connection. Finally, in chapter 7, we test a model of our theory.

CHAPTER THREE

Action Space in Chicago and New York

In this chapter, we explore the late twentieth- and early twenty-first-century school reform histories of Chicago and New York. Schooling in these cities underwent massive change during this period, and reform efforts there proved influential across the United States. But stories of these efforts—even those we tell here—can lend themselves to a simpler reading than is warranted. This is one in which evidently good leadership and winning arguments seem simply to have carried the day. We advocate a more complex reading by the light of the theory of action space laid out in chapter 2. By this light, arguments seem more plentiful than they otherwise might, and also more contested and less ready-to-install. Indeed, nothing in these stories happens because of a right argument or a wrong one, but rather because of what actors on the ground make of multiple arguments. By this light too, reformers' work seems more complicated and changeable. Try this theory-informed reading. Notice how multiple leaders in these cities worked over this period to reframe beliefs, and in the process catalyze professional capacity, civic capacity, and money. Consider how they managed (or not) to keep these capacities in balance. Finally, consider the implicit roles in these stories of collapse and connection. Use your sense of these to extrapolate beyond where the stories leave off.

Chicago

Founded on transportation and commodity transfer as well as manufacturing, Chicago had better success in becoming postindustrial than its

Midwestern counterparts among big cities—for example, Milwaukee,
Detroit, and Cleveland (Ehrenhalt, 2012; Jargowsky, 1996). Although
it too lost an astonishing proportion of its manufacturing jobs (an estimated 32 percent between 1969 and 1983 alone), it more easily replaced
them with jobs in other sectors, especially finance (Ehrenhalt, 2012).
One consequence of its success in this regard was a great spread of gen-
trification, starting at the city's core and fanning out along its commuter
rail axis, capturing some neighborhoods in the process that had seemed
permanently poor. Alan Ehrenhalt calls the process "inversion"—poor
and affluent exchanging places between the "inner city" and the less-
inner city or even the suburbs. "Between 2000 and 2010," he writes,
"Chicago became a whiter city with a larger affluent population" (2012,
p. 45). The change led in turn to increased isolation among other people, who felt pushed to the margins, and also to class and racial tension
(Lipman, 2004). In terms of schooling, Chicago had 675 public schools in
2011–2012, serving 404,000 students, of whom 87 percent came from low-
income families. Overall, 42 percent were African-American, 44 percent
Latino, and only 9 percent white in a city whose overall population was
then about 46 percent white (American Community Survey, 2010; Chicago Public Schools, 2012).

An Action Space Forms

Politically, Chicago has long been famous not only for its contentious-
ness but, paradoxically, also for what Dorothy Shipps calls its "consolidated political culture" (2006, p. 87). It is a city that tends toward mayoral regimes, business compacts, grand civic coalitions, mass organizing
at the grassroots level, and collaboration among foundations. All five of
these phenomena have played roles in the recent history of school reform there, as this first story of action space illustrates.

    In 1987, then US secretary of education William Bennett pronounced
the Chicago Public Schools (CPS) the worst in the nation (Hess, 1991).
He focused especially on the system's management. Inheriting generations of consolidated political culture, the central office had swollen with
political patronage, and had also become "corporate" in a stodgy mid-
twentieth-century sense. It was byzantine and insulated, Shipps suggests,
its insulation having proved effective in warding off decades of civil
rights complaints. Bennett's remark might well have merely reinforced a
discouraging belief about the incorrigibility of a city school system, but it

did not. The remark was uttered just at the moment when the city's first black mayor, reformer Harold Washington, had begun to turn his attention to the schools. Elected to a second term by a small plurality composed largely of blacks and Latinos, Washington seemed ready to turn a quarter century of black and Latino grievance against the CPS into a strategy for change, and Bennett's attack helped. So did complaints by corporate leaders about the work-preparedness of CPS graduates, and so too did the fury of parents who had just endured a monthlong teachers' strike—the fourth since 1980 (Lipman, 2004).

Less than a month after Bennett's visit, however, Mayor Washington suddenly died. His loss demoralized reformers at first, though it also lent passion to the continued construction of the civic coalition for school reform he had championed. It included school reform activists, community organizers, business interests, and foundations. The combination of elite and grassroots reformers, of money sources, and of groups with professional school reform expertise formed a significant action space. Within this space, over the course of the next year, the coalition helped secure passage by the Illinois legislature of the landmark 1988 school reform act.

The 1988 coalition was inspired by both emerging corporate ideology and grassroots organizing culture. It aimed, on the one hand, to make the system smarter, particularly with respect to money; and it aimed, on the other hand, to empower the system's core constituents, especially parents. The law enhanced the authority of the business-dominated School Finance Authority (SFA), founded a decade earlier as part of a bankruptcy rescue operation, and it established a School Board Nominating Committee to constrain the century-old power of the mayor to appoint board members. It also established elected local school councils (LSCs) in every Chicago school. Composed of a majority of elected parents and community members, plus a minority of teachers, the LSCs were granted significant budgetary authority under the new law—namely, control of discretionary federal dollars passed through the state, averaging between half and three-quarters of a million dollars per school. The LSCs were also granted a significant degree of academic oversight, namely the authority to review and approve the annual school improvement plans the law mandated. Finally, the LSCs were granted the power to hire principals on four-year performance contracts, and to fire them if their performance proved unsatisfactory. Principals already in place lost their tenure under the law, though all principals gained more authority in hiring teachers and other staff (Hess, 1991; Shipps, 2003, 2006; Shipps, Kahne, & Smylie, 1999).

The advent of the LSCs in Chicago was heralded nationally as an assault on bureaucratic stagnation in big-city schooling (Shipps et al., 1999). But it is important to note that the strategy embodied distinctly different theories of action. Community advocates within the 1988 coalition viewed both the LSCs and the heightened powers of the SFA as mechanisms for community control of schooling, and a bulwark against the reassertion of bureaucratic and mayoral control. However, corporate advocates within the coalition viewed the LSCs as mechanisms for "customer-oriented business planning," and saw a more powerful SFA as a kind of corporate board (Shipps, 2003, p. 20). Such differences in theory of action within a coalition (though, on one level, a valuable outcome of negotiation) often lead to later splits, and such would prove to be the case here. In fact, a newly recentralized, but also reinvigorated, Chicago Public Schools would soon emerge, one more closely aligned with the vision of the corporate interests.

Still a successful coalition, however fractious, has momentum, and this one had a number of achievements. For example, it produced the $98.4 million Chicago Annenberg Challenge (CAC), one of the first Annenberg-backed projects to launch. In chapter 5, we offer a close-up story of the CAC. Here, we merely point out that it was launched within an action space the coalition expected to last, and it sank within another one for which it was badly suited. (We will discuss that quick shift of action space in the next section of this chapter.)

Meanwhile, other achievements of the 1988 coalition proved more enduring. One is easy to overlook but has proved crucial to later school development in Chicago. The 1988 reform introduced a novel combination for Chicago of school-level control of discretionary funding, LSC principal hiring, and annual school-level planning; and this combination diversified Chicago schooling over time—changing a lockstep and leaden system. New reform arguments and idiosyncratic theories of action took hold across Chicago in the years that followed (Bryk, Sebring, Allensworth, Luppescu, & Easton, 2010; Hess, 1991; Shipps et al., 1999). Those who imagine singular and definitive solutions to the problems of urban schooling might regard such diversity as problematic. Others, however, take a longer view. David Tyack and Larry Cuban (1995), for example, see the "tinkering" characteristic of such environments as conducive to achieving well-grounded reform. This only happens, however, under conditions that allow for the systematic study of innovations. As it turned out, the 1988 coalition also helped to establish such conditions, with the creation in 1990 of the Consortium on Chicago School Research (CCSR) at the University of Chicago. CCSR has continued ever since to supply Chicago schooling with independent and technically strong studies that are developed in collaboration with the Chicago Public Schools and used to guide ongoing reform efforts. The 1988 coalition also played an important role in the development of an independent newsmagazine focused on school reform. Published in both English and Spanish, and backed up by online guides to schools and links to CCSR as well as other sources of information, *Catalyst Chicago* is a venture of the faith-based Community Renewal Society. Founded in 1882, the society is emblematic of a Chicago civic infrastructure dedicated to social justice, built originally on settlement house activity, then strengthened through Depression-era organizing and the civil rights movement—an exemplar of what we call connection. Reaching a broader audience than CCSR, and especially attuned to neighborhood interests, *Catalyst Chicago* is an unusual organ of grassroots civic capacity.

A Second Action Space Forms

Even as the 1988 coalition was developing, a countercoalition surfaced in Chicago, trumpeting a different set of arguments and professing (to the reform community, though not to the public at large, as we will see) the need for a different action space. Mayor Richard M. Daley, first elected in 1989, was dubious about both the value of local school councils and the need for a School Finance Authority. And he was continually annoyed by the School Board Nominating Committee's propensity, in his view, to send him unqualified nominees (Shipps, 2003). Furthermore, he thought the CPS central office *could* be made to work efficiently and well—William Bennett, the Annenberg Challenge, and all other detractors notwithstanding. The key would be placing it under more direct mayoral authority and ensuring that it followed good business practices. It was the latter part of this claim that carried the most political weight locally, but it was the argument about mayoral control that gained national attention and proved influential in Cleveland, Detroit, New York, Philadelphia (briefly), Baltimore, Providence, Washington, DC, and elsewhere.

In 1995 this countercoalition convinced the Illinois legislature to pass a second Chicago school reform act. Coming just seven years after the decentralization law, the new law recentralized Chicago schooling—though in a way quite different than before, and with considerably more efficiency. Daley became the second big-city mayor in modern times (after Boston's) to assume effective control of the city's school system. Under the terms of the new law, the School Finance Authority was suspended and the School Board Nominating Committee abolished. The mayor gained the right to choose directly and without oversight a five-person board and its president, as well as a *chief executive officer*. This CEO replaced the more familiar *superintendent*, a terminological shift that was meant to reflect a change from early twentieth-century business influences to late twentieth-century ones. Under the 1995 law, which remains in effect, the CEO of the Chicago Public Schools sets the course of study for the system and oversees all schools—with the power to identify failing schools, to intervene in their operations in unprecedented ways, to put them on probation, or to reconstitute them (requiring all staff to reapply for their jobs and face termination). The local school councils were preserved under the new law, though it specified that the CEO may dissolve an LSC as part of reconstitution, and may evaluate and terminate principals independent of LSC wishes. The new law also froze the amount of discretionary funding that LSCs control at 1994 levels, reserving the rest for central management. Moreover, by consolidating previously separate and categorical funding streams, the law handed central management unprecedented fiscal clout (though, as in 1988, no new monies overall) (Shipps, 2003; Shipps et al., 1999).

Mayor Daley sold the new law as merely an adjustment to the 1988 law, and as a result, the public for the most part perceived continuity rather than discontinuity in the new policy system. After all, both the 1988 and the 1995 laws served to legitimate Chicago schooling in the wake of Bennett's excoriating remark. Both confronted dramatically the discouraging belief that Chicago public schooling was incorrigible, and both were perceived as making schooling more accountable—in the first case to parents and community, in the second to the mayor (Shipps et al., 1999). But Mayor Daley clearly wanted a different action space than the one he had inherited, and he explicitly let the reform community know as much, especially the foundations. He appointed a corporate-style board chaired by his chief of staff, Gerry Chico, and appointed his budget director, Paul Vallas, as CEO. Vallas became the first of what would become a string of big-city school leaders across the United States with little or no previous experience as professional educators. Today, some of the nation's largest school systems have or recently have had such leaders—including Washington, DC, New York, San Diego, Seattle, and Los Angeles. Collectively they have challenged (though hardly routed—even in Chicago, it would turn out) a century-old conception that top district leaders need substantial experience in teaching and school leadership. Derived from the encouraging belief that business can show the way to school reform, the new conception holds that managerial experience in general trumps educational experience—and indeed, that managerial experience in schooling alone may actually be detrimental in a big-city school leader.

Surprising skeptics, Vallas got the operations of the Chicago Public Schools to run accountably for the first time in decades and promoted the fact adroitly, thereby improving public confidence in the schools nearly immediately. He outsourced many service operations—taking advantage of a feature of the new law that lifted all restrictions on outsourcing. This set an additional precedent for other places, and not incidentally gave other sectors of Chicago's economy tangible interests in the school system's success (Shipps et al., 1999). Vallas proved a precedent setter too in his scorn for what he called "social promotion," though the way Chicago measured readiness for grade promotion during his administration had serious psychometric flaws—including a disconnect between the city's curriculum and its high-stakes tests (Shipps, 2003). Finally, Vallas introduced a continuum of district-school relations based on these same test scores. Some high-performing schools were largely free of district control, the next 60 percent were required to implement mandated curricula, and the final 20 to 25 percent were put on probation. This would prove a precedent for the sanctions built into the federal education law called No Child Left Behind, as well as for innovations in other school districts.

Vallas was CEO for six years—a long run among district chiefs—but then he ran out of political steam. Poor results for both the probation/reconstitution scheme and the student retention policy—studied by the Consortium on Chicago School Reseach and reported by *Catalyst Chicago*—played a role in his departure, as did poor relations with the Chicago Teachers Union and the political toll over time of his own combative style (Hendrie, 1999; Johnston, 2001; Shipps, 2006). He left to pursue a campaign for governor of Illinois, though he lost in the Democratic primary. The action space for Chicago school reform did not, however, deflate in his absence. This is because Mayor Daley owned it, even if

Vallas was for a time its face. Indeed, throughout the Vallas years, it was
Daley who had kept the action space intact. Relieved of School Finance
Authority oversight, he used the city's tax authority to get more money
to the schools, and he used his connections with business elites to lobby
the Illinois legislature for more state aid. He used his strong connections
with the city's unions to gain labor peace—including a four-year contract
with the teacher's union, plus an early renewal. And he used his ties to
the city's financial infrastructure to raise the city's bond rating and enable a significant amount of new school construction, which he used in
turn to consolidate grassroots civic support, neighborhood by neighborhood (Shipps, 2003). It may seem merely academic to hold that Daley's
actions in one instance (1995) involved a change of action space, whereas
in another instance (six years later) it did not. But one of the values of
having a theory of action space, with its emphasis, among other things,
on the rise and collapse of particular constellations of reform effort, is
that it calls attention to the role in reform of both continuity and discontinuity. Reform is, after all, situated on a continuum between conserva-
tion and revolution, but reformers often need, for various reasons, to emphasize one pole over the other.

On the other hand, reformers have different levers they can use within
the same action space. Thus, in this instance, although Daley kept the
resources flowing and the action space intact, he also recalibrated the
tenor of Chicago school reform through his appointment of Arne Duncan as the Chicago Public Schools' next CEO. Duncan had been Vallas's deputy, but the mayor likely knew that he would bring his own fresh
perspective to the top job. At the time of his appointment, Duncan was
an articulate and affable thirty-six-year-old former professional basket-
ball player (Australian league), as well as Harvard graduate who had for
years assisted his mother at her after-school program serving African-
American youth on Chicago's south side. Sure enough, Duncan took
a more conciliatory stance as CEO toward the LSCs, exercised somewhat more caution in the use and interpretation of testing, and showed
more interest in alliances with civic organizations (both grassroots and
elite). He also introduced new reform arguments into the theory of action. A number of these arguments involved changes in the district's professional capacity, or what Duncan and his allies called its human capital systems. Some changes involved drawing on new sources of talent
through relationships with "new reform" organizations like New Lead-

ers for New Schools, Teach for America, and the New Teacher Project.[1] Others involved efforts to improve talent already in place—for example, working with the New Teacher Center to mentor early-career teachers or with the National Board for Professional Teaching Standards (NBPTS) to develop a pool of outstanding veteran teaching talent in the city. Indeed, the Duncan administration increased dramatically the number of teachers in Chicago certified by the NBPTS (to 863 by 2008, working in nearly half of Chicago's schools—the largest concentration anywhere working with poor students) (Hart, Sporte, Ponisciak, Stevens, & Cambronne, 2008; Williams & Forte, 2008). In many of these talent development efforts, the Chicago Public Schools teamed with the innovative Chicago Public Education Fund (see chapter 5). In filling higher leadership positions in his administration, Duncan also abandoned what Charles Payne calls the long-established tradition in the city of rewarding "cronyism, butt-kissing, and time-serving," favoring principals who had demonstrated success in turning around challenging schools (2010, p. 177). The problem, however, as Payne points out, is that some of these turnarounds were not yet strong enough to weather a leadership change.

Another argument characteristic of the Duncan years involved the creation of new schools to replace failing ones—across three major initiatives. The first involved a major grant from the Bill and Melinda Gates Foundation to create small high schools in the city, part of a $2 billion national effort. The Gates small-schools theory of action held—too simplistically, it would turn out—that the personalization small schools afford (to know students well) fosters academic engagement, which leads in turn to high achievement (Toch, 2003). An entity called the Chicago High School Redesign Initiative (CHSRI) served as intermediary between the Chicago Public Schools and the Gates Foundation (and other collaborating foundations). Beginning in 2001, CHSRI opened three dozen new small high schools, and researchers from the Consortium on Chicago School Research closely studied the effort. Indeed, as the theory of action would have it, the researchers found that juniors in the CHSRI schools (after three years of experience with the innovation) experienced a statistically higher level of what CCSR calls "academic press"—greater expectation to engage and learn—in combination with more academic and social support. However, they also found that while smaller school size appeared to contribute to collegiality and collaboration among teachers in a sample of the schools studied qualitatively, the collaboration was typically focused on helping each other deal with everyday routines and responsibilities. Rarely was it used to address core instructional practices or to work on improving them. Smallness alone is insufficient for instructional reform, the researchers concluded, though they also pronounced the effort promising (Kahne, Sporte, de la Torre, & Easton, 2006; Stevens & Kahne, 2006).

A second new-schools initiative, launched in 2004, combined the Gates Foundation argument concerning the power of personalization with one articulated by Paul Hill (2006) and others concerning the value of a *portfolio* approach to school governance. Like funds in a portfolio of investments, schools that failed to meet goals should, this argument holds, be replaced by better performing ones. It's not size alone that matters, but size plus choice. This time, the initiative involved elementary as well as high schools. Mayor Daley announced the initiative at the elite Commercial Club of Chicago as an effort to shake up the system. Leaders from business, education, philanthropy, and community activism were at his side in a major demonstration of Chicago's consolidated culture (Gewertz, 2004). Called Renaissance 2010, the initiative set out to close sixty failing and under-enrolled elementary and secondary schools, and to open a hundred new autonomous high-performance small schools of choice by 2010. By the end of 2008, it had opened seventy-five (and closed forty-four). Many of the new schools had extended days and years, and most were run as charters or by educational management organizations on contract.

Renaissance 2010 attracted lots of critics—particularly among educators and families affected by the school closings. These were on the predominantly poor south and west sides of the city and especially concentrated in neighborhoods also affected by the demolition of public housing (Kelleher, 2004). Some of the critics described Renaissance 2010 as an effort by the city to gentrify neighborhoods by first closing their schools, then replacing them with a choice system that middle-class families are best equipped to navigate (Lipman, 2005). This characterization of the portfolio argument would later migrate to other places, where it also animated opposition—for example, Washington, DC, Newark, Philadelphia (as we discuss in chapter 4), and New York City (chapter 6). *Catalyst Chicago* documented the difficulties associated with the introduction of school choice in a school district with limited busing and a long history of neighborhood school assignment (Myers, 2008). Some also criticized

Renaissance 2010 for further eroding the civic capacity achieved through local school councils (charter schools and contract schools in Chicago are not required to have LSCs) (Lipman, 2005).

In a 2009 paper, researchers from the Consortium on Chicago School Research examined the impact on students displaced by school closings. Most of these students ended up in schools just as academically weak as the ones that had closed. However, the researchers also found some evidence supporting the rationale for the effort. Although only 6 percent of the displaced students they studied (using a comparison group of similar students whose schools did not close) ended up in the top quartile of Chicago schools, these students scored higher on tests a year later than displaced students who enrolled in other receiving schools. The price they paid for this advantage, however, was to travel farther to school each day, to and through other neighborhoods—a sometimes dangerous practice in a city full of gang boundaries (de la Torre & Gwynne, 2009).

By 2007, resistance to the school closing strategy had led the district to emphasize a "turnaround" strategy instead—one that keeps the students in place but displaces the principal and some or all of the teachers (de la Torre et al., 2013; Paulson, 2008). A CCSR study compared these schools with similar schools not "turned around" and found that elementary and middle schools made significant improvements in test scores over time (though not at first); while high schools did not show significant improvements in the measures used at that level, namely decreased absences and increased numbers of ninth graders on track to graduate. Still, the researchers reported that a small number of later high school turnaround efforts, which paid greater attention to capacity building, showed signs of improvement over their earlier counterparts (de la Torre, Allensworth, Jagesic, Sebastian, Salmonowicz, Meyers, and Gerdeman, 2013). These are the kind of findings that researchers call "mixed," and that reformers who had hoped for the success of particular strategies often find disappointing—indeed, disappointing enough to draw them toward different arguments. We would say, by contrast, that such findings are helpful—in this case, alerting reformers to the differential impact of the small-schools argument, prompting a closer look at outliers, and encouraging some tinkering with theories of action. Such a reaction is all the more possible under circumstances where local research capacity stays intact.[2]

When Arne Duncan was tapped to be President Barack Obama's secretary of education, he had served as CEO of the Chicago Public Schools for seven years—one year longer than Paul Vallas. The specific arguments that Duncan carried to Washington are reflected in the evaluation criteria for his and the president's Race to the Top competition among states: adoption of proposed national standards and assessments (worth 70 points in the competition); creation of policy conditions friendly to the formation of charter schools (40 points); "turning around" low-achieving schools (50 points); improving teacher and principal effectiveness (138 points); and improving data systems (47 points) (US Department of Education, 2009). In instituting this program, Duncan did his best to dispel a discouraging belief that money doesn't matter, calling the Race to the Top competition American school reform's "moonshot" (McNeil, 2009).

Back in Chicago, Mayor Daley moved promptly to replace Duncan with Ron Huberman, the thirty-seven-year-old chief of the Chicago Transit Authority—yes, the transit authority. Huberman was also Daley's former chief of staff and a former member of the Chicago Police Department. As chief of staff, Huberman had pressed for the adoption of private-sector and data-focused performance management systems by all the city's agencies and departments; as transit chief, he introduced substantial efficiencies to a formerly low-performing system. However, a number of prominent Chicagoans—including the president of the Chicago Teachers Union, and civil rights leader Jesse Jackson—criticized Huberman's appointment on the basis of his lack of experience as an educator (Gewertz, 2009). In his first year as CEO, Huberman scaled back Renaissance 2010 and for the first time opened new schools only in neighborhoods saturated by underperforming old ones (Myers, 2009). He also put even greater emphasis on the human capital strategy that his predecessor had introduced—investing especially in the selection and retention of high-quality principals and teachers. Finally, he promoted data-focused school management and, with substantial funding from the Dell Family Foundation, introduced a Chicago "dashboard" data retrieval system for principals (Harris, 2010a, 2010b). In these initiatives, he was following powerful new arguments in the air, sown by an encouraging belief in the usefulness of business strategies in education. Huberman remained in the job for less than two years, however. He left in late 2010, not long after Mayor Daley's surprising announcement that he would not run again for reelection. The city schools had by then experienced several changes of CEO, but all within the continuity provided by a single mayor in charge for more than twenty years. In the days following the mayor's announcement, one could almost sense a collective shiver in the city's consolidated culture.

Action Space Thrown off Balance

Ordinarily, action space punctuates longer periods of normal operations. But the tug of encouraging beliefs is powerful today, and the need for school improvement in Chicago still manifest—even a quarter century after William Bennett's blast. Thus it seemed clear that Daley's successor as mayor—Rahm Emanuel, a former Chicago congressman who moved back to the city following three years as President Obama's White House chief of staff—would seek to keep the Chicago action space inflated. And indeed he did, despite facing a billion-dollar budget gap and an overall district enrollment decline of thirty-four thousand students since 2003 (*Chicago Tribune*, 2012). Emanuel broke with Daley tradition, however, by appointing an experienced educator and non-Chicagoan, Haitian-born Jean-Claude Brizard, as the city's next schools CEO, and he also upset the Daley tradition of cooperating with the teacher's union. Indeed, the rancorous relationship between Mayor Emanuel and the Chicago Teachers Union (CTU) led in September 2012 to the first Chicago teachers' strike in twenty-five years. The strike focused at one level on the classic issues of pay and the length of the workday, but at a deeper level on teacher evaluation, school closures, the role of charter schooling in the city, and other reform matters (Sawchuk, 2012). Poor relations between the combative Emanuel and assertive CTU president Karen Lewis (who called the mayor a liar and a bully) also played a role (Davey, 2012). During the strike, the two fought each other in the press, while Brizard—with whom Emanuel reportedly had a strained relationship—kept a low profile, and interim chief education officer Barbara Byrd-Bennett negotiated with the teachers (Ahmed-Ullah & Mack, 2012; Rossi & Fitzpatrick, 2012). A week after the strike was settled, Byrd-Bennett replaced Brizard—effectively merging the CEO (executive) and CAO (academic) roles for the first time in seventeen years. African-American, an experienced and reportedly collaboratively minded district superintendent (in Cleveland, Detroit, and New York's Chancellor's District), Byrd-Bennett faced daunting challenges: the budget shortfall, the aftermath of the acrimonious strike, the irascible mayor, and the need to persuade a community deeply distrustful (of CPS) to accept up to 120 school closings (Byrne & Dardick, 2012).

New York City

New York City is the largest and most densely populated city in the United States, with a 2010 census count of 8.2 million people. It is the hub of a megalopolis that runs along the Atlantic coast from southern New Hampshire and Boston on the north to Washington, DC, in the south, and stretches westward to eastern Pennsylvania. In the 1970s and early 1980s, it seemed that this hub might implode through the combined effects of bankruptcy, crime, and general civic despair. By the 1990s, however, the city was faring well as a world capital of finance and headquarters for media, the arts, fashion, and other areas of a globalized economy. When it managed as well to reduce its crime rate dramatically, the city also became one of the world's biggest tourist destinations. Remarkably, all of this survived the terrorist attack of 2001, which killed more than three thousand people. Moreover, the city's core industry, namely finance, survived the intense and worldwide recession that began in 2008—ironically so, given the role that industry had played in causing the recession.

Of special interest to us is the fact that in the first decade of the twenty-first century, New York City's public schools moved from being one of the world's most derided school systems—querulously and opaquely governed—to being an innovative and influential system. It educates nearly 1.2 million students today in close to fifteen hundred schools—an enrollment roughly twice that of Los Angeles Unified, the next biggest US school district, and more than three times that of Chicago.

When we began our work in 1995, New York had thirty-two elected community school district boards overseeing K–8 education, a politically fractious central board of education, and a chancellor appointed by this board to oversee central operations as well as several citywide subdistricts (for high schools, specialized schools, and poorly performing schools). The majority of central board members were appointed by the city's five borough presidents, and the rest by the mayor. The creation of New York City's community school districts in 1970 followed what Diane Ravitch (1974) calls a "school war" between advocates of strong centralized control and those committed to radically decentralized control of schooling. The advocates of centralization included the United Federation of Teachers, which had only won collective bargaining rights in 1962 and was determined to keep them citywide, while the decentralization advocates included community groups rooted in the civil rights movement, for whom having a say in the running and staffing of their neighborhood schools was a close-to-the-bone issue.

As the community school districts developed, some proved corrupt. Others, while not corrupt, proved inefficient and ineffectual. One might say that they were unable to tap into the civic resources their communities offered; unable to attract, raise, or sustain high levels of professional capacity; and for both these reasons, unable to beat the odds that poverty had laid on the children they served. A few districts, however, proved atypical in these ways. They also proved influential nationally. Indeed, they were important shapers of several major late twentieth- and early twenty-first-century school reform arguments.

Community School District 13 in Brooklyn, for example, contributed substantially to an argument about school reform that emphasizes tight centralized management, curriculum prescription, a strong focus on test-based accountability, and (in some instances) strong parent and community involvement (Lewis, 2006). The district had a succession of African-American superintendents and associate superintendents who eventually moved on to other important posts—people like Jerome Harris, who became superintendent in Atlanta; Argie Johnson, who became New York's deputy chancellor as well as Chicago's last superintendent (her successor was CEO Paul Vallas); and Beverly Hall, who served as New York deputy chancellor, then as superintendent in both Newark and Atlanta. Hall's long tenure in Atlanta was at first celebrated as an exemplar of what might be called the strong-superintendent argument, and implicitly a refutation of the discouraging idea that big-city school districts are hopeless in terms of boosting student achievement. Later, however, as evidence accumulated that the decade-long rise in Atlanta test scores was substantially due to cheating, Hall's tenure became instead an exemplar of what happens when one presses an argument too hard. State investigators found that the cheating (involving, for example, teachers' and principals' "corrections" of students' answer sheets) was the consequence of unrealistic targets, unreasonable pressure, and "a culture of fear, intimidation, and retaliation" (Bowers, Wilson, & Hyde, 2011, p. 350). For her role in the scandal, Hall was indicted in 2013 on charges including racketeering, theft, and conspiracy (Winerip, 2013).

Yet the strong-superintendent argument has had other successes that have held up. For example, it is the argument that informed the design of another nationally influential New York subdistrict, the Chancellor's

District. This was a citywide collection of some of New York's worst-performing schools, removed from their original community districts in 1995 and run directly by Chancellor Rudy Crew. A retrospective longitudinal comparison of student test-score gains in the Chancellor's District with those of other New York City schools listed by the state as poorly performing showed significant gains for the subdistrict, and well before pressures to raise test scores became as intense and pervasive as they are today (Phenix, Siegel, Zaltsman, & Fruchter, 2004). The Chancellor's District has been replicated in a number of other districts, including twice in Philadelphia, where it registered some success under two different district leaders (Useem, Christman, & Boyd, 2006). And one of the Chancellor's District superintendents, Barbara Byrd-Bennett, would later become CEO of the Chicago Public Schools.

Meanwhile, three other New York subdistricts became influential nationally—all of them associated with the leadership of Anthony Alvarado. Community School District 4 under Alvarado's leadership was the site of an effort beginning in the 1980s to transform what was then New York's lowest-performing district through the creation of innovative small schools sharing large buildings. Sy Fliegel and James MacGuire (1993) tell the story of this effort in *Miracle in East Harlem* (See also Fruchter, 2007). District 4's influence on school reform, both within and beyond the city, depended on its demonstration that urban schools, like many urban households, can effectively share large buildings even when they comprise notably different designs, cultures, and grade levels. This demonstration project became the foundation of New York's small-schools movement.

When Alvarado became chancellor in 1983, he founded a citywide subdistrict called the Alternative School District. It incorporated experimental and specialized schools founded earlier and also became over time a major incubator of small schools—especially small high schools. We look more closely at this district's work and its long-term influence on New York high schooling in chapter 6. This is where we also explore the Annenberg Challenge project in New York City, which began to scale up small-school development.[3] Here we merely point out that by means of visits, writing, the migration of educators, and eventually large-scale government and philanthropic investments, the designs and curricula of these schools influenced high school reform—and to some extent, school reform in general—in Chicago, Philadelphia, Oakland, Boston, Denver, and other districts large and small.

Alvarado's chancellorship was derailed by a scandal after only a year. In 1987, however, he managed to return to a leadership position in New York, this time as superintendent of Community School District 2, which encompassed most of Manhattan below Harlem. In 1988, the district's average achievement level ranked it near the middle of New York's thirty-two community school districts. By the time Alvarado left the district eleven years later, however, it had climbed to second best, behind a substantially middle-class community school district in Queens. Putting aside arguments on either side of the question of whether District 2 can be compared to other school districts given its Manhattan context (and opportunity to amass elite civic capacity and draw young-professional capacity), it is clear that the benefits of the reform that Alvarado and his colleagues launched and sustained in District 2 spread well beyond the district's most advantaged children.[4] Analyses by NYU's Institute for Education and Social Policy found that even the schools with the most disadvantaged students made significant gains, and that the proportion of students reading below the 50th percentile districtwide dropped from 47 percent to 35 percent in the elementary grades and dropped even more dramatically in the middle grades (Fruchter, 2007). Stein, D'Amico, and Resnick (2001) point out, moreover, that even the percentage of students reading in the lowest quartile dropped significantly—indicating that the initiative did more than pick low-hanging fruit.

Beginning with literacy, and later moving on to mathematics, District 2 engaged in international benchmarking. It identified what it took to be best teaching practices worldwide, then hired people who were able to coach others in these practices. In literacy, it adopted an approach called Balanced Literacy, hiring as consultants many New Zealanders and Australians who had helped develop it (New Zealand Ministry of Education, 1996). Hubbard, Mehan, and Stein (2006) point out, however, that the district's view of adoption in this case was different than the norm—that for the next dozen years, Balanced Literacy in District 2 was regarded as a dynamic and continually evolving project. Hundreds of teachers, principals, and staff developers continually studied children, absorbed influences from diverse expertise in literacy, and—to use Tyack and Cuban's phrase—*tinkered* with instructional design. Indeed, Hubbard and her colleagues say that the success of Balanced Literacy in District 2 was attributable to the fact that it "was negotiated over time, not proclaimed from above" (Tyack and Cuban, 1995, p. 47). The tinkering produced a district-wide instructional culture by accretion, one that proved highly distinctive and also highly directive. Few teachers or schools eluded its influence (Elmore & Burney, 1997b; Ravitch, 2010; Weiner, 2003). It was a culture focused on teacher learning as well as accountable teaching, and its tools were common planning, interclassroom visitation, access to external expertise, critique and reflection, and what Elmore and Burney call the "intentional blurring of the boundaries" between school management and professional development (1997b, p. 8). Alvarado and his lean district staff worked to align all of the district's resources—human and financial—toward the creation of this culture, and their work proved influential within and beyond New York (Elmore & Burney, 1997a). Indeed, in the absence later on of district-wide curriculum designs in New York, the District 2 design became in a majority of schools the default design—an influence that remains strong today. The design also became the blueprint for a notable action space in San Diego—one that collapsed prematurely for a variety of reasons, including the want of the patient rolling out characteristic of District 2 (Cuban & Usdan, 2003; Darling-Hammond, Hightower, Husbands, LaFors, Young, & Christopher, 2005; Hess, 2005b; Hubbard, Mehan, & Stein, 2006).

Despite its success and influence, however—and ironically, also because of its success and influence—District 2 (as Alvarado had shaped it) came to an untimely end. This happened soon after Mayor Michael Bloomberg managed to convince the state legislature in Albany that New York City should follow Chicago and implement mayoral control of schooling. Control in hand, Bloomberg appointed Joel Klein chancellor in 2002. At the time of his appointment, Klein, a former member of the Clinton Justice Department, was CEO of Bertelsmann, Inc. Bloomberg moved the newly named *Department* of Education from 110 Livingston Street in Brooklyn to the Tweed Courthouse, just behind City Hall in Manhattan.[5] In a deliberate contrast with the closed-door culture of 110, the building was outfitted with the corporate bullpen working arrangements favored by the mayor, founder of the financial data and communications company Bloomberg LP. Meanwhile the old board of education was disbanded, and replaced by a thirteen-member Panel for Educational Policy, of whom eight are appointed by the mayor. The distinction between the politically powerful old board and its replacement became firmly established in the public imagination when, in March 2004, the mayor fired two of his own appointees to the panel on the eve of their planned vote against his recommendation to institute a grade-retention policy for third graders (Archer, 2004).

Under Bloomberg and Klein, old fractious school politics abruptly shifted to sleek on-message politics. Blackberries replaced faxes as the principal means of control, and a systematic effort was launched to rout old-boy and old-girl networks. Tweed filled up with people from such fields as investment banking, law, corporate accounting, and management consulting—all eager to play out an encouraging belief about what business can teach education (Herszenhorn, 2004). The impact of their work over nearly a decade was huge. It included a new human capital and talent management system, a data-driven performance system for principals and teachers, and a massive accountability system for the schools themselves. Indeed the pace of change was at least triple that of before, and was accompanied by unprecendented (and *planned*) structural instability.

Tweed also recruited veteran educators, albeit ones of a certain innovative stripe. Some were veterans of the leading community school districts, though most of these stayed only for what turned out to be the phase 1 reforms. Others—more iconoclastic—like Eric Nadelstern who eventually became chief schools officer, were veterans of the Alternative School District. Many of these stayed on to mastermind the phase 2 and phase 3 reforms. Tweed recruited younger educators too, again entrepreneurial ones, who had typically gained their early experiences in the city's most inventive schools and school networks, including those serving the neediest students. Many of these educators found a route through the new, privately funded Leadership Academy into principalships as well as leadership posts within the support organizations that would later develop. Finally, Tweed recruited seasoned innovators who would serve as short-term staff or consultants. There was James Liebman from the Columbia Law School faculty, who oversaw the deep overhaul of accountability systems; Michelle Cahill from the Carnegie Corporation, who partnered with Bob Hughes of the intermediary New Visions for Public Schools to effect a remarkable transformation of New York high schooling (see chapter 6); and Sir Michael Barber, partner at McKinsey and Company, who had been British prime minister Tony Blair's senior advisor on school reform.

In the early days of the Bloomberg action space—or what would later be termed the first phase of Children First—all the city's community school districts and citywide subdistricts were superceded by ten instructional regions plus six regional support centers. The boundaries were drawn such that poverty was not concentrated in particular regions. Instead, every region took a share. This ensured too that professional capacity (which in the old system had been drawn to the more economically prosperous community school districts) was also better distributed—at least at the leadership level. The boundaries were drawn also to minimize civic influences that were perceived to be corrupting ones—for example, neighborhood politics, community school district cultures, and local parent organizations.

Thus District 2 merged with three much poorer districts, and its leadership was charged with spreading the famous District 2 professional capacity from the original 43 schools to an astonishing (and ultimately impossible) 126 more. The district's influence was also pronounced in the city's first-ever citywide adoption of curricula—with Balanced Literacy in the forefront, and literacy and math coaches appointed for every school. This mandate settled uneasily over schools that were used to more curricular autonomy or (depending on their district) less demanding curricula in terms of teacher learning (Gootman, 2004; Gootman & Herszenhorn, 2004). Responding to negative feedback from parents and teachers in some already successful schools, Klein allowed exemptions for schools that could make a good case that they were doing well with other curricula. The exemptions proved a harbinger.

Near the beginning of Bloomberg's second term, and after the relatively short tenures of two successive deputy chancellors for instruction who had championed both the new structures and District 2–inspired mandated curricula, there came an abrupt shift of argument (though not, we would say, of action space). The mayor and the chancellor called it the second phase of Children First, though it would shortly involve the complete dismantling of the first phase. They invited principals to withdraw their schools from the instructional regions and to become "empowerment schools." Nearly a quarter of the city's principals accepted the offer, making their schools collectively the fifth largest school district in the United States (just behind Dade County, Florida). This was not a district in the ordinary sense, however. Principals who signed performance agreements (and thus weakened their own job protection) were promised substantial exemption from system requirements—including curriculum and professional development mandates, scheduling constraints, even attendance at meetings. They also received significant increases in their budgets (with the money subtracted from the regional budgets), and substantially increased discretion in spending. The schools were loosely linked in nongeographical networks of twenty schools each, supported by four-person support teams and backed up by a central service center. Reversing nearly a hundred years of hierarchical management in New York, the principals were given authority to retain, dismiss, and even give cash bonuses to members of their network support teams. For their part, the support teams were urged to "follow up relentlessly when the system doesn't respond or performs unsatisfactorily, and 'filter' or 'block' other requests that may burden principals" (New York City Department of Education, 2006, p. 9). The regions—some of them reeling from the loss of funding as schools withdrew—were urged to reinvent themselves as fee-for-service providers, and efforts were made (with limited success) to revise cumbersome procurement policies so that the newly empowered schools could more easily shop for services.

At about the same time, the city began to introduce a new accountability system. The system featured measures of student achievement against a citywide horizon group with similar demographics; measures of school environment based on attendance as well as parent, teacher, and student surveys; measures of school quality based on reviews by educators trained in an adaptation of English school inspection;[6] and a menu of customizable no-stakes interim assessments. The system also included new tools to help schools understand and act on the data the measures produced. One of these was ARIS (Achievement Reporting and Innovation System), a management information system that cost more than $80 million to build, proved difficult to implement, and ultimately was eclipsed in many schools by more innovative technology. Another was Children First Intensive Inquiry Groups, piloted briefly in the empowerment schools, then rolled out to every school in the city during the 2007–2008 school year (a scale-up pace typical of this action space). In these groups, teachers track over time a specific group of struggling students by means that include monitoring data in ARIS and observing the students in class (Talbert, 2011).

Then, before even a year of the experiment with empowerment had passed, and before the accountability system was fully in place, the mayor announced and Chancellor Klein implemented yet another astonishing change: the dismantlement of the regions. In the spring of 2007, each principal in the city elected one of three alternative support structures: (1) empowerment, (2) a private support provider drawn from a list of approved bidders, or (3) a nongeographical community support organization overseen by one of four former regional superintendents. The latter most resembled the regions, but all of these support organizations were, as the term suggests, *support* providers, not supervisory structures. In a speech to the Partnership for New York City, a group of two hundred CEOs who constitute the city's chamber of commerce and also a major economic investment arm, Klein said that the change was possible because of the "systemwide coherence" and "streamlined management structure" achieved by the first phase of Children First. "Our efforts, then and now," he said—in a blizzard of negatives—are based on four fundamental "rejections": (1) of the idea that challenges to urban education are insurmountable, (2) of the idea that principals should be told what to do rather than given discretion to act as they think best, (3) of the idea that practices of accountability in business are inapplicable to education, and (4) of the idea that reform in education is necessarily incremental. He went on to express his disdain for "tinkering," and framed the changes he was announcing in urgent and tragic terms. "Delay," he said, "is measured in human lives" (Klein, 2007).

The "second phase" characterization of what was actually a complete turnabout seems political spin—an effort to assure stakeholders that an emerging political calculus is actually the unfolding of a master plan. This interpretation is supported by David Herszenhorn's (2006) account of the considerable number of (privately raised) dollars that went into rethinking the premises of the first phase. The discontinuity also seems to have been calculated with the intention of destabilizing the system. Jack Welch, former CEO of General Electric and an advisor to Chancellor Klein, advocates periodic organizational destruction in order to condition the organization to continuous change and to drive out traditionalists (Tichy & Sherman, 1993; Welch, 2005).

On the other hand, as between the later phases in Chicago, examined above, we see more continuity here than discontinuity. Despite a complete overhaul of arguments, the capacities supplying the action space stayed relatively constant in their sources, volume, and characteristics. So did Mayor Bloomberg's and Chancellor Klein's leadership. For example, the action space remained thick throughout with nontraditional professional capacity. At the same time, Tweed remained dismissive of more mundane professional capacity—with targets ranging from the United Federation of Teachers to all but a handful of the city's experienced educational leaders. Similarly, the action space remained thick with elite civic capacity and new sources of money. The philanthropically active Bloomberg and the well-connected Klein applied their considerable drive to the task of ensuring support from foundations and corporations, cultural and artistic institutions, the Partnership for New York City (the site of Klein's speech quoted above), and other elite civic and financial sources. And they raised millions of dollars through a new philanthropic arm of Tweed called the New York City Fund for Public Schools. At the same time, they vastly overhauled the internal accounting systems supporting schools. For example, teachers were accounted for at their actual salary cost rather than as uniform units of cost—in the process, giving principals more budgetary discretion and more incentive to hire young. By contrast, Bloomberg and Klein did little to support or increase grassroots civic capacity. Indeed, they tended to spurn grassroots civic capacity as unsophisticated at best and corrupting at worst. Although they instituted a system of parent coordinators for every school, they also disempowered the community school boards and offices that had been the principal channel for parental voice and participation. Moreover, the continual restructuring of district offices and the geographical diffusion of the support organizations left parents and other community stakeholders confused about who held the power to address their questions, concerns, and grievances. Increasingly, many turned to community organizing as a way to regain an effective voice—a phenomenon we explore in chapter 6.

Mayor Bloomberg was the first New York mayor elected under term limits. However, he used the recession that began in 2008 as a rationale to suspend the limits on a one-time basis. His financial acumen was needed, he argued, to help the city weather the fiscal crisis. Although term limits had been established by direct vote in two successive referenda, the law permitted the city council, with the mayor's signature, to abrogate them. Amid much controversy, the council obliged. During his reelection campaign, Bloomberg emphasized his record in educational reform. He also spent more personal money on the campaign than any American candidate for office at any level had ever before spent—a whopping $90 million. Despite polls in the final days of the campaign that indicated as much as an 18 percent lead for the mayor, he won by only 5 percent. Exit polling reported by the *New York Times* attributed roughly half the votes against him to his manipulation of term limits and his lavish campaign spending (Chen & Barbaro, 2009). A *Times* analysis also claimed that the mayor's loss of two boroughs—Bronx, the poorest, and Brooklyn, the most populous—suggested that he had a more complicated relationship with New Yorkers overall than either he or others had previously realized (Barbaro & Chen, 2009).

Soon after the election, Chancellor Klein announced another radical restructuring of New York schooling. This time the Office of Teaching and Learning—the bureaucracy's instructional arm—was dismantled (Cramer, 2010). The change signified a complete abandonment of the school reform argument that had most distinguished Klein's earliest efforts—namely the development of citywide curricula. This restructuring also expanded the empowerment system to every school—keeping the partner-sponsored networks but eliminating the support organizations headed by former superintendents, which had served as the last outpost of the old districts and regions. It eliminated as well the regional support centers, assigning their functions to the networks, now called Children First Networks. The CEO for empowerment, Eric Nadelstern, became the chief schools officer.

Again, these were all big changes, though ones that left the action space intact in the most important respects—namely, the kinds of capacity that constituted it, and the overall theory of action that informed it. The latter might best be described as creative disruption. It would result in the biggest distinguisher of the Bloomberg action space—namely, the decentralization of New York public education across a vast "portfolio" of schools, some of them charter schools, some of them design-based schools managed by private partners, many of them "co-located" in buildings with other schools, most of them competing for customers within various configurations of family choice (depending on neighborhood and schooling level), each of them stretched to varying degrees of opportunity and peril by an intensely experienced autonomy and accountability, and all of them supported to varying degrees of effectiveness by non–geographically based support networks or privately funded parnerships (Brill, 2011; O'Day, Bitter, & Gomez, 2011; Ravitch, 2010). We will have more to say about the portfolio argument in chapter 4.

In the fall of 2010, Mayor Bloomberg announced Chancellor Klein's resignation. Klein would join Rupert Murdoch's News Corporation, where he hoped to oversee the development of a new educational initiative related to his interest in the ways technology might individualize learning. As it turned out, he also became chief advisor to Murdoch in his dealing with a phone-hacking scandal (Peters, Barbaro, & Hernandez, 2011). Overlooking Nadelstern, Bloomberg chose New York's first female chancellor, Cathleen P. Black, previously the chairwoman of Hearst Magazines. Indeed, her entire career had been spent in publishing. Bloomberg dismissed protests from some educators and community groups that Black's nearly complete absence of educational and governmental experience, or even involvement in educational issues, should disqualify her. His dismissal invoked more fervently than anyone had before the argument that successful big-city school leadership does not require substantial prior educational experience. It is enough, he said, to have had successful large-scale managerial experience in any field. This is an argument rooted in the encouraging belief that business acumen can show the way in education reform. In this case, however, it proved to be not enough. Black lasted only ninety-five days in the grueling job. Afterward, she told the *New York Times* that "it was like having to learn Russian in a weekend, and then give speeches in Russian and speak Russian in budget committee and City Council meetings" (Barbaro, 2011). Black's replacement was longtime deputy mayor Dennis Walcott, who had briefly been a kindergarten teacher, and also—perhaps more significantly—head of New York City's Urban League. He settled comfortably into the Bloomberg action space, though in a lower-key way than had Joel Klein. With the end of Bloomberg's third (and last term) approaching, the whole city wondered—as had Chicago when Daley stepped down—what might come next.

CHAPTER FOUR

Action Space in Context: Philadelphia and the Bay Area

In this chapter, we explore action space over time in two more cities: Philadelphia and the Bay Area. Here, however, we give more emphasis than in chapter 3 to the role played by political and cultural contexts beyond the action space. Our camera goes wider here, so to speak. In particular, we pay attention to the role of the state in school reform and school finance. Of course, the states mattered in our chapter 3 stories about Chicago and New York too, but our storytelling there downplayed them in order to highlight factors like the politics and cultures of the cities themselves and the shifting chemistry of action space. Here we go the other way.[1]

In the United States, education is constitutionally under the control of states and also financially dependent on them. Yet the characteristics of this control and this dependence vary considerably across states. Our Philadelphia and Bay Area stories illustrate two of many possible patterns of variation. Together, however, they illuminate the need for school reform leaders to manage as best they can whatever pattern they encounter—always within the additional constraints of an action space that requires a balance of professional capacity, civic capacity, and money. The stories also demonstrate that this is a very challenging task even for the bravest and most clear-eyed reformers.

Philadelphia

On our watch, beginning in the mid-1990s, Philadelphia experienced a rapid economic dislocation, a major phase of a long decline—moving

from regional industrial and financial powerhouse to back-office operation for multinational corporations. Within the same time frame, the city
also became a national model for big-city school reform *twice*—with different arguments reigning and different configurations of action space.
Today, some in the city are pushing to create yet a third action space
for school reform, and they have a "blueprint" in mind as described below. At this point, however, it remains unclear whether they will overcome the misgivings of others for whom the earlier two rounds of reform
proved chastening—particularly against the background of a persistent
shortfall of funding for ordinary operations.

The First Action Space

The first action space took shape when Philadelphia still had downtown
corporate headquarters, and corporate leaders joined Mayor Ed Rendell in recruiting David Hornbeck to be the city's new superintendent of
schools. He succeeded Constance Clayton, a district insider whose super-
intendency had lasted more than a decade. By contrast, Hornbeck was
very much the outsider, and he was inexperienced in school-district leadership. He was nonetheless highly regarded as a chief state school officer
(Maryland), an educational consultant to the National Business Round-
table, an architect of Kentucky's influential Education Reform Act, and a
national champion of a then waxing argument for school reform focused
on standards-based systemic reform. This argument calls for aligning standards, curriculum, instruction, assessment, and school and district policies; and it advocates the use of rewards and sanctions for educators based
on the performance of their students. Today its influence is pervasive—
from federal law to classroom practice. But then it was still a new argument, untested at the level of a big-city school system. Hornbeck was eager
to make the test. He brought diverse personal experience to the task—not
only as state-level policymaker and policy consultant, but as lawyer, or-
dained minister, longtime youth advocate, and passionate civil rights advocate. More than any other leader we studied, Hornbeck brought a balance
of professional and civic capacity to his reform work. Very importantly
too, he brought considerable expertise in school finance. He not only understood the role of money in creating special opportunity for school reform—or what we call action space—but had a record of championing and
engineering fair funding for ordinary schooling operations. And he saw
the latter as crucial for Philadelphia—indeed, a key objective of reform.

The year before Hornbeck arrived as superintendent, Pennsylvania's Democratic governor, Bob Casey, had frozen state funding for schools, and altered the formula for distributing it so that rural and urban poverty, as well as inadequate tax bases, were no longer taken into account. The change with minor adjustments would stay in place under the next two governors, both Republicans. Meanwhile, Philadelphia grew poorer, and because it serves as its own county, it lacked all access to a metropolitan tax base. By contrast, Pennsylvania's other major city, Pittsburgh, was able to share some costs with Allegheny County. Throughout Hornbeck's tenure as superintendent (and well beyond), a lack of what Hornbeck and other fiscally focused school reformers call *adequate* state funding would bedevil Philadelphia school reform. This is funding measured not just on a per-student basis, but on a weighted basis that takes account of poverty and other special student needs. In a 2009 memoir, Hornbeck complains that Pennsylvania has not only failed over a long period to take account of Philadelphia's exceptional needs but that it also claims falsely that the only problem with available funding is the city's inefficiency in using it (Hornbeck & Conner, 2009).

When Hornbeck became Philadelphia's superintendent in 1994, the vast majority of the district's 215,000 students lived in poverty. Meanwhile, in a pattern highly correlated across schools with the schools' poverty levels, only 15 of 171 elementary schools scored at or above average on nationally normed reading tests; and fewer than 50 percent of students entering high school in 1989 graduated four years later. The city also had the lowest per-pupil funding in the metropolitan region (Corcoran & Christman, 2002). Hornbeck knew that the support of the mayor and of downtown business would not be sufficient to deal with such distress, though he knew it was necessary. Indeed, their support proved persuasive in attracting the support of foundations like the Pew Charitable Trusts and the Annenberg Foundation. In February 1995, Philadelphia became the first announced recipient of an Annenberg Challenge award. The city thereby gained $50 million over five years, plus a pledge by the CEOs of Greater Philadelphia First to raise $100 million more in matching funds. Hornbeck hoped that the new combination of local support and national prominence would catalyze state support on the order of the kind that had advanced systemic reform in Kentucky and Maryland. The Challenge dollars launched a reform effort that Hornbeck called Children Achieving. It aimed, in the words of its action plan, to help "a large proportion" of Philadelphia's young people "achieve at high levels" (School District of Philadelphia, 1995, p. i). The words seem modest given the rhetoric of reform today, but the scope of arguments that Children Achieving incorporated was quite bold—including a call for a massive increase in state funding.

In the end, however, Children Achieving required more professional capacity than the city could easily come by, more civic capacity than it could sustain, and lots more money than it would be able to obtain from the city, state, or private sources—the Annenberg gift and match notwithstanding (Corcoran & Christman, 2002; Corcoran & Foley, 2003; David & Shields, 2001). One obstacle arose early in Hornbeck's tenure: a Republican sweep of the statehouse and both houses of the legislature, installing in Harrisburg both a budget-cutting agenda and a different argument about how to pursue school reform—namely through state-supported vouchers to allow students to attend private schools, plus charters to enable for-profit and nonprofit entities to run privately operated but publically funded schools. A second obstacle developed later: the loss of downtown business support as a consequence of globalization (Corcoran & Christman, 2002). As a Hornbeck associate put it later, "David believed that you could make a social compact with the business community, but he looked up and they were gone" (quoted in Boyd & Christman, 2003, p. 109). Finally, a third obstacle developed gradually: general exasperation with Hornbeck's perceived ineptness in dealing with key constituencies—especially the teacher's union, the city's principals, and the state (Boyd & Christman, 2003). He seemed averse to negotiation, principled to a fault. In fact, he regarded the job he had tackled as a monstrously complex one and expected big fights, though he also expected steadier support and cover from the business community and the politicians who had recruited him. We tell the story of the Children Achieving action space in more detail in chapter 5—both what it attempted and why it collapsed.

A Second Action Space

Children Achieving raised very high expectations even while selling itself as common sense. When common sense proved unreliable, the stage seemed set for a radical shift of argument, and Pennsylvania governor Tom Ridge and the state legislature were ready with one. They argued in the late 1990s that what Philadelphia schooling needed was not reform of the system but abandonment of it, and the substitution of market-based schooling. Ridge steadfastly opposed any increased state funding for Philadelphia, even in the face of Hornbeck's charge that the current state funding formula amounted to racism. Ridge also successfully championed charter schooling, and proposed (three times, though unsuccessfully) a statewide school voucher plan. As increasing financial stress enveloped Philadelphia schooling, the Pennsylvania legislature passed two laws permitting the state to seize control of districts under certain circumstances and to outsource their management (Useem, Christman, & Boyd, 2006). These laws were waiting when Hornbeck threatened to close down the Philadelphia schools rather than cut the budget for Children Achieving. When the school board dealt with a large budget gap in 2000 by cutting his budget, Hornbeck resigned, saying that he would not preside over the dismantling of Children Achieving.

The budget cuts averted the immediate crisis but failed to correct what was clearly a structural deficit, and the specter of state takeover surfaced again in the summer of 2001. In the face of it, a new mayor, John Street—who had supported Hornbeck but also clearly wanted to move beyond the feud with the state—signed a memorandum of understanding with Governor Ridge. It gave the governor the authority to commission an analysis of the district's financial and educational situation. Street did not know at the time that Ridge would ask Edison Schools, a for-profit educational management organization (EMO), to perform the analysis (Boyd & Christman, 2003). By the time Edison delivered its report in October 2001, Ridge had left Pennsylvania to become the first US secretary of homeland security. His successor as governor, Mark Schweiker, issued a takeover plan, based largely on the Edison analysis, that put Edison itself in charge of sixty low-performing schools, as well as many central-office functions. However, the move provoked immediate and substantial grassroots civic backlash. Students were particularly vocal in their opposition. *Education Week* published the photo of a student who had written "not for sale" on her forehead (Gewertz, 2001). The protesting students were joined by the Philadelphia Federation of Teachers, other city unions, parent groups, and some elected officials. The resulting undercurrent of resistance to school "privatization" would persist in Philadelphia for the rest of the decade and beyond.

Although Mayor Street wanted the takeover because of the extra state funding attached to it, he wanted it on more favorable terms. The protests helped him negotiate what was called a "friendly" takeover. A School Reform Commission (SRC) was created in December 2001, with two members appointed by the mayor and three by the governor; the state and the city shifted millions to cover the deficit; and the city issued a $317 million bond (Boyd & Christman, 2003; Christman, Gold, & Herold, 2006).

Governor Schweiker appointed James Nevels as chairman of the SRC. This African-American leader of a multibillion-dollar suburban investment group proved an adept manager of the political turbulence that continued to attend the takeover, orchestrating a demonstration of the commission's independence from the governor with a string of consensus votes. Yet his instinct in the crisis proved emblematic of a closed-door governance style that persisted even after things had calmed down. It kept the peace, but at a cost. It discouraged public conversation and critique concerning reform priorities and strategies, and in the process crimped the development of the kind of civic capacity that can help sustain reform over the long haul (Gold, Simon, Cucchiara, Mitchell, & Riffer, 2007). In effect, it stored up discontent for later.

We date the beginning of the second action space to Nevels's recruitment in 2002 of none other than Chicago's Paul Vallas to be the new Philadelphia superintendent. Together, Vallas and Nevels negotiated a rejection of the Edison plan in favor of a "diverse-providers model." The model involved Edison (in a much reduced role) but other EMOs too, all joining the district itself as managers of a set of Philadelphia's low-performing schools. They would draw in the process on additional per-pupil funding provided by the state. The EMOs collectively managed forty-five elementary and middle schools. This made Philadelphia the site of what was then the nation's largest experiment in privately managed schooling, a fact that attracted much national notice and scrutiny from the education press and policy researchers. Philadelphia was a national model again—despite declining money for ordinary operations and despite, as we mentioned above, an undercurrent of civic dissent.

Three of the EMOs, including Edison, were for-profit companies. Two others were nonprofits with community activist histories, while two more were universities (Temple and the University of Pennsylvania). Of the forty-five EMO schools, Edison managed twenty from the start, and eventually gained two more. Meanwhile, the district—through an entity called the Office of Restructured Schools—directly managed twenty-one low-performing schools. These were academically and demographically similar to the EMO-managed schools, though not as seriously failing.

The district's strategy in the twenty-one "restructured" schools combined leadership team development, ongoing instructional coaching in literacy and math, and coaching in the use of data. In effect, Philadelphia created a competition between the EMO schools and the restructured schools, and used, as a kind of control group, yet another set of schools (dubbed the "sweet 16"), which received only increased funding—no other intervention (Christman et al., 2006; Gill, Zimmer, Christman, & Blanc, 2007; Useem et al., 2006). It is important to note here that families did not choose which school their children attended. Thus the effort was not a demonstration of the argument that would later seize the policy imagination in New York and Chicago (and eventually Philadelphia too)—namely, that big cities should develop a portfolio of different kinds of schools within a choice-based school assignment system (Center on Reinventing Public Education, June 2012; Hess, 2005a; Hill, 2006; Hill, Pierce, & Guthrie, 1997). Moreover, the process of how schools and EMOs were paired was neither transparent nor publicly discussed. The lack of transparency extended also to how the EMOs were assessed, and how one was terminated at the end of the first year (Gold et al., 2007).

Nor was the school assignment process the only vestige of traditional district authority in Vallas's Philadelphia. For example, all schools—including EMO-managed ones—followed the district hiring model, as well as the citywide teachers' contract. They were all subject to Vallas's new zero-tolerance discipline policy and to the K–8 elementary school configuration he initiated (Christman et al., 2006). Most schools also followed the new core curriculum and diagnostic assessments he introduced (Useem et al., 2006). Vallas called the mix of centralizing and decentralizing strategies "thin management." In fact, the EMOs were pleased to be themselves "managed" in some respects. For example, they liked not having to hire their own employees and not having to deal with potential union problems (OAAI, 2007). They also welcomed Vallas's curricula—particularly those EMOs whose own curricular ideas were less developed than Edison's. The Philadelphia Federation of Teachers welcomed the curricula too; they had disliked Hornbeck's expectation that teachers design curriculum themselves in response to the new standards.

As he had in Chicago, Vallas worked hard to instill public confidence in the competence of the district. This had waned in the turmoil of Hornbeck's final years. In this regard, Vallas dismissed the need for Edison to play a role as lead district advisor as originally proposed in the takeover plan. That would be *his* role, he said (Polaneczky, 2002; Useem et al., 2006). Finally, Vallas followed the penchant he had shown in Chicago for irascible top-down decision making—something that jibed well with the closed-door decision making characteristic of the School Reform Commission under Nevels (Christman et al., 2006; Useem et al., 2006).

Meanwhile, the state's accountability system based on standardized test scores, as well as the No Child Left Behind federal policy framework (about which Vallas was notably enthusiastic), exerted considerable centralizing influences too. Researchers from Research for Action, leading a multiyear effort to track the impact of the state takeover in Philadelphia, reported that "what appeared on the surface to be a radical experiment with privatization ended up looking more like a public-private partnership." The "externally managed schools actually became part of the more centralized system in practice" (Useem et al., 2006, p. 16). Indeed, the system under Vallas resembled the one Hornbeck had imagined, albeit with many public-private partnerships in place. The partners went well beyond the EMOs to include numerous groups overseeing the city's charter schools and an unprecedented number of other organizations that became contractors to the city's schools. These ranged from small nonprofits to the Microsoft Corporation. A study conducted by Research for Action on the impact of the state takeover on civic capacity concluded that it had turned stakeholders into consumers, contractors, vendors, and audiences—a range of participation, the researchers noted, that excludes the kind of voice and oversight characteristic of citizenship (Gold et al., 2007).[2] One result was that the next crisis found too few constituents ready to trust the people in charge.

Indeed, the financial crises that had dogged Hornbeck caught up with Vallas too. Just as Children Achieving needed more money than was readily available from either city or state sources, so did a diverse-provider Philadelphia School District (Gold, 2006). The extra state funds that had launched and sustained the work with low-performing schools, plus the bond issue and sale of district property that had defused previous budget crises, had not eliminated the underlying structural deficit (Gold et al., 2007). Still Vallas's announcement in November 2006 of a projected $73 million shortfall took both city and state by surprise, and his reputation for competence was damaged. The deficit also put the governor on the spot—again a Democrat, and none other than former Philadelphia mayor Ed Rendell, who had joined Hornbeck in pressing for more state funding.

Meanwhile, into the budget crisis reprise dropped an evaluation of the diverse-providers model by the Rand Corporation in association with

Research for Action.[3] The report concluded that while student achievement had substantially improved between the 2001–2002 school year
(just before the state takeover) and the 2005–2006 school year, a comparison of these gains with those of a statewide set of low-performing
schools showed no significant difference except in eighth-grade reading
(Gill et al., 2007). As often happens in the outyears following the introduction of a new high-stakes test, nearly everyone was doing better in
Pennsylvania. When the researchers looked for differences within Philadelphia alone, however, they did find an interesting one. They measured
the longitudinal achievement gains between 2001–2002 and 2005–2006
of individual students in the EMO, restructured, and "sweet 16" schools,
then they compared these trends with those of other Philadelphia students.[4] In none of the four years after takeover did the EMO schools
show any statistically significant effects, positive or negative—either in
reading or math. The same was true of the "sweet 16" schools. Only the
district-managed or restructured schools showed effects: statistically significant and positive effects in math for all four years, and in reading for
the first year (Gill et al., 2007).

But evidence is hardly sufficient to unseat an argument once it gains
a hold. Community activists urged the School Reform Commission to
heed this research: Why spend money on contracts that did not boost
student achievement? Others pointed to a broader issue—the number of
outsourcing contracts that the school district had initiated under Vallas.
A quarter of the school district's budget by 2005 was taken up by such
contracts, often issued on a no-bid basis (Gold et al., 2007). Still, the
SRC announced that the contracts with EMOs would be renewed for at
least another year, though at a reduced cost, and they remained largely
in place until the effects of the 2008 recession became apparent.

Early in 2007, Vallas announced that he would be leaving to become
the new state-appointed superintendent of schools for the Recovery District of Louisiana. This special statewide district was established in 2003
to turn around the state's lowest-performing schools. In the wake of
Hurricane Katrina in 2005, the Recovery District absorbed a hundred
New Orleans schools damaged or destroyed by the storm, and became
a demonstration site and talent magnet for reformers pursuing the argument for portfolio management of schools. At a meeting hosted by the
New Schools Venture Fund and New Leaders for New Schools (both major contributors to the effort to remake American schooling on the basis of an entrepreneurial business model), Vallas called New Orleans the

site of the greatest experiment in choice, charters, and the reinvention of what it means to have a school *system* (Hendrie, 2007). In June 2007, James Nevels announced his departure too. He said he thought a new SRC chair should oversee the hiring of a new CEO, though the *Philadelphia Daily News* reported that Governor Rendell had ushered him out (Russ, 2007). Though the city had only briefly experienced mayoral control of its schools, it had now achieved gubernatorial control by a man who had once been mayor.

In his first term, facing a hostile legislature, Rendell managed to get only small funding increases for education, but with a Democratic House in his second term, he had greater success. The result was a new, "targeted" funding formula that increased the state's share of funding for Philadelphia and other high-poverty districts and expanded early childhood education and full-day kindergarten programs. But then the recession hit, seriously crimping the governor's capacity to reach his avowed goal of "adequate" funding for all districts. A 2007 study he had commissioned said that this would take an overall increase of $4.4 billion in funding—including $1 billion for Philadelphia alone (Venkataramanan & Mezzacappa, 2010). Instead of overseeing this expansion of funding, Rendell found himself using federal recovery dollars just to avoid massive cuts. In the process, the actual state share of funding for schools dropped. In an interview with *Philadelphia Notebook* reporters near the end of his second term, Rendell expressed exasperation with this circumstance and complained that both of the candidates vying to succeed him favored some version of vouchers over increased state funding as a solution to the persistent fiscal and achievement shortfalls in Philadelphia. "The problem with vouchers is not that they don't work," Rendell said, "but that they only work for a small percentage of students . . . [and take] the kids with the most focused parents out of the system" (Mezzacappa & Venkataramanan, 2012, p. 20).

In early 2008, Arlene Ackerman became Philadelphia's new school superintendent. She had formerly served as school superintendent in Washington, DC (three years), and San Francisco (five years). In Philadelphia, Ackerman accelerated the chartering efforts of her two immediate predecessors, launching in the process a Renaissance Schools "turnaround" initiative that contracted with private managers like Green Dot America, a union-friendly charter management organization based in Los Angeles, and Philadelphia-based Mastery Charter Schools. As Vallas had done earlier, Ackerman also created the district's own turnaround design to complement—even compete with—the private contractors. Called Promise Academies, the design featured longer school days and calendars, uniforms for students and teachers, and detailed curricula focused on reading and math (Herold, 2010a, 2010b). An eighteen-month interim evaluation of the Renaissance/Promise initiative by Research for Action found positive results. Most notably, student achievement and attendance in the initiative's schools improved to a significantly greater degree than in a set of comparison schools, though the initiative's high schools fared slightly worse. Moreover, there was no statistical difference in achievement or attendance between the district-run Promise Academies and the charter-managed Renaissance Schools (Gold, Norton, Good, & Levin, 2012). Apparently, the ingredients of their early success were available in both sectors.

Despite the draw in these data, however, enrollment in charter schools continued to accelerate in Philadelphia (reaching 25 percent of citywide enrollment by 2011–2012, and projected to increase to 40 percent by 2016–2017). About two-thirds of this enrollment involved the transfer of students from public schools. These transfers, plus an overall decline in the city's population, soon created large amounts of excess space in Philadelphia's public school buildings (whose overall footprint had stayed largely the same since the 1970s) (Penn GSE, 2012). The excess space entailed, of course, real costs—lighting, heating, even to some extent staffing—costs that had to be covered by more thinly spread per-pupil funding. Exacerbating the problem was the fact that the other third of the growth in charter school enrollment involved students transferring from the city's and suburbs' parochial and other private schools. For each charter student residing in Philadelphia, the district had to transfer on average $10,400 of city and state funding—a completely new expense in the case of the private school transfers. Accounting for both the unused space and the new student costs, the Boston Consulting Group (2012) estimated that each charter school student added roughly $7,000 to the district's annual budget. BCG also pointed out that the Renaissance effort ameliorated this added expense significantly by tying the development of some number of charter schools to school closures.

Yet, as had happened previously in Philadelphia, the Renaissance/ Promise initiative's early success was achieved against an increasingly tumultuous fiscal and political crisis. In the 2010–2012 period, following the end of federal recovery funding and the rollback of Rendell's targeted funding formula by his successor, Republican governor Tom Corbett, there were severe budget cuts. The climax of the cutting came in the summer of 2011, when the SRC cut $629 million for the new school year—an unprecedented amount, resulting in many teacher layoffs, including at Promise Academies (Gold et al., 2012).[5] Then in August, the Renaissance champion, Superintendent Arlene Ackerman, resigned. She had clearly been caught by the same structural fiscal and political problem that had dogged her predecessors, Hornbeck and Vallas. Like her predecessors too, she faced criticism of her management style. She was also hurt by a Pulitzer Prize–winning series in the *Philadelphia Inquirer* on violence in the Philadelphia schools (Samuels, 2012).

Call for a Third Action Space

After additional cuts to school budgets and central-office operations in 2011–2012, the Philadelphia School District still faced a projected deficit for 2012–2013 of nearly $300 million. The School Reform Commission (whose members were almost all new) and the chief recovery officer and interim superintendent, Thomas Knudsen (a former gas industry executive), prepared to go to the bond market. To obtain a favorable rate there, they commissioned the Boston Consulting Group (BCG)—one of the world's largest business consultants—to conduct a study of the district's prospects for fiscal recovery *under the presumption of* a school portfolio management system. Then, before the study was released, the district issued a five-year "blueprint" proposing just such a system (School District of Philadelphia, 2012). Associated with school reform in New Orleans, New York City, Denver, Chicago, and some other big cities, the portfolio argument features the following: diverse school designs; school autonomy with thin central management and support by independent networks; full family choice in school assignment; pupil-based funding for all schools (including charters and even private schools in some formulations); and performance-based accountability that involves a regular process of closing down some schools and opening others (Center on Reinventing Public Education, June 2012). Though the district did get a favorable bond rate, the bond nonetheless added another $22 million in annual debt service to district budgets through 2034 (Herold, 2012).

As directed, the BCG laid out the contours of a portfolio system for Philadelphia in August 2012. The report recommended aggressive school closings (forty to fifty schools in the short term, fifteen to twenty more over the next five years); outsourcing of many jobs currently under union contract with the district (especially maintenance); dramatic downsizing and reconfiguration of the central office; and the envelopment of charter schools into a new sort of "system"—one that follows the Renaissance pattern of using charters as a tool for overall educational development in the city. At the same time, the report acknowledged the costs of mounting what we call in this chapter a third prospective action space for Philadelphia school reform. These costs are associated with recruiting and staffing new talent in financial operations, human resource operations, and leadership; the development of a new information technology infrastructure; and the development of new school choice operations, new school accountability operations, and new public information initiatives (Boston Consulting Group, 2012). They likely include as well the costs of continuing design consulting—probably lots of it (the BCG analysis alone cost $5 million, covered largely by the William Penn Foundation) (Mezzacappa, 2012). Kate Shaw, executive director of Research for Action, pointed out in a *Philadelphia Daily News* op-ed article that New York City had spent some $3 billion between 2003 and 2010 on its efforts to build a portfolio system of schools. Where, she asked, would Philadelphia obtain anywhere near this kind of money, given the fact that it faces a projected five-year deficit in ordinary operations of $1.1 billion, according to the BCG's own calculations (Shaw, 2012).

This was among the key questions facing Philadelphia's new superintendent, William Hite, amid continuing resistance to "privatization" (Hangley, 2012; Hing, 2012). Meanwhile, Hite proceeded with the blueprint plan for closing schools—with a startling twenty-three closures announced in early March 2013 (Herold, 2013; Hurdle, 2013). Just two weeks later, the Chicago Public Schools beat this Philadelphia milestone by announcing fifty-four school closures (Rich & Hurdle, 2013).

The Bay Area

The Bay Area is, of course, not a city as Chicago, New York, and Philadelphia are cities. It is instead a region that includes three major cities—San Francisco, Oakland, and San Jose—but also incorporates suburbs, small towns, and rural stretches. Moreover, even in its urban manifestations, with the notable exception of San Francisco, most of the Bay Area seems *new* in the way that much of California does, but Chicago, New York, and Philadelphia emphatically do not. For example, most of the Bay Area is fully reliant on automobiles, characterized largely by single-family and owner-occupied housing, with businesses more dispersed than concentrated, and elite civic capacity less visible than in our other three places. The Bay Area is a metropolitan area, though one without a single city center. One could describe it as an emerging city, though only in some imaginable twenty-first-century sense, pending a prospective shift in the Bay Area or California idea of municipality. Should such a shift occur, it would be comparable to the one that led to the expansion and consolidation of Philadelphia in 1854, or of New York in 1898—though on a far vaster scale.

The Bay Area became one of the places we studied because the Annenberg Challenge funded something called the Bay Area School Reform Collaborative, or BASRC. This novel school reform effort surfaced amid a larger initiative that privileged big cities (the White House announcement of the Challenge had declared the nation's ten largest cities the principal candidates for funding). BASRC directly and successfully challenged that privilege—claiming professional capacity equivalent to or greater than that available in exclusively urban places, substantial access to money for reform, and a civic capacity different from but as potentially powerful as that available in places like Chicago, New York, and Philadelphia.

BASRC pursued a school reform argument that is now more commonly articulated than it was in those days—namely, that school reform requires the assistance of an intermediary organization. The founders of BASRC thought this especially true for California, with its weak and fractional school districts, on the one hand, and impetuous and intrusive state policymaking, on the other. The BASRC action space was conceived as a temporary intermediary organization with special capacity to advance big changes. It aimed to seed the Bay Area with influential schools functioning as professional learning communities, engaged in ongoing inquiry and evidence-based decision making, and networked across the region. Funded in large part by the Hewlett and Annenberg Foundations as one site of the Annenberg Challenge, BASRC raised and regranted more than $100 million between 1996 and 2006.

The California Context

We cannot tell the BASRC story without considerable background information on California. The nation's largest and arguably most culturally influential state may be the most challenging when it comes to hosting a school reform action space. Stanford researchers Susanna Loeb, Anthony Bryk, and Eric Hanushek spell out why in a 2007 report from their study of California education governance and finance. They note, for example, that the California Education Code, which combines state statutes with ballot initiatives affecting education (the latter being frequent in California, and the bluntest of policy instruments), consisted at the time of their research of 1,250 separate articles, contrasted with New York's 115 and Illinois's 60. This outsize code is one consequence of the state's habit of imposing detailed policy prescriptions—whether by legislation, referendum, or executive order—in matters that are generally settled elsewhere with a substantial degree of local discretion. A good example of this is Governor Pete Wilson's decision in the summer of 1996 to channel a hefty budget surplus into a statewide K–3 class-size reduction. Although the move was popular politically, it caused schools throughout the state to scramble for teachers as well as mobile classrooms, and led teachers in poorer communities to move massively and precipitously to higher-paying positions in wealthier districts (Johnston, 1996; CSR Research Consortium, 2002). Another example is the passage in June 1998 of Proposition 227, which suddenly and massively affected the instruction of English language learners in a state that educates a third of the nation's English language learners. In an odd combination of definitive and ambiguous language, the proposition declared that such learners must be taught "overwhelmingly in English, through sheltered/structured English immersion, during a temporary period not normally intended to exceed one year." The result was political consternation, great amounts of confusion, and highly uneven implementation, but—according to evaluators from the American Institutes for Research (2006)—little other practical impact.

An irony of overreaching policy prescription is that its effects can vaporize in millions of necessary (or not) adaptations on the ground. In the process, some stakeholders who see the perverse (or washed-out) effects of mandated reforms become infected with the discouraging belief that reform is pointless, mere churn, and even that state policies generally should be ignored. Why is California prone to overreaching? Loeb, Bryk, and Hanushek (2007) attribute it to a sense on the part of the state's politicians that they need to regulate a system that is substantially state-financed. As with most states, the federal government contributes roughly 10 percent of the education budget in California—

mostly through aid to poverty-impacted districts. An additional 62 percent comes from the state, generated by business and personal income taxes, sales taxes, special taxes, and proceeds from the state lottery. Local property taxes make up the difference—roughly 23 percent of the budget. In California, however, the legislature and governor decide for the most part how local property taxes will be distributed. The purpose of this central control is equalization. Thus property tax increases at the local level do not result in school budget benefits. In most cases, the increased revenue just reduces the state's share of funding. Meanwhile, a third of all school financing in California—regardless of its source—is earmarked for special purposes or categories of students (for example, the funds mentioned above that were earmarked in 1996 for class-size reduction). Only two-thirds of school financing is general purpose—for salaries, building maintenance, supplies, and so on. High salaries (due to the state's high cost of living) plus low general-purpose funds make for a poor margin of discretionary funds, whether for reform or any other purpose. It also makes for some of the worst ratios of staff to students of any state in the United States (EdSource, 2009).

Over the course of the twentieth century, as financing for schools increased in nearly every state, so did the role of state policymaking (Meyer & Scott, 1983). For California, however, the process was less gradual. First, a complex 1970s court case, *Serrano v. Priest*, held that substantial reliance on local property taxes to finance schools violated the state constitution. The state responded to Serrano with formulas to equalize spending across districts. This equalization was accelerated substantially in 1978 with the passage of a statewide referendum (Proposition 13) that severely restricted local taxing authority, rolling back assessments to 1976 levels, then, during a time of substantial inflation, limiting annual increases to 2 percent. Still regarded as politically unassailable for the protection it affords homeowners in a state where real estate values have historically been high, Proposition 13 hitched California schooling to the fluctuating intake of statewide income and sales taxes. During the deep recession that began in 2008, with California unemployment at a sixty-year high of 12.2 percent and taxpayers coping with the fallout of a huge tumble in stock-market valuation, the state had a $24 billion two-year budget gap (Steinhauer, 2009a; Medina, 2011). Since school spending accounts for 37 percent of overall state expenses, the schools took a big hit (Maxwell, 2009; Steinhauer, 2009b).

Although California schools gain more or less automatically in boom times, the gain is shaped in large measure by the political ambitions of governors, who set budgets, and legislators, who enact categorical spending grants. Similarly, drops in funding—as in the searing recession—are apportioned within an overall budget more constrained by mandates than in other places. Meanwhile, the mandates burden spenders and cutters alike with detailed compliance reporting. Furthermore, as policy researcher and policymaker Michael Kirst told education journalist John Merrow for *First to Worst*, his documentary about California school finance, the diminution of funding obligation and spending discretion at the local level has resulted in an erosion of local ownership of schooling. And local ownership is a crucial ingredient of what we call civic capacity for reform (Learning Matters, 2008). Of course, civic capacity affects the maintenance of adequate ordinary operations too.

In its Quality Counts 2009 report card on the states, *Education Week*, using prerecession data, gave California an A– for equity in school finance but an F in spending weighted for regional costs. The state was then eleventh best in the United States in terms of how equally it spread money for schooling, with a differential of only $3,770 between districts at the 5th percentile in per pupil spending and districts at the 95th percentile. However, it spent only $7,571 on average per pupil, which was $2,392 below the national average, $2,216 below Louisiana, $1,064 below Mississippi, $5,493 below New York, and $7,568 below top spending Vermont (Hightower, 2008). When this ranking is adjusted for regional costs, California ranked next to last. When the immediate impact of the *Serrano* decision plus Proposition 13 cut local funding for schools by half, the state rode to the rescue, Kirst told Merrow, but it leveled *down*, not *up*, and created an equity of mediocrity (Learning Matters, 2008).

What California gets for its low funding are low rankings in average student achievement. In the 2011 National Assessment of Educational Progress (NAEP), in eighth-grade math, California earned roughly the same score as West Virginia, Tennessee, New Mexico, Alabama, Mississippi, and Louisiana. Only Washington, DC, was below this pack. It was roughly the same story in the eighth-grade reading results, except Tennessee broke higher. In fourth-grade reading and math, California was again in the bottom pack of states, though the pack was bigger (National Center for Educational Statistics, 2011). Of course, the huge diversity of California often masks such low averages, and California schools and districts make it to best as well as worst lists.

Bay Area Action Space

The Bay Area is a large coastal metropolis encompassing nine counties, some seven thousand square miles, a massive bay (named at one end for San Francisco, at the other for San Pablo), hundreds of municipalities, and even more school districts as we discuss below. It has three major cities: San Francisco, San Jose, and Oakland. In contrast to Greater Los Angeles or the New York metropolitan area, however, none of the cities dominates the region. While San Francisco looms large culturally and is the financial capital of the west, San Jose, as the capital of Silicon Valley, is at least as responsible for the fact that the Bay Area overall has the third highest concentration of Fortune 500 companies in the United States. Meanwhile, Oakland, with its massive shipping business, is no economic slouch, and it is also a major shaper of the Bay Area's spunky urban culture—including its own brand of hip-hop. There are more than 6 million people living in the Bay Area, of whom roughly 3. 4 million are white, 1. 4 million Latino, 1.5 million Asian, and 407 thousand black. Almost two million are foreign-born, and an astonishing 42 percent report living in homes where English is not the only language spoken. This last statistic beats all of our other places, including New York at 37.3 percent (American Community Survey, 2008).[6]

The BASRC founders called themselves an ad hoc group working to create an ad hoc organization. They were not out to create some kind of regional school district. Indeed, the action space they hoped to build was hardly organizational at all in conventional terms. It makes sense to think of the BASRC founders as early social networkers. They imagined that reform organizations and funders, as well as districts and schools across the diverse Bay Area, might develop a common vision for schooling and its improvement, and that they might learn to share their expertise in the service of this vision. They hoped to draw the capacities they would need for action space from the region's passion for innovation, its cultural edginess, its wealth, and its considerable professional talent—educational, technological, and entrepreneurial. They hoped to buffer reform-oriented schools and school leaders from bureaucratic cultures and constraints associated with some Bay Area districts—without actually supplanting the cultures or lifting the constraints. Finally, they wanted to insulate these schools and leaders from what they perceived as an increasingly dysfunctional state policy with its boom-and-bust cycle.[7]

The founders included such veterans of state-level school reform as Merrill Vargo, who would become BASRC director, and former state superintendent Bill Honig; veteran promoters and networkers of school reform like Eric Schaps of the Developmental Studies Center and Amy Gerstein of the Bay Area Coalition of Equitable Schools (a regional branch of Ted Sizer's Coalition of Essential Schools); and reform-involved foundation staff like Ray Bacchetti of the Hewlett Foundation and Eleanor Clement Glass of the San Francisco Foundation. The group was influenced by the perceived failure of major state-led systemic reforms in California during the 1980s and early 1990s to penetrate practice at the level of schools themselves. This failure was captured in a much circulated and discussed article by policy researcher David K. Cohen (1990). It portrays a California teacher he calls Mrs. Oublier, who claims to have been deeply influenced by the state's large-scale effort to reform the teaching of mathematics. The effort had employed statewide standards, textbook revisions, teacher networks, and much professional development assistance. Mrs. Oublier loved it, but as Cohen crouched in the back of her second-grade portable classroom in what he called a dusty corner of southern California, he saw only superficial impact on her teaching. One can loosely translate Mrs. Oublier's name from the French as either *she who forgot* or *she who has been forgotten*. Either way, the name calls attention to the role of deep teacher learning in school reform, and limits on the capacity of state-directed reform to affect it. BASRC director Merrill Vargo had experienced this limit as director in the early 1990s of a state-level reform initiative called the School Restructuring Demonstration Program—better known by its legislative tag SB 1274. Aimed at high schools, the initiative supported such efforts as reorganizing the schools into houses, devising new schedules, and gaining waivers from district or state rules. Judith Warren Little, who studied the project, concludes that in its "preoccupation with structural aspects of reform . . . [it] inadvertently drew attention away from the underlying conditions of teaching and learning that would be required to make the new structures effective" (Little, 1999, p. 39; see also Little & Dorph, 1998).

How better to foster teacher learning? To Vargo and other BASRC founders, organizing for district-directed reform seemed initially as futile as organizing (again) for state-directed reform. The reason is what Vargo calls the "jurisdictional dissonance" of California schooling (Vargo, 2004, p. 577). Over the course of the twentieth century, California, like most other states, pressed for school district consolidation. In 1932, the state had 3,579 separate school districts, by 2005, only 979. Still this vast reduction did not have a proportional impact on jurisdictional dissonance. One reason is that of the 979 districts, 562 consist of elementary schools only, 88 include only high schools, leaving only 329 that are "unified" K–12 (California Department of Education, 2006). Another reason is that at one point in the long history of legislation meant to reduce districts overall, county school districts were empowered to help, though they added still another jurisdictional level. And a third reason is that fast-growth cities like San Jose expanded their municipal boundaries at a pace that school district annexation with its difficult politics simply could not match. Thus, while its older urban counterparts, San Francisco and Oakland, both have citywide unified school districts, the city of San Jose incorporates nineteen school districts—including one that is called San Jose Unified. The result is fractured civic capacity and professional capacity. In the six Bay Area counties that BASRC focused on (including all but the substantially rural Sonoma, Napa, and Solana Counties), there are 118 school districts, which together serve a population one million fewer than New York serves with a single district.

To substitute for weak local and state capacity to lead (or fund) school reform, BASRC set out to become a third-way public education reform action space for the Bay Area. It wanted to work outside jurisdictions and also between them. BASRC's chief tool—at least in the first phase of its work—was the same one that New York would adopt more than a decade later—namely, teacher inquiry groups participating in what BASRC called a "cycle of inquiry." In contrast to New York's 1,500 schools, BASRC worked initially with 233 "member schools," though it focused almost entirely on a subset of 86 of these that were dubbed "leadership schools." These had been selected following a portfolio-based peer review of their capacity to engage in focused school-based inquiry. The leadership schools received supplemental funding of $150 per student, while neither the membership schools nor the forty school districts that signed on to collaborative membership received any funding. Other members of the collaborative included most of the reform support organizations operating in the region (for example, the Bay Area Writing Project, the Developmental Studies Center, and the Bay Area Coalition of Equitable Schools). These too had to undergo peer review of portfolios to gain membership. Those approved gained the opportunity to work on a fee-for-service basis as "support providers" to the leader-

ship schools. BASRC also formed a reform funders group that included
the Stuart Foundation, the San Francisco Foundation, and the Hewlett
Foundation (Jaquith and McLaughlin, 2009).

Various configurations of these participants worked out a vision of
Bay Area reform as equity-oriented, evidence-based, school-focused,
network-supported, and network-accountable. BASRC developed a set
of cross-network activities designed to achieve this vision—for example,
intervisitations and other peer-review activities to foster accountability,
affinity groups to promote cross-network learning, a collaborative assembly for governance and learning, and public advocacy to raise civic
support. Impressive in conception, this infrastructure never functioned
well—a victim of such diverse factors as travel time across the vast region (more significant then than it might be today, given Web 2.0 tools),
a lack of clarity among collaborative participants about their roles and
responsibilities, and a weak commitment overall to the very idea of a regional collaborative for school reform (Jaquith and McLaughlin, 2009).
Thus, phase 1 of BASRC settled down quickly into building and tend-
ing professional learning communities in the leadership schools—a small
canvas relative to a vast landscape. Each school focused on an improvement target (for example, literacy), worked on obtaining or developing
data relevant to meeting the target, and analyzed and acted on the data
in a "cycle of inquiry." These leadership schools were to be demonstra
tion sites for the larger network, suggesting a kind of contagion-based
change model, though the means for spread, as we have suggested, was
weak (McLaughlin & Talbert, 2002; Jaquith & McLaughlin, 2009).

It is useful to consider BASRC's theory of action in light of the three
encouraging beliefs we explored in chapters 1 and 2. The belief that
school reform can redress social inequality was fundamental (Talbert,
Wood, & Lin, 2007). BASRC focused directly on "the achievement gap"
at a time when this phrase—referring to race-based differentials in standardized test scores—was not yet widely in currency. BASRC insisted
on disaggregating school achievement by race some seven years before
the federal education law No Child Left Behind required it. Important
to BASRC, too, was the encouraging belief that school reform can take
useful cues from business. BASRC pressed for the application to school
reform of certain practices of the knowledge-based economy then rap-
idly enveloping the Bay Area. For example, there was the practice that
John Seely Brown, chief scientist at the Xerox Research Center in Palo
Alto, and Estee Solomon Gray portrayed in their now classic 1995 *Fast*

Company article called "The People Are the Company." It tells the story of how Xerox copier repair technicians informally share their knowledge in "communities of practice," and how Xerox, having learned about this from Brown's research, attempted to network these and the other communities of practice.[8] Xerox was joined in such efforts by other corporate pioneers of what is now called knowledge management (Nonaka, 1998; Wenger, McDermott, & Snyder, 2002). They include Hewlett-Packard, whose cofounder William Hewlett helped bankroll BASRC. BASRC assumed that schools can learn to work smarter—as corporations like Xerox and Hewlett-Packard had—by sharing and leveraging the explicit and tacit knowledge they collectively harbor, and by developing school-based and network-based systems for continuous inquiry and evidence-based practice (Vargo, 2004).

BASRC was a progenitor of a school reform argument that would later deeply affect American school reform nearly everywhere—one borrowed from business, honed as a reform strategy in medicine, and accelerated by No Child Left Behind and other federal school reform initiatives. We refer to the systematic use of data (Talbert et al., 2007). Today, the idea of using data to guide reform as well as teaching seems almost mundane, but one of us, Milbrey McLaughlin, recalls vividly a Bay Area teacher in the late 1990s asking her what the word *data* means. It is important to note that in advancing the data argument (which necessarily involves educating educators about what data is and how to weigh it), BASRC addressed more squarely than many later reforms what Ball and Forzani (2007) describe as teaching's inescapably interpretive dynamics. These are the consequence of the fact that teaching happens in a complex set of interactions among the teacher and what he or she knows, students and what they know and need, and content and its challenges (McDonald, 1992; Cohen, 2011). Many reforms wish away these interpretive dynamics as if they were the noise associated with teachers who have been insufficiently motivated and directed. BASRC, by contrast, aimed to inform these interpretive dynamics with data (at a time when teachers were unaccustomed to data) and to tune the dynamics as well to the best available professional knowledge across the region (Vargo, 2004; Talbert et al., 2007).

The Center for Research on the Context of Teaching (CRC) closely followed the development of BASRC's theory of action—not just what it aimed to do but what it designed for and the impact of these designs on practice across two phases of BASRC work. CRC's report on

BASRC's first six years found some success at the school level. The leadership schools outperformed the control group of schools on the statewide basic skills assessment, and those serving large populations of high-poverty students did consistently better on this assessment than did similar schools in the region. However, the leadership schools did not do as well as other Bay Area schools on BASRC's key reform target—closing within-school achievement gaps. For many leadership schools, even three or four years practice with school-based inquiry was insufficient for teachers to master the technical skills involved, or to adopt the norms and mindset essential to effective use of data to improve practice. Meanwhile, the high-poverty leadership schools, pressed by other demands on their time and energies, had too little capacity left to take advantage of BASRC activities and support. And negative context factors intruded: personnel churn, shortage of competent support providers, lack of district support, and the development of a new state accountability index that distracted schools from their original learning goals. In fact, the increase in attention to accountability at state and federal levels proved at times an unhelpful prod toward the kind of accountability BASRC was pushing. Both state and federal policy pushed evidence-based programs but not evidence-based practice (Talbert et al., 2007).

Meanwhile, BASRC's strategy of using the leadership schools as demonstration sites generally failed. While many of these schools opened themselves to visitors and shared their experiences at BASRC events, most never figured out how to "lead," or lacked sufficient time, resources, or other capacity to do so. Nor were "followers" much in evidence. And the communication strategies and structures that BASRC actually put in place remained too underdeveloped to become the knowledge management vehicles BASRC intended them to be. Again, though this was the Bay Area, it was also the pre–Web 2.0 era. Crucially too, the considerable civic capacity of the Bay Area never coalesced around BASRC to a degree proportionate to the money BASRC raised or to the professional capacity it managed to network (McLaughlin & Talbert, 2002). One reason was that advocates of regional economic planning and development had not yet awakened fully to its educational dimensions— except with respect to research universities like Stanford and Berkeley. Another was that in pursuing its intermediate, third-way school reform strategy, BASRC had made itself politically inert.

On the other hand, CRC found that BASRC was not on its own everywhere. For example, there were two BASRC-member districts that matched BASRC's emphasis on an evidence-based learning stance toward reform. There the leadership schools gained power to boost achievement and equity, and also proved influential on other schools—not through contagion, but through the district's mediating efforts. In describing this effect, McLaughlin and Talbert write that the experiences of these districts "move debate beyond centralization/decentralization dichotomies." They highlight the question of "how to be tactical about what decisions are made where and how responsibilities follow"(2003, p. 22). When equity issues are at stake, they suggest, districts may be in most circumstances better positioned than schools themselves or the state to make smart and effective decisions about the distribution of resources. Yet these two districts proved exceptional among BASRC's member districts. Most of the rest were either indifferent to the reform agendas of their BASRC leadership schools—one might say by design, given the BASRC theory of action—or actually functioned as obstacles (McLaughlin & Talbert, 2003).

Beginning in the 2002–2003 school year, BASRC altered its design in order to leverage district professional capacity. This was BASRC phase 2, but as in our Chicago and New York stories, the name somewhat belies the sharpness of shift in theory of action. One factor in the shift was a new emphasis at the Hewlett Foundation on standards-based reform and the role of districts in implementing this. In any case, the shift involved a radical scaling back of regional ambition. BASRC phase 2 focused, after an initially broad reach, on just six "focal" districts, and two to four schools within each. It also emphasized working directly with schools and districts, rather than through other "support providers." Finally, it involved a new core strategy—simultaneous school and district coaching.

The consequences of these changes in direction proved disappointing. Reporting on the results of BASRC phase 2, Porter and Snipes (2006) say that leadership coaching at the district level did not, for the most part, penetrate practice at the school level, and ended prematurely in half the districts. School-level coaching faded even earlier. Predictably, the overall impact on student achievement was negligible: reading achievement in the focal districts improved, though no more than in the comparison districts.

A major factor that weighed against the overall success of phase 2 was BASRC's need to create a new organization from scratch. This was complicated by the time it takes—even across only five districts and

twelve schools—to create a cadre of new coaches and a consistent practice of coaching. Indeed, time was a culprit in many respects: time for
the schools that had not participated in phase 1 to learn the cycle of inquiry and other tools, in the depth to which BASRC aspired; time for the
districts to build an effective data infrastructure as well as what Kath-
ryn Boudett, Elizabeth City, and Richard Murnane (2005) would later
call a data-wise culture; and, finally, time for them also to evolve internal capacity in the form of "knowledge activists," people who know how
to ferry knowledge both ways between district and classroom (Talbert
et al., 2007).[9] Jaquith and McLaughlin conclude that BASRC had an organizational design flaw that bedeviled it in both phase 1 and phase 2: it
was a *temporary* intermediate organization that needed more time than
it had available "to evolve a way of working with schools and districts
that provided both consistency of vision and opportunities for local adaptation" (2009, p. 22). To put this in terms of action space, BASRC was
on its own in dealing with collapse. It had no Chicago or Philadelphia
public school district to fall back on, no mayor to appoint a new reform-
minded leader, no incoming superintendent to carry on.

Even as they document in intimate detail the challenges that BASRC
faced (institutional, technical, organizational, professional, and political), Talbert, Wood, and Lin (2007) maintain, nonetheless, that BASRC
was on the right trajectory. In the end, the researchers point out that
the few schools and the one focal district that actually learned the inquiry practices that BASRC taught (as measured by five years of tracking by survey and observation) also made significant progress on student
outcomes. The Alameda Unified School District (AUSD) in the East
Bay adjacent to Oakland achieved substantially greater improvement
in student outcomes than did the other focal districts, and exceeded
mean gains in language arts and mathematics scores for all other Bay
Area and California districts. Most importantly, given BASRC's mission, AUSD made significant progress in closing the test-score gap between Alameda's socioeconomically disadvantaged students and others, and between its English language learners and others. Success in
closing the latter gap is particularly rare in California. "BASRC's efforts
to leverage and support district reform were inadequate," the researchers write, but this does "not imply that its theory of action about how
districts and schools can improve their performance is wrong" (Talbert
et al., 2007, p. 8).

Still, in 2005 BASRC disappeared—the name, the regional identity, and the action space. It had, after all, intended to disappear, and it was pressed by the Hewlett Foundation to reconstitute itself as a fee-for-service entity following ten years of foundation funding. Today it is known as Pivot Learning Partners—a not-for-profit company with some $7.5 million of revenue in 2012, providing professional support to school districts *statewide* in the form of school coaching, data tools, redesign consulting, and professional development seminars. Merrill Vargo is still in charge, and some other BASRC actors are involved as well. Indeed, the current organization's roots in BASRC are acknowledged on its website and in its annual reports. Other BASRC connections also survived the collapse of the BASRC action space. Inventive practices and tools were honed across Bay Area schools and Bay Area education careers and passed along to others—often without, but happily sometimes with, attribution. But this was, of course, a different kind of leadership than BASRC had intended, individual rather than organizational

Meanwhile, reform amnesia remains endemic in the Bay Area, as elsewhere. For example, a report by the Bay Area Economic Forum, issued in 2006, just a year after BASRC ended, describes a threat to the region. Having long been "a talent magnet, drawing creative, educated people from all over the planet," the report says, the Bay Area finds itself today losing more and more of its foreign-born scientists and engineers to careers in other countries (p. 8). The answer to the problem, it suggests, is to grow native talent, and it recommends that Bay Area schools reduce or eliminate the achievement gap. The report does not suggest how they might do this—whether alone or together—and never mentions BASRC, which had been launched a decade earlier to do exactly this.

CHAPTER FIVE

Learning from Collapse in Philadelphia and Chicago

One of us teaches a course on educational reform called "Why Reform Fails." Mark Smylie begins the course by asking students to read *Dead Reckoning*, a book whose coauthor was a longtime medical examiner in New York City (Baden & Roach, 2001). The centerpiece of the book is an intimate account of an autopsy. The book begins with the line, "A good body bag gives up no clues" (p. 14). Later, as the narrator begins the autopsy, he says to himself, "My mind has to be very clear now." He means *clear of* the potentially distracting and misleading information that the detectives in the room press on him (the body is that of a homicide victim), and *clear about* the framework within which he will make his examination. This is a framework constructed of knowledge from anatomy and the forensic sciences. Smylie asks his students to read this fascinating though grisly text because he wants them to enter his course clear of the tendency of educators to dismiss the learning opportunities provided by failure, and clear about the analytical framework he provides them for engaging in their own reform work and analysis.

We take a similar stance in this chapter. We highlight collapse, give it its due, and lay it out on the table, so to speak, in the form of cases from Chicago and Philadelphia. The cases are accounts of the Annenberg Challenge projects in each city—action space we explored for other purposes and in less detail in chapters 3 and 4 respectively. Here we want to see what can be learned from the collapse of these projects. We think that learning from collapse is foundational to passing on knowledge from one (collapsed) action space to the next. We call this *connection*.

To learn from collapse, we must, paradoxically, steer clear for the moment of connections, just as the medical examiner does. And in this moment we must be clear about our framework. For our purposes, the framework is the theory of action space as an inflatable/collapsible arena, one constructed of money, civic capacity, and professional capacity. A good theory is "a machine to think with," David Olson writes, "a device for organizing and interpreting events with the aim of bringing other questions and other forms of evidence into conjunction" (1994, p. xvii). It narrows what we see now in order that we may discover more later. We use our thinking machine in this chapter to examine and explore collapse, though we are interested too in how action space inflates in the first place and in the connections that may survive collapse. It is this other interest that requires in the end a reattachment to past and future. Thus, at the conclusion of each of our cases, we step back from the table to talk with the detectives.

Philadelphia

From the two-decade sweep of Philadelphia school reform we traversed in chapter 4, we zoom in here on the first action space: David Hornbeck's Children Achieving. As in a nineteenth-century Russian novel, the idealists here sought to do too much all at once. They thought that by moving quickly and broadly, they could create a groundswell of support for change and a steady rise in resources. Instead, they got opposition and apathy. Initial support from the business community evaporated and civic leaders became exasperated with the intractability of the reform plan and of its leader. The massiveness of the reform created fatigue and resistance among teachers and inadvertently disempowered principals. For their part, the reform leaders failed to attend sufficiently to the human capital dimension of reform. Real understanding of what change requires proved rare. Poor implementation proved common. And powerful groups proved unwilling to cooperate with each other. Meanwhile, the city took a major step in a long decline, one that deeply affected the reform's prospects.

Built with great publicity in 1995, the Children Achieving action space collapsed dramatically in the summer of 2000. As a result, we will never know if the reform would have produced the performance gains that its principal architect, Superintendent David Hornbeck, envisioned — namely average student achievement at the proficient level or higher in math, reading, and science in every Philadelphia school by 2008. This seems unlikely, however, given the data trends of the first five years, and the very low starting point—only 29.9 percent of all students scoring at the basic level on the baseline tests (Corcoran & Christman, 2002; Corcoran & Foley, 2003). And even if Children Achieving had survived and met its goal, the goal itself would have been swamped some seven years before its due date by the much higher expectations mandated by No Child Left Behind. This is ironic since Children Achieving was one of the first major reforms to insist on testing all students.

The Children Achieving Strategies

Children Achieving's complicated theory of action incorporated eight strategies, which we explore in turn below. Some of the strategies focused explicitly on raising money, professional capacity, and civic capacity. Others advanced arguments that were then in the air, and still are in the air. Examining the Children Achieving strategies in retrospect, we can better understand why the spectacular action space they helped shape fell so hard. We can see how much the strategies taxed the city's existing professional, civic, and financial resources, and how weak these resources were to begin with. We can also see the gaps that emerged between what was envisioned and what was designed.

FAIR FUNDING.   Children Achieving sought increased funding and a new state funding formula at a time when Philadelphia's tax base was shrinking and state government was coming under the control of a politics gripped by the discouraging idea that money cannot make a difference in urban education. The ensuing struggle between state and city leaders over Philadelphia school finance overwhelmed discussions about the progress of instructional reforms. Hornbeck took a calculated risk in making fair funding a central strategy. He thought that the other strategies would quickly demonstrate their impact in rising test scores and that he could use this evidence to sustain the overall effort before money from the Annenberg Challenge ran out. He counted on the hefty leverage that he thought a comprehensive approach to urban school reform could bring. He had seen that work in both Kentucky and Maryland, where he had previously been a school reform leader (Hornbeck & Conner, 2009). When the leverage failed to materialize in Philadelphia, he pushed hard anyway, even taking the state to court. The moral outrage he expressed in the effort—including only barely veiled charges of racism that enraged the governor—ended up sucking the air out of the Children Achieving action space. It alienated supporters and shut down meaningful discussions between district and state leaders. It made funding the primary focus of the district staff and drained time and energy from the hard work of improving teaching and learning. In the process, it gave those opposed to Children Achieving a way to shift attention from the needs of the schools and children to complaints about the superintendent's leadership style (Corcoran & Christman, 2002). At the same time, however, it highlighted a real problem of inequity, one that remains in place today.

STANDARDS.   The architects of Children Achieving were pioneers of an argument then beginning to sweep the states, one that by the end of the first decade of the twenty-first century had not only fundamentally changed state policy everywhere but had become a central argument of federal policymaking too. It urges the adoption of content standards that define what students should know and be able to do at certain checkpoints in their education (in Children Achieving, at the end of grades 4, 8, and 10, and with respect to core subjects as well as "cross-cutting competencies" like technology and multicultural competence). According to this argument, content standards guide teachers' planning and expectations; are the basis for assessing student performance; and when assessed, motivate all parties (including students themselves) to improve as needed. Children Achieving used standards in both an "empowering" and "controlling" way with respect to teachers. The latter were given more latitude than before about what to teach and how but also were told as never before what learning goals to target. It may seem odd to hear that Philadelphia teachers had never before been told what learning goals to target, but the oddness is an artifact of the impact of the standards argument on American schooling over the last twenty years. Though it hardly seems possible now, it was indeed once common for schools, school districts, and states to devise curriculum without specifying learning outcomes, and even without expecting that the curriculum would have a substantial impact on *all* students' learning.

The process used to create the Philadelphia standards was inclusive and brought together teachers, administrators, parents, principals, and community members who served on committees that met over several months before reaching consensus and presenting their work for school board approval. As the committees worked, their members learned much about other efforts across the country to promote standards-based education and about the implications of standards for school and classroom practices. In the process they became committed to the standards strategy. However, the committees were disbanded upon completion of the standards documents and the district never capitalized on their members' knowledge, advocacy, or leadership. Most teachers ended up using the new standards merely as checklists to monitor the content they covered, rather than as guides for their detailed planning and frames for their expectations regarding student performance. Indeed, many teachers said they found the standards too general to guide teaching in any serious way. Rather than feeling empowered, they felt confounded by the standards or even abandoned in terms of the teaching direction they felt they needed.

To its credit, the district heard this complaint and responded by developing curriculum frameworks. These articulated the instructional theory underlying the standards and provided examples of how to enact the theory, including sample activities and model units.[1] The recommended practices, however, did not always rest on solid evidence of effectiveness. Moreover, they made overconfident assumptions about teachers' knowledge of subject matter and their pedagogical skills—including, crucially, their skills in classroom management. Researchers evaluating the reform found that the frameworks were useful for teachers who already held high expectations for their students, who were competent in classroom management, and who also had other exposure to instructional innovation. But the majority of teachers the evaluators studied did not fit this profile, and for these teachers, the framework proved a weak spur to improvement (Corcoran & Christman, 2002).

ACCOUNTABILITY. Children Achieving's accountability strategy launched a major cultural shift in Philadelphia schooling. It focused everyone's attention on student achievement and school improvement. It provided incentives for school staff to seek out and adapt innovations that they might have otherwise ignored or resisted. Initially it also satisfied business, government, and other civic leaders' insistence that the district make data about student performance accessible to the public. At the core of the accountability strategy were biennial school performance targets with accompanying rewards and sanctions (cash versus interventions). Something called the Performance Responsibility Index (PRI) was used to set these targets and track each school's record in meeting them. It was a forerunner of the accountability indexes that would later become ubiquitous when mandated by the federal education law called No Child Left Behind (NCLB). The PRI combined several indicators of performance, including promotion rate to the next grade level in elementary and secondary schools; proportion of ninth-grade students graduating from high school in four years; student and teacher attendance; and math, science, and reading scores on a standardized test called the Stanford Achievement Test, ninth edition (SAT-9). Children Achieving also introduced one of the most inclusive testing programs in the United States, as if anticipating NCLB. It included nearly all students, even those who were lowest-performing and those with learning difficulties and language differences. Indeed, from 1996 to 1999, Philadelphia increased by 16 percent the proportion of eligible students it tested, yet nonetheless made some performance gains—a notable achievement. In those days, it was common for schools and school districts to increase average test scores by excluding many students from the testing.

Despite some success, however, the accountability strategy did not promote a student-focused, district-wide culture of continuous improvement, as the Children Achieving reformers hoped it would. One problem was that the SAT-9, an off-the-shelf test, was not constructed to align with the new Philadelphia standards. Using it nonetheless as the primary measure of student performance caused teachers—on quite rational grounds—to teach to the test rather than to the standards, and of course it oriented whatever learning communities developed in response to the accountability strategy in this same direction. Exacerbating this limitation on the test's validity, Philadelphia used the same form of the SAT-9 each year. Despite strong efforts by the district to maintain test security, researchers studying Children Achieving found copies of the test in circulation within the schools (Corcoran & Foley, 2003). Meanwhile, the PRI had serious flaws too. One was that it measured only cross-sectional progress in student achievement (for example, how fourth-grade scores this year compare to those from last year), rather than individual students' learning gains from one year to the next. Thus it took no account of students' backgrounds or their entering levels of achievement, and yielded little benefit in terms of cuing instruction for individual students. This flaw was typical of early accountability systems and has only recently begun to disappear as states have moved toward what are called value-added assessment systems (Ballou, Sanders, & Wright, 2004; Hill,

Kapitula, & Umland, 2011). Second, the PRI failed the transparency test—a common occurrence among indexes today as well. The complex calculus it used to determine targets and whether schools met them was not easily understood by parents or the public, and educators perceived a false precision in it. Indeed, the problem proved more than a matter of perception. The increase on the PRI required to reach the improvement targets set for schools was often smaller than the statistical error present in the calculations of the index. In other words, schools might fail to reach their targets or might surpass them because of statistical flukes. Finally, the PRI biennial timetable was flawed. It left too little time for schools to implement significant reforms in curriculum and instruction. Schools received their first-year (of the cycle) PRI scores at the beginning of the second year, but they then had only seven months before students were tested again. Meanwhile, their second-year budgets were already set, and the summer professional development period was over. The short time frame for corrective action reinforced the tendency to focus on test preparation as the best strategy for reaching the PRI target (Corcoran & Christman, 2002).

SUPPORT FOR EDUCATORS.   This started out as one of Children Achieving's major strategies but lost out in a crowded field of them, and in the face of enormous tension between the Philadelphia Federation of Teachers and the central office. Evaluators studying Children Achieving reported that "in four years of meeting with and interviewing central-office staff and PFT representatives, we seldom heard positive comments from members of either group about the other, and frequently encountered distorted interpretations of the other party's motives" (Corcoran & Foley, 2003, p. 109).

Although Children Achieving increased professional development opportunities for Philadelphia teachers, these opportunities were often superficial, especially in the early years. This was partly because the reformers had so many other things to plan and implement at the same time, partly because professional development resources were spread too thin and partly because of an implicit assumption in Children Achieving's theory of action that the standards combined with serious accountability pressures would beneficially shape new teacher behaviors even without professional development. As discussed above, this assumption proved unfounded. Content standards and accountability measures offer a foundation for instructional change, but they produce results only if teachers are provided considerable learning time and support. For many teachers in Philadelphia, the gap was wide between the standards, on the one hand, and the teachers' existing professional capacity to implement them. It did not help that their union was outspokenly hostile toward the reform. Nor did it help that the architects of Children Achieving decided against incorporating several preexisting Philadelphia teacher-learning networks in the support design, though they did incorporate two others. As it turned out, teachers associated with these two—the National Science Foundation–funded Urban Systemic Initiative, and a Balanced Literacy project—proved more amenable to the Children Achieving reform than their colleagues in general did, and they proved more likely also to implement standards-based practices (Corcoran & Christman, 2002).

It is important to note that the kind of instructionally targeted, ongoing professional development opportunities that many Philadelphia teachers needed are hard to provide without support and leadership from principals. Yet few Philadelphia principals in these days saw themselves as instructional leaders or saw professional development as part of their jobs. Nor did the reform's leaders make the point: nowhere in the espoused theory or design of Children Achieving was the role of principals as site-based instructional leaders recognized or developed (Spiri, 2001). Thus principals received little or no professional development to help them learn how to turn around poor instruction, even as they experienced new pressures from the public release of the PRI scores to be accountable for it. In general, they ended up feeling disempowered and demoralized, and their turnover rate proved high (Corcoran & Christman, 2002). Arguably, turnover is a good thing among poorly performing professionals, though we would argue that trying professional development first is more economical.

SERVICES AND SUPPORTS FOR STUDENTS. The Children Achieving reformers understood the negative effects of poverty on children and their capacity to learn. Hornbeck put it plainly from the very start:

> Community services and support can make the difference between success and failure. Children who are unhealthy, hungry, abused, ill-housed, ill-clothed, or otherwise face the kinds of problems outside the school born of poverty will not achieve at high levels. Therefore it is imperative that initia-

tives be dramatically expanded to provide the necessary services and supports to reduce the impact of these major barriers to learning. (Quoted in Foley, 1998, p. 4)

Given the scarcity of funding, however, Hornbeck could not direct the
district itself to provide these services and supports. Instead he chose
an indirect path: a component of Children Achieving called the Family Resource Network (FRN) would work to strengthen the impact on
schools of services and supports provided by other government agencies and community groups. Using advocacy to increase services, coordination between the district and outside providers, and consolidation
of existing supports and services, the FRN aimed to improve student attendance, student health, school safety, and family and community involvement. However, communication about FRN and its function was
inadequate, and most teachers and principals—hearing only such state-
ments as Hornbeck's quoted above—thought that the FRN role would
be direct, not indirect. There was confusion even within the FRN itself,
as staff struggled to decide what should be done by the district and what
could best be handled by outside groups. Some leaders of these outside
groups praised the FRN, saying that they felt they had a focused point of
contact with the district for the first time. But others expressed wariness
about working with a district bureaucracy that seemed confused about
whether its role was delivery or coordination.

Nonetheless, the FRN made progress. It installed truancy courts in
schools to address chronic tardiness and absence, and these improved
student attendance. It also helped to increase student immunizations
and eye exams, even access to health insurance. In the end, however, inadequate financing undermined the FRN even in its indirect role. Successive budget cuts eliminated many positions. This added to the perceptions of teachers and principals that they were not being well supported
in areas that the rhetoric of Children Achieving had pronounced crucial
(Corcoran & Christman, 2002).

DECENTRALIZATION.   Theories of action in large-scale school reform
typically incorporate multiple arguments. This increases political support, though it can also threaten coherence. Children Achieving exhib-
ited, on the one hand, certain centralizing tendencies—for example, a
strong superintendent not shy about using the bully pulpit, common standards, and an accountability index with teeth. On the other hand, it was

also to a remarkable extent (for its time) a decentralized effort—at least on paper, and for a while. The reform architects introduced two new structural features to give schools more authority over decision making. *Small learning communities* reduced big schools to subunits serving typically fewer than four hundred students. They aimed to strengthen relationships among teachers and students, and to personalize schooling. Children Achieving inherited this approach from an immediately preceding Philadelphia action space focused on high schools, and it scaled up the approach—though, as is typical in school reform, with little acknowledgment of the source and little effort to explore what might be learned from the earlier experience.[2] Nonetheless, the evaluators of Children Achieving found that where small learning communities were well implemented, teachers reported higher levels of professional community, and the evaluators found a positive relationship between strength of professional community and student performance gains in elementary schools (Corcoran & Foley, 2003).

The second decentralizing feature involved what were called *clusters*. These were vertical groupings of schools meant to reduce the big-city system to something approximating a small-town system. Children Achieving divided Philadelphia into twenty-two clusters, each consisting of a comprehensive neighborhood high school and the middle and elementary schools that feed into it. However, the newly established cluster offices faced a formidable set of tasks. They were directed to provide focus for improvement initiatives in the schools, to mobilize resources to support improvement, to build a responsive relationship with neighborhood organizations and community members, to provide professional development for teachers, to coordinate social services, and to strengthen K–12 curriculum, instruction, and assessment.

From the beginning, central-office staff members seemed unclear about how to operationalize these decentralizing initiatives, and they also seemed ambivalent about the possible impact of them in terms of diminishing their own roles and responsibilities. For their part, school staffs were unready to assume as much responsibility as the decentralizing strategies seemed to demand. In particular, many lacked the capacity to take on peer leadership roles at the same time that they were struggling to make changes in their own classroom practice as demanded by the standards strategy. Nor did they have access to professional coaching or models of decentralized schooling.

A turning point for the decentralization strategy came in 1998, when reform leaders viewed with dismay disaggregated district test data that showed, for example, that the four-year graduation rate was almost 30 percent lower for students in families on welfare than for all students. Central-office staff were concerned that the reform's equity objectives were being neglected, and they concluded that they had to take a more prescriptive approach to schools concerning what and how to teach (Foley, 2001). However, as they retreated from decentralization and began to give more direction to school staff, they failed to articulate the policy shift and its rationale. This is not untypical of large-scale school reform efforts. They must, on the one hand, make adjustments in their theory of action *in action*, even as they work to sustain public faith in their theory of action as espoused. In this case, schools felt a loss of autonomy as new mandates piled up, yet district leaders continued to frame the reform in terms of decentralization. In the end, Philadelphia became a confused and muddled amalgam of centralization and decentralization (Corcoran & Christman, 2002).

INVESTMENTS OF CIVIC CAPACITY.   Children Achieving was championed initially by the Philadelphia business and philanthropic communities, other elite civic leaders, and Mayor Ed Rendell. They saw standards, accountability, and decentralization as commonsense ideas. The downside of this was that they did not think of them as arguments that would need to be adjusted to complicated contexts. When the arguments proved more difficult to implement than they had imagined, the business leaders in particular became disillusioned with the reform and with its leader, Superintendent Hornbeck. Some worried that too much of the Annenberg Challenge money was being spent on administration—for example, the new cluster offices. Some complained that the superintendent had failed to negotiate sufficient changes to the teachers' contract when it came up for renewal in 1998, and that he refused to negotiate with the governor over the latter's plan to improve Philadelphia schooling through vouchers, which many of them found attractive. Some were also frustrated by the failure of Children Achieving to outsource more of the district's service needs to private companies. Moreover, throughout this time, the mayor kept a low profile, saying almost nothing in support of Children Achieving (Boyd & Christman, 2003). Meanwhile, as we noted in chapter 4, the entire culture of business in Philadelphia shifted as major downtown businesses were taken over by multinationals. The result was a relatively sudden and almost complete disappearance of elite civic support.

By contrast, grassroots civic leaders remained stalwart champions of the reform. They expressed pride and gratitude that Philadelphia had a plan, something they felt other cities lacked. Many saw economic inequality and racial discrimination as the most significant problems confronting the schools. Thus, Hornbeck's persistent fight for fair funding and his references to racial disparity made him a hero for these grassroots leaders even as support crumbled for him in the business sector. Still, when the reform began to falter as discontent among teachers and principals surfaced and test scores flattened, many grassroots leaders hoped for modifications in the reform strategies. However, political circumstances forced them into a defensive posture. Constructive criticism could be misconstrued, they thought, and might give ammunition to those who wanted to discredit the reform and drive off Hornbeck.

As for parents, the Children Achieving leaders worked to make them partners in the reform—for example, seeking to engage them in school leadership roles. However, they tended to underestimate how hard it is for schools in low-income and racially isolated neighborhoods to build trusting collaborative relationships with parents, how much skill this requires of principals and parent leaders, and the range and number of resources it demands. A few schools successfully worked with intermediary organizations to enable parents to identify their concerns, raise controversial issues, work through conflicts, and address issues that had an impact on their children. But these instances were rare (Corcoran & Christman, 2002).

ALL AT ONCE. This last of Children Achieving's eight strategies announced that all the others would be pursued simultaneously and at full force, starting now. No staging, no phasing. Like the fair funding strategy, the all-at-once strategy had a devastating impact on the others. For one thing, staff in many schools were overwhelmed and confused by the various demands made on them *all at once*: new curriculum, new assessments, new structures for working together, new leadership arrangements, and new procedures for obtaining services for students. What made sense to reform leaders in theory was perceived as "hell on the ground" by principals and teachers, as one Philadelphia educator told the evaluators (Corcoran & Christman, 2002, p. 31).

Gaps between what is espoused and what is enacted are not unusual
in a complex reform. Strategies that seem aligned on paper prove mis-
aligned and even incoherent as they are turned into concrete designs in
real places, as they impinge on people's ordinary practice, and as they
undergo interpretation and resistance. Reformers must prepare for and
deal with this predictable misalignment—particularly when the ideas
about teaching and learning they espouse are as different from prevailing
ones as the Children Achieving ideas surely were. Yet dealing with such
differences takes time, and there was too little time and too much striving all at once. Overloaded by reform, many Philadelphia school professionals were unable to focus their efforts on learning—though learning
(theirs as well as the children's) was the largely unacknowledged heart of
this reform. In particular, the all-at-once strategy stripped the reformers
of *their* opportunities to learn. It seemed to preclude tinkering. Moreover, the pace and moral tone of the reform made it difficult to give or
receive feedback. One civic leader who supported Children Achieving
but nonetheless favored midcourse corrections in its theory of action
crystallized the problem: "The completeness of his [Hornbeck's] vision
wasn't amenable to questioning. You couldn't tamper with any part of it"
(Corcoran & Christman, 2002, p. 28).

Stepping Back from the Case

What can we learn from the collapse of the Children Achieving action space? Our answer to this question begins with the response of the
Cheshire cat to a similar question from Alice: "That depends a good deal
on where you want to get to." If you are leading a particular action space
here and now, and want to act to optimal effect for as long as you can,
the lesson you might fairly draw from Children Achieving is to be wary
of outstripping capacities and to be less comprehensive, less aggressive,
and more politic than Hornbeck was. Hornbeck himself, however, drew
a different lesson. Here's how he put it in his 2009 book, *Where There's a
Will, There's a Way*:

> Many will argue that my biggest mistake was confronting political leaders
> with their failure to fulfill their responsibility to the children of Philadelphia.
> However, this is not something I would change if I had it to do over. The "pol-
> itic," realistic strategies had been tried for years before I came, and have been
> tried again since my departure—and have failed miserably. Behaving as if we

are asking favors when we advocate for adequate and equitable public education is neither appropriate nor effective. My mistake was in not being more
aggressive. (Hornbeck & Conner, 2009, p. 303)

Clearly Hornbeck drew another lesson too, as did several of his colleagues. It is about working over the long haul to build the capacities
that Children Achieving lacked. After stepping down as superintendent,
he founded an organization called Good Schools Pennsylvania. With
funding from several foundations, Good Schools Pennsylvania mobilized groups of citizens to demand fair funding and education reform,
and supplied substantial civic capacity to the cause for more than a decade. Vicki Phillips, a key architect of Children Achieving and leader of
the Children Achieving Challenge (its Annenberg arm), seems to have
taken into her next jobs a lesson about the role of professional capacity building in making schooling more equitable—again over the long
haul. These jobs include two urban superintendencies and stints as chief
state school officer in Pennsylvania and chief education officer of the
Bill and Melinda Gates Foundation. In a speech to the Council of Great
City Schools, Phillips said, "If we could distill everything we've learned
about education into one sentence [and here it seems fair to assume that
this *we* is really *I*], it would probably be this: Nothing is as important
as an effective teacher" (Phillips, 2009). Warren Simmons, also a key
architect of Children Achieving in his role as director of the Philadelphia Education Fund, went on to become the long-serving director of
the Annenberg Institute for School Reform, where he focused the institute's work on urban school districts serving disadvantaged children,
an emphasis he traces back to the 1990s and the Annenberg Challenge.
He also calls for smart education systems where reform and reinvention
are linked to community engagement and development—or as we would
put it, where professional capacity and civic capacity are teamed (Simmons, 2009). Finally, there is Ed Rendell, mayor of Philadelphia during
Children Achieving. As we suggested above, he was frequently missing
in action during Hornbeck's struggles, apparently unwilling to risk political capital on fair funding when he had his eye on running for governor. During his second term as governor, however, he fought hard for
adequate, equitable, and predictable state funding, and made progress—
though as we point out in chapter 4, not enough (McHugh, 2008).

The Children Achieving reform project is considered by most policy
pundits today to have been a failure—as is the Chicago Annenberg Chal-

lenge (discussed below) and the New York Networks for School Renewal (discussed in chapter 6). But failure and success are highly contingent on perspective, and both can have a slow incubation and a long reach.

Chicago

We begin by imagining the story of the Chicago Annenberg Challenge as presented by a made-for-TV movie. Here are selected scenes (all depicting actual events):

> *Scene 1.* In the Roosevelt Room at the White House, a billionaire philanthropist announces the largest gift to public schooling in the history of philanthropy and challenges the ten largest cities in America to mobilize their resources to make a plan to reform schools for the sake of their children. The press release calls it the Annenberg Challenge.
>
> *Scene 2.* Hearing the news on the radio in Chicago, an education professor (formerly on the FBI's most-wanted list for being a member of the 1970s Weather Underground) calls two friends. The first is the education officer for one of the city's largest foundations. The second runs a cross-city campaign for school reform. All three were champions of the 1988 Chicago school reform act.
>
> *Scene 3.* Over lunch the same day, the three plot how to mobilize the city's resources for reform. They plan an Annenberg proposal to strengthen the city's five-year-old school reform action space. The space is still viable, one of them says, "if less energetic." What it needs, they agree, is an infusion of money plus professional capacity (from networking the many external partners working with Chicago schools).
>
> *Scene 7.* A raucous but hopeful meeting of a new working group is convened, cochaired by the education professor and numbering some seventy-three community and school reform activists. At the meeting, the activists form a collaborative to advance school reform in the city by using Annenberg Challenge funding to attack problems related to time (too rigidly apportioned in most schools to support real learning), size (schools too big to know their students well), and isolation (too many barriers to cooperation among people within and between schools, and between schools and their communities). "We'll be a foundation of a different type," the education professor says. "We don't want ordinary accountability. We want to reward networks for showing the right impulses."

Scene 15. A middle-aged white woman, who heads an important foundation pledged to match some of the $49.5 million in Annenberg funds awarded to Chicago, lunches with a young black lawyer (formerly a community organizer). She asks him to chair the new board of the Chicago Annenberg Challenge (CAC). "Your own life's story," she tells him, "can serve as testimony that lower-income and minority children can thrive when given access to good schools."

Scene 18. Shortly after the 1995 passage of the law granting mayoral authority over Chicago schooling, The mayor sits in a large City Hall office with his former budget director, now CEO of the Chicago Public Schools. They talk about their plans to reform the schools. Referring to the CAC, the mayor suddenly erupts, "I have accountability for the system. I'm the one whose career is going to be made or broken with this commitment, and I want to have access to that money."

Scene 35. At a battered conference table, now piled with proposals from prospective CAC networks, a businessman member of the CAC board (and a leader of the effort to pass the 1995 mayoral control law) sits with the CAC executive director. The businessman points at the proposals with a disgusted look. "These by and large were awful," he says, "which is what you could have expected. You were getting people that didn't know anything about developing or implementing programs. You got this whole 1995 reform business going on, and then you've got 'time, size, and isolation.' It's a parallel universe."

Scene 109. A glum-looking executive director and other CAC staff sit at what is now a really battered conference table with members of their evaluation team. One evaluator says, "Our analysis is not yet complete, but the research seems to indicate that student outcomes in CAC schools were much like those in demographically similar non-CAC schools. Among the schools it supported, the CAC had little impact."

Scene 116. [Seven years later in Alaska] At a press conference, the Republican Party candidate for vice president of the United States accuses the Democratic candidate for president of "palling around with terrorists."

Scene 117. [Quick cut to] Web ad playing on a computer screen. A voice-over asserts: "Ayers and Obama ran a radical education foundation together that distributed more than $100 million to ideological allies with no discernible improvement in education."

Scene 118. A special collections librarian at the University of Illinois at Chicago wheels out boxes and boxes of evaluation papers and other documents from the Chicago Annenberg Challenge to waiting news reporters and photographers.

Scene 119. [Words on the screen] Epilogue: Thus it happened that what appeared until then to be among the most forgettable efforts in American school reform history became one of the most noticed. Reporters from across the world scrambled to read every word of the thousands of documents released by the University of Illinois. Bloggers everywhere descended on the documents released simultaneously on line by the Annenberg Foundation. The Wikipedia entry on the Chicago Annenberg Challenge filled out overnight with hundreds of details and footnotes.[3]

Inside the Movie

The biggest drag on learning from collapse is forgetfulness, and the Chicago Annenberg Challenge was indeed, until 2008, among the most forgettable of all the action spaces that we write about in this book. Sadly, the 2008 reporting, blogging, and Wikipedia authoring focused exclusively on the CAC as a political wedge issue, not a rich opportunity for learning about school reform. Thus CAC remained forgettable even after the one-time chair of its board became the forty-fourth president of the United States.

Timing is everything in the design of action space. The CAC design was based on a passing action space in Chicago school reform, and it opened just as a distinctly new and different space opened up: one that replaced community control with assertive mayoral control and acted on the encouraging belief that business perspectives can save even what one US secretary of education called the worst school district in the nation. We told this story in some detail in chapter 3. Here it is important merely to note that as the new action space unfolded, a relic of the old one—namely CAC—persisted beside it. Indeed, CAC had been designed to sit beside the district, though the designers imagined that the district would continue to be dysfunctional. Instead, the district was soon transformed (Smylie & Wenzel, 2003).

The Chicago Annenberg Challenge, technically an intermediary between the Annenberg Foundation and the Chicago Public Schools, functioned as actual foundations often did in those days: soliciting and evaluating proposals, working to support grantees in such areas as strategic planning and communication, organizing some opportunities for grantees to share their work with each other, and requiring detailed activity and budget reports twice a year. And while it consulted with the mayor and the CEO of the Chicago Public Schools (CPS), it pursued the original plan to fund networks of schools—in effect, to go around the CPS. Meanwhile, in this work with the networks, it did not articulate specific improvement goals for the schools or even advocate particular approaches on the part of the networks and the community partners who ran them—beyond the initial press to focus on time, size, and isolation, then later (in the face of disappointing results with the first approach) on "whole-school change." CAC believed in trusting the schools to set their own goals, solve their own problems, and invent their own solutions to local needs (Sconzert, Smylie, & Wenzel, 2004). Its theory of action went something like this: CAC funding (matched by local school council funding) would purchase the power of networking and support from an external partner, and these, together with the reform momentum already generated by the 1988 reform (for example, the collective power of staff and parents to set a reform vision and hire the right principal to implement it), would supply the schools with the money, professional capacity, and civic capacity they would need to improve the school and the learning of the students who attend it.

CAC made two types of grants in its first four years, and many more overall than it had first anticipated. First it made small one-year planning grants to schools and external partners to develop networks and network-facilitated school improvement plans. Then it followed up with renewable multiyear implementation grants to external partners, forty-five in all, each working with a network of schools (generally four or five schools). About 90 percent of these schools were elementary schools, and they constituted approximately 40 percent of all schools in the Chicago Public Schools system. They resembled the others in average enrollment size, level of academic achievement, racial and ethnic composition, and percentage of low-income students (Smylie & Wenzel, 2003).

In terms of added funding for reform, what CAC delivered to these grantees varied over time. Average CAC funding grew from $15,000 in 1995 to a peak of about $47,000 in 1999. While no principal would scoff at having an additional $47,000 in his or her budget even today, this amount represented only about 1.2 percent of the annual operating budget of a Chicago elementary school in 1999. From a network perspective, the CAC granted the typical network of five schools and its external partner enough dollars to provide salaries, benefits, and support to two professional staff members (for example, what we might today call school coaches). Following its peak, however, CAC funding dropped precipitously on average: from $47,000 in 1999 to $29,000 in 2000 and a mere

$2,600 in 2001, the last year of CAC. The main reason was a new system of differentiated funding introduced in 1999. CAC would continue to support two hundred schools, but it selected eighteen to receive significantly more funding than the others based on an analysis of their improvement trajectories. These "breakthrough schools" were selected on the basis of network progress reports, school visits, and records of school participation in CAC activities. The process put particular emphasis on the schools' commitment to professional development for teachers and on strong school leadership. In a departure from the original theory of action, the schools were intended to serve as cross-network models, with funds going directly to the schools rather than through their external partners—about $100,000 per school over the last two years of CAC (Smylie & Wenzel, 2003).

In the end, however, the difference between the breakthrough schools and the other CAC schools proved negligible in terms of student outcomes. Yet there was an interesting difference in terms of school improvement—one that challenges the discouraging idea that money doesn't matter. The breakthrough schools became noticeably stronger on most measures of teacher professional community, and somewhat stronger on measures of school leadership as well as teacher-to-principal and teacher-to-teacher trust (Smylie & Wenzel, 2003). These are all measures of what we would call professional capacity. The finding is, of course, not surprising, given the fact that the schools were selected on the basis of an apparent tendency in this direction. However, the breakthrough schools are nonetheless noteworthy for what they signify strategically—namely a shift of emphasis away from both 1988 and 1995 strategies. As Shipps, Kahne, and Smylie (1999) point out, both the 1988 and 1995 phases of Chicago school reform were "predicated on the notion that change is best achieved through external political influence over and control of professionals, either by a coalition of grassroots activists and business leaders, or by a central management bureaucracy with allegiance to the local political leadership" (p. 536). In making deliberate investments in professional capacity—albeit late in the game and in a small number of schools—the CAC prefigured what we described in chapter 3 as the modifications of the Arne Duncan years.

The CAC external partners were a diverse bunch organizationally. More than a third were institutions of higher education—among others, DePaul University, Chicago State University, and the Erickson Institute. Twenty-three percent were cultural institutions—for example, the Chicago Symphony Orchestra and the Whirlwind Performance Company. Another 28 percent were explicitly school support organizations, though with a wide range of practices; these included the Success for All Foundation, the Great Books Foundation, and Facing History and Ourselves. A final 14 percent were community organizations such as the North Lawndale Learning Community and the Beverly Area Planning Association. As these examples may suggest, the partners overall were also diverse in their experience with the kind of long-term, collaborative improvement efforts implicitly required by the CAC theory of action. Although CAC put an initial emphasis on networking itself—the presumed power of schools to build their expertise collectively—it shifted early on to an emphasis on the role of the external partner as a source of expertise, and over time increased its expectation that this expertise could lend professional capacity to the networks (Smylie & Wenzel, 2003). The universities and school support organizations among the partners typically were best positioned to deliver on this expectation. Most also had experience working with the schools in their networks. The community partners also had established relationships with their schools, though as sources of civic capacity rather than professional capacity—for example, helping them communicate with parents or the local business community. In the context of their CAC work, they felt pressure to import expertise in such areas as curriculum and instruction. The cultural organizations as a whole were the least prepared to deal with their networks in the way that CAC implicitly intended—not just because of an absence of school reform expertise (beyond, say, enriching the arts curriculum), but also in most cases because of a lack of previous relationships with their network schools.

Not surprisingly, the emphasis of the networks' efforts in the end varied considerably. About 55 percent of the networks focused especially on curricular and instructional improvement, 16 percent on learning climate and social services, 13 percent on parent and community support, and only 16 percent on what we called in the preceding Philadelphia story *comprehensive* support (Sconzert et al., 2004). In any case, at the height of the CAC action space in 1999, the CAC evaluators found no statistically significant differences in effects among these network focuses. However, in a move that would powerfully affect what we can learn now from the Chicago Annenberg Challenge, the evaluators then shifted their attention to within-network variation. They hypothesized that the impact of partnering and networking might be highly mediated by school-level circumstances and capacities (Smylie & Wenzel, 2003). More about this in our story's epilogue.

Meanwhile, as the CAC unfolded, the district, under the leadership of Mayor Richard Daley and CEO Paul Vallas, built a different action space. We told the full story of this action space in chapter 2. Here we simply recall its grip on schools, including CAC schools. It declared that all students in third, sixth, and eighth grades had to meet certain cut scores on the Iowa Test of Basic Skills (ITBS) or face summer school and possible grade retention. Schools with fewer than 15 percent of their students scoring at or above national norms on the ITBS were placed on academic probation, threatened with reconstitution, and given a probation manager to direct their improvement efforts. Schools in a middle tier of ITBS results were required to adopt what was quickly termed a "scripted" curriculum, fitted to the test.[4] At the height of the CAC, in 1999, 54 of its 206 schools were on academic probation. Of these, about 20 worked with their CAC external partner as their probation partner, while the other 34 worked with two different partners (Smylie & Wenzel, 2003).

How did the Chicago Annenberg Challenge turn out? For one answer, see scene 109 of the movie above, which includes a clause that laces the evaluators' final technical report: "Any improvements were like those occurring in demographically similar Chicago schools." The impact of CAC overall was negligible with respect to student outcomes: ITBS scores, academic engagement, classroom behavior, students' sense of self-efficacy, and social competence. And with the partial exception of the breakthrough schools noted above, the CAC impact was also negligible with respect to school improvement: quality of classroom instruction, student learning climate, school leadership, teacher professional community, parent and community support, instructional coherence, and relational trust (teacher-principal, teacher-teacher, teacher-parent, and teacher-student). Thus, as a school reform device (albeit one designed for a different kind of action space than it ended up part of), the Chicago Annenberg Challenge proved weak. Based on their research, the evaluators explain the weakness as likely the consequence of the following factors working in concert (though, of course, variably across the many CAC schools):

• *Broad goals and vague strategies.* By and large, the CAC left the determination of intermediate goals (below the level of "improve schools and student learning") to the external partners, networks, and schools it funded. This diffusion weakened its reach. CAC did the same with regard to strategy. Some grantees pursued effective strategies, while others did not—effectively washing away overall impact.

- *Too few resources for too many schools.* Michael Fullan and Matthew Miles join many other researchers in asserting that school reform is "resource hungry" (1992, p. 750). The CAC decision to spread its resources across two hundred–plus schools and forty-five external partners proved ill-advised. However, it was politically difficult to avoid, given the public profile of the initiative and the scale of the problems in the city. Nor was the resource scarcity just about money. The CAC schools and their networks needed more advice and feedback than CAC central was equipped to provide.
- *Weak levers for change.* Research on school reform emphasizes two kinds of levers—on the one hand, reculturation and knowledge building, on the other hand, incentives and accountability for changing practices (Elmore, 2000; Fullan, 2001; Hess, 2004; Payne, 2010; Spillane, 2004). CAC was weakly positioned in both respects. It never sufficiently articulated or pressed its directive to reculture schooling through attention to time, size, and isolation. Its emphasis on increasing professional capacity through teacher professional development came late. Finally, the size of the grants it made provided insufficient incentive to make the kind of change it aimed for, and the mere threat to withdraw the grants (rarely carried out) instilled too little accountability.
- *Lack of capacity among the external partners.* The CAC initiative was founded on the assumption that Chicago external partners collectively possessed a sufficient supply of the professional capacity and civic capacity that the CAC schools would need to improve themselves and their outcomes. While this may or may not have been true (probably *not*), the actual CAC grantmaking and the plans that the grantees created proved too poor a distribution device.
- *Lack of capacity among the schools.* In the 1997 teacher surveys, a substantial proportion of CAC schools scored in the weakest categories of available human and social resources to support school development: 24 percent reported minimal principal support for change; 17 percent reported minimal orientation of the school toward innovation; 36 percent reported a weak capacity for joint problem solving; 33 percent said that collective responsibility was limited or very limited; and 54 percent said that there was either minimal or no teacher-to-teacher trust. Some measures of human and social resources grew stronger between 1997 and 1999, but in almost all cases the improvements vanished when the funding declined after 1999 (Smylie & Wenzel, 2003).

- *Lack of commitment to reform goals.* There was substantial variation among CAC schools on such measures as principals' assessment of the centrality of the CAC to their schools' work and teachers' participation in CAC activities—both the number of teachers involved and the frequency of their involvement. The lack of commitment was exacerbated in many schools by staff turnover, and the loss of key leaders—including staff hired by external partners. Finally, it was exacerbated by two other factors: low expectations of students, and high levels of competing reform activity in the schools. In 1997, only 48 percent of CAC teachers thought that their students had at least a 75 percent chance of graduating high school, and only 21 percent thought they had at least that much chance of going to a two- or four-year college. And in 1999, fully 80 percent of CAC principals agreed with the statement "The Annenberg Challenge is just one of many programs we have at this school" (Smylie & Wenzel, 2003).
- *Countervailing reform forces in Chicago.* In 2001, 36 percent of CAC principals agreed with the statement "Central Office priorities often conflict with those of our network"; and in 1996, one-fifth of external partners who were asked a similar question in interviews had cited conflicts. Moreover, the evaluators found that such conflicts were usually resolved in ways that compromised the CAC side. Nor were conflicts exclusively philosophical or policy-focused. External partners complained, for example, that with little advance notice, the district would call principal or teacher meetings that forced cancellation of CAC meetings scheduled far in advance (Smylie & Wenzel, 2003).

Stepping Back from the Case

It is the function of a case study to reduce complex situations embedded in long and continuing histories to simple, time-bound terms. Thus one can say that the Chicago Annenberg Challenge failed for underreaching, while Philadelphia's Children Achieving failed for overreaching. But as we suggested in stepping back from the Philadelphia case, one can also take a longer view.

The longer view in Chicago is easier to take than in Philadelphia. One reason is that the Chicago Annenberg Challenge ended at about the same time that Mayor Daly shifted emphasis in his school reform action space from the combativeness characteristic of the Paul Vallas era to the rapprochement characteristic of the Arne Duncan era—rapprochement with civic groups and, by means of substantial investments in the city's professional capacity, rapprochement with educational groups too. The consequence was that what started out as an orthogonal effort moved closer to CAC in its theory of action. Or, as the CAC evaluators put it in their final report: just as it closed down, CAC got a district it could work with (Smylie & Wenzel, 2003).

In a sense, however, CAC never completely closed down. The arguably least memorable of all the Annenberg Challenge projects has had among the longest and most far-reaching effects—both within Chicago and beyond—and we are not referring to a presidential campaign here. First, with its last $2 million, CAC transformed itself into Chicago's first Public Education Fund. In distinct contrast to the conventional kind of foundation, after which CAC had originally fashioned itself, the new Chicago Public Education Fund operated from the start as a venture philanthropy (and still does). It raises unrestricted capital through gifts and pledges (with substantial amounts of it donated by the fund's own directors, who include major business and other elite civic leaders). And it establishes what it calls "funds" to invest this capital strategically, with the hands-on attention and prowess of a venture capital firm—tracking performance data, consulting on management (here drawing on the directors' intellectual capital), and conducting management reviews. Meanwhile, having learned from experience, the fund does all this in close consultation with the mayor and the CEO of the Chicago Public Schools. In particular, it has become an important civic support for building professional capacity, but its use of "funds" enables it to shift emphasis nimbly among CPS priorities—investing, for example, in the preparation of national-board-certified teachers and in the overhaul of human resource management systems during the Arne Duncan and Ron Huberman years and, more recently, in the development of transformative leaders for schools and networks. Although it does not trumpet a connection to the Chicago Annenberg Challenge, to our ears its current focus on "time, technology, and talent" has roots in the old CAC focus on "time, size, and isolation."

Second, the Chicago Annenberg Challenge provided the crucial research base for one of the most important products (and tools) of early twenty-first-century research on school reform—namely, the essential-supports model of the Chicago Consortium on School Research (Bryk, Sebring, Allensworth, Luppescu, & Easton, 2010). The "essential supports," as the CCSR researchers evaluating the CAC first defined them, are ambitious and coordinated instruction; a student-centered learning climate; leadership; a professional community; and parent-community ties. These collectively and interactively contribute to instructional coherence across the school and to the development of an organizational phenomenon the model calls relational trust (between principal and teachers, between parents and teachers, and among teachers themselves). In their later elaboration of the model, Anthony Bryk and his CCSR colleagues (2010) consider in rich detail not only how the model works within the context of a school, but also how the model interacts with the social context that surrounds the community and the social capital available there. They have found, based on data that especially includes CAC data, that the presence of essential supports is highly correlated with such measures as religious participation, a sense of collective efficacy, personal ties beyond the neighborhood, low crime rate, and low density of child abuse and neglect. They have found, too, that schools located in communities with low social capital have to compensate with high levels of essential supports in order to make progress in student learning. In short, the researchers describe a complex, multifaceted, interactive, and contextually dependent process of school improvement—one not easily engineered by a reform initiative that is simple, singular in its argument, or oblivious to its surround.

The CAC evaluators used the original model of essential supports not only to assess the overall impact of CAC but also to interpret what they saw from what they called their "Annenberg window"—the twelve field research schools they studied closely for five years (Smylie & Wenzel, 2003, p. 92). Here they were able to see the dynamics behind the impact (as well as lack of impact). To the question of what is worth remembering about the Chicago Annenberg Challenge, our answer especially is *these dynamics*. They are apparent in four patterns of development with respect to essential supports. The researchers describe them graphically in the figure we reproduce here as figure 4.

Two of the twelve schools (Group 1) started out relatively high on measures of essential support in 1997 and stayed high over the five years. Two other schools (Group 2) developed continuously on one or more of the essential supports between 1997 and 2001. Four schools (Group 3) developed on one or more of the essential supports between 1997 and 1999 but then regressed when the money declined, with a corresponding impact on the external partner's support. The final four schools (Group 4) started off low on measures of essential supports and stayed low.

To account for these patterns, the researchers analyzed voluminous field research data. When schools focused on a single essential support

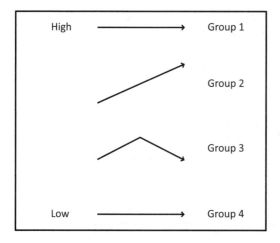

FIGURE 4 Patterns of development among field research schools. *Source*: Smylie and Wenzel (2003, p. 82).

or on multiple supports in an uncoordinated way, the researchers concluded, they made very little progress overall (Group 4). Similarly, when they shifted their focus from multiple supports to only one, or when their efforts lost momentum or coordination, early improvement declined (Group 3). By contrast, the schools that focused in a coordinated way on the development of several related supports seemed to create a synergy that promoted or sustained overall school development (Groups 1 and 2) (Smylie & Wenzel, 2003).

These findings highlight the importance of action itself, rather than just the presence of action space. Resources are not enough. They require intelligent and coordinated deployment by leaders who apply what the researchers call "strong maps or theories of school development and change," or what we would call adequate theories of action (Smylie & Wenzel, 2003, p. 104).

Still, resources matter a lot—though in more complicated ways than is often presumed or acknowledged among reformers and by reform arguments. What distinguished Groups 1 and 2 from Group 4, for example, was not the simple presence of entrepreneurship in the search for resources. It is true that two of the Group 4 schools had relatively few resources overall, and this severely constrained their development. However, the other two Group 4 schools had substantial resources, though ones that had been acquired and deployed in a strategically feckless way.

By contrast, Group 1 and 2 schools not only knew how to keep resources flowing but how to hunt for them and deploy them with a specific reform agenda in mind. Group 3 schools fell apart because they could not replace resources even though they could use well the ones they were handed (Smylie & Wenzel, 2003; Sebring, Hallman, & Smylie, 2003).

Finally, this window on success and failure deep within the Chicago Annenberg Challenge reveals a complication about leadership, or more particularly about what makes leadership strong. Schools that made or sustained progress with regard to the essential supports cultivated strong, *distributed* leadership (Smylie & Wenzel, 2003). The evaluators contrast this with authoritarian leadership of the kind associated with principals who delegate little, fail to elicit or value colleagues' and clients' voices, and fail to mobilize commitment to a common vision and effort.

CHAPTER SIX

Learning from Connections in New York

To force collapse out into the open in chapter 5, we began with a reference to autopsy and compared our storytelling to a Russian novel and a made-for-TV movie. But we ended each case study of collapsed action space with a reflection on the connections that survive collapse. In this chapter, we reverse emphasis, highlighting connections from the start. This is where they are hardest to perceive. First, we identify three themes in one old New York story—a story that initially seems to have nothing to do with school reform. But perspicacious actors in this 1980s action space thought otherwise, as we point out. In this chapter, we acknowledge their perspicacity retroactively. We do so by pulling three themes like connecting threads through two later New York stories—ones that clearly involve school reform, but from very different perspectives. The first involves the Annenberg Challenge in New York, and other action space that created the extraordinary phenomenon of small high schooling there. And the second involves community organizing for school reform—a strategy increasingly common in other places too. Our storytelling takes us to the summer of 2013, on the verge of a mayoral election, with an important question looming about school reform in the city. Our shorthand names for the connecting threads we draw through the three stories are *scale*, *partnership*, and *attitude*. By *scale*, we mean optimal institutional size for assembling sufficient expertise and accomplishing necessary work in an action space. In our stories, the word applies to communities, schools, and reform-oriented agencies. By *partnership*, we refer to collaborative relationships between and among those who provide the necessary inputs to action space: funding sources, professional experts of various kinds, and civic stakeholders. Finally, by *attitude*, we mean a refusal on the part of the actors in action space to accede to disempowerment. Where power differentials are rife, it is crucial to have some leveling mechanism, and attitude is an excellent one.

The purpose of our storytelling here is to alert reformers to the fact that making connections is hardly a sentimental activity. It is instead a strategic opportunity, a way to gain political leverage in the incessantly political work of keeping action space inflated and effective.

Story Number 1: The Bronx Is Burning

The name *South Bronx* rarely appears on maps. It signifies a social construction that is more about race and poverty than geography (Jonnes, 1986, 2002; Onishi, 1995). It was originally used in a lowercase way to refer to four neighborhoods in the southeastern tip of the only New York City borough that is physically attached to the rest of New York State. But the name spread north and west as low-income black and Latino families began to replace higher-income Jewish, Italian, and Irish ones (as well as some middle-class black and Latino families) throughout the southern half of the borough, beginning in the 1940s. The whites were lured to the suburbs by better housing, and helped in their moves by prosuburban and inherently racist government policies (Caro, 1975; Worth, 1999). The name South Bronx signified the change. It distinguished the spreading domain of the "other." Some of New York's poorest residents were pushed into the area. Subsequently, other city housing policies had a devastating impact there, leading to landlord neglect, abandonment, and arson (Worth, 1999).

A northern boundary for this South Bronx was set by the construction of the Cross-Bronx Expressway—beginning in the 1940s and continuing into the 1960s. Jill Jonnes calls it "a seven-mile-long, six-lane-wide ditch hacked through one solid Bronx neighborhood after another . . . across 113 streets, avenues, and boulevards" (2002, p. 120). An *expressway* in New York parlance is a road that trucks can travel. The construction of the Cross-Bronx Expressway—involving the emptying and dynamiting of hundreds of buildings—prepared the Bronx for the massive depopulation and arson fires that were a mere decade away. Four expressways frame the South Bronx today, and the diesel fumes they produce are often blamed for the region's high asthma rate (Fernandez, 2006).

Images popularized the association of the South Bronx with the discouraging idea of intransigent urban blight. The film *Fort Apache, the Bronx*, starring Paul Newman, portrayed a desolate crime- and drug-infested South Bronx Police Precinct (Richards and Petrie, 1981). During home games for the Yankees in the 1977 World Series, cameras frequently cut away from Yankee Stadium to nearby arson fires while sportscaster Howard Cosell intoned, "The Bronx is burning" (Freeman, 2000). Jonathan Mahler's popular history of New York captures the view that Cosell referred to:

> In the area surrounding the stadium, more than twelve hundred buildings had been abandoned. Empty lots were covered by shoulder-high weeds. Ten blocks from the ballpark, an unfinished five-million-dollar low-rise housing development, abandoned for lack of funds in 1972, was a thriving heroin den. When Charlayne Hunter-Gault, the first Harlem bureau chief of *The New York Times*, visited the Samuel Gompers Vocational-Technical High School in the South Bronx, she was confronted by charred classrooms and broken blackboards. Students passed around a bottle of wine during class. "It's very difficult to generate enthusiasm," one teacher told her, "when you feel everything is terminal." (Mahler, 2005, p. 30)

Between 1977 and 1997, two US presidents and one prospective one visited the South Bronx in order to make image politics. All three, accompanied by cameras and reporters, focused on a particular block of Charlotte Street in the Crotona Park East neighborhood. President Jimmy Carter came to Charlotte Street, he said, to witness the effects that changes in policy and the economy had had on the physical and social fabric of New York City, and to see how federal dollars might make a difference (Dembart, 1977; Fernandez, 2007b; Grogan & Proscio, 2001). What he saw, according to the *New York Times*, was "a Gothic landscape of destruction and concealed menace, the burned-out remains of 40,000 arson fires" (Grogan & Proscio, 2001). In the early 1960s, more than three thousand people lived in fifty-one apartment buildings on Charlotte Street and the adjacent Wilkins Avenue and East 172nd Street. By the time Carter arrived, there were only nine buildings still standing, and only one was occupied (Rooney, 1995).

Carter was followed by candidate Ronald Reagan in 1980, running (successfully, as it turned out) against Carter's reelection. Reagan compared what he saw on Charlotte Street to a war zone: London after the

Blitz. He used the image before the cameras to claim that the Carter strategy had accomplished nothing, and he offered a different argument: use tax incentives to encourage private investments. Off-camera, however, Reagan seemed less certain that money from any source could make a difference. He wondered quietly where the human agency and motivation were going to come from. Referring to some neighborhood people he had briefly met, he told an accompanying *New York Times* reporter, "You think of them back there in all that ugliness and they have no place to go. All that is before them is to sit and look at what we just saw" (*New York Times*, 1980, p. A16). He thus manifested the then widespread assumption—at least among outsiders—that South Bronx people were helpless. Otherwise, why would they still be living there? Reagan thought they could contribute zero civic capacity. But he overlooked the fact that the people he met briefly on his visit to Charlotte Street were organized. They had turned up to protest his visit. In fact, through a bullhorn, he had actually argued with them (Worth, 1999; Raines, 1980).

By the time President Bill Clinton came to Charlotte Street in 1997, the "inner city" rubble of the Blitz had disappeared and the neighborhood had taken on a "suburban" look. What he saw were single-family, ranch-style houses with tidy green lawns. Indeed, Clinton reprised the presidential tradition of visiting Charlotte Street to exploit the surprising turn of image and to point out that a discouraging belief had been reframed on this street. This could happen elsewhere too, he said (Yardley, 1997). In fact, replacing fifty-one apartment buildings with eighty-nine ranch houses was—and remains—a controversial move in housing terms, and the move proved a rarity among the many South Bronx housing efforts that followed (Rooney, 1995). Still, few dispute its impact. To unfix distinctions between inner city and outer city, between urban and suburban, was to challenge forces that helped depopulate the South Bronx and then nearly burned it down. To this day, visitors who come to the South Bronx want to see Charlotte Street, and it is the *scale* of it (in the context of its history) that moves them. A *New York Times* reporter, writing about the street thirty years after President Carter's visit, captures the scale in simple details: a hammock in the backyard, a chipmunk ornament on a lawn, the sound of a water sprinkler *and* of an elevated train (Fernandez, 2007a). *Partnership* is part of the Charlotte Street story too—in this instance, involving city government, downtown banks, local grassroots groups, community organizers, housing experts, elite organizations in the city, and others. Crucially, the partnership involved an equal mix of financial capacity, professional capacity, and civic capacity. Finally, what we call *attitude* is part of the story. Remember the organized protestors who greeted Ronald Reagan, and whom he perceived as feckless? Just a few years later, organized voices became rife across the South Bronx—sometimes on both sides of an issue. Jill Jonnes (2002) reports a verbal skirmish that happened even at the dedication of the Charlotte Street project in 1984. A man in the crowd yelled out, "These houses will be torn down in a week!" and Mayor Ed Koch yelled back, "The people who bought them will defend them with their lives" (Jonnes, 2002, p. 376).

Over the course of two decades, the arguments that Carter, Reagan, and others made about how to transform places like the South Bronx were wrestled to the ground by many people. In the process, the action space they created drew not only the public dollars that Mayor Koch budgeted in the face of Reagan's federal housing cutbacks, but also the private investment dollars that Reagan argued for, and that the Ford Foundation and Surdna Foundation and David Rockefeller's New York City Housing Partnership (later the Partnership for New York City) cleverly coaxed out of downtown. This action space drew on the professional capacity of urban planners, builders, housing finance experts, bankers, local entrepreneurs, elite power brokers, church leaders, and community organizers. Uptown civic capacity partnered with all this downtown and uptown professional capacity, and downtown money, to create nonprofit community development corporations (CDCs). Then the Koch administration turned an enormous amount of abandoned and city-seized property over to the CDCs—a public policy gamble that paid off well. The CDCs worked as the grounded partners of foundations, governments, and banks—all big organizations that, along with big government, had by the late 1970s amassed a bad record in urban renewal. The CDCs, by contrast, were of the right scale; they were able to contribute firsthand knowledge of the neighborhoods to grow locally savvy professional expertise, to raise and contribute sweat equity, and to heighten the confidence of more distant investors through their willingness to shoulder some of the commercial risk themselves.

Early CDCs include the Mid-Bronx Desperados, Father Gigante's SEBCO Houses (South East Bronx Community Organization), the Bronx Shepherds Restoration Corporation, Banana Kelly (named after a crescent-shaped street saved from arson by tenant activists), and SoBRO (the South Bronx Overall Economic Development Corporation). And they include organizations that will pop up in one or both of the other stories in this chapter—for example, South Bronx Churches, ACORN (Association of Communities Organizing for Reform Now), and New Settlement Apartments. As these names suggest, many of the CDCs had roots in religion, community organizing, or both.

The reconstruction of housing in the South Bronx depended ultimately on a willingness among both uptown and downtown leaders to challenge the discouraging belief that the South Bronx was disposable. These leaders insisted instead that the fate of the city was implicated in the fate of the region. Reconstruction also depended on a partnered willingness—despite many political battles—to take arguments in the air (for example, about private versus public investment) and wrestle them into novel theories of action, including the use of CDCs. The success thereby achieved, evident in the changed landscape of South Bronx neighborhoods today, kept attitude alive over time and had a massive influence on New York, including New York schooling.

Eventually, like all action space, this one collapsed, though gently, as with an inflatable device a swimmer no longer requires. Luis A. Ubinas, who grew up in the South Bronx and later became president of the Ford Foundation, referred indirectly to this gentle collapse in announcing a $200 million investment by Ford in a project meant to spur metropolitan development within and around Detroit, Michigan, and Gary, Indiana. Here is an excerpt from his speech:

> Last month, I walked with a friend from 138th Street in Mott Haven to Yankee Stadium. It's about two miles. There were no burned out buildings or vacant lots strewn with trash. No syringes on the sidewalk. No acrid smells from the previous night's fires. What we saw was a place where hard working people send their kids to decent local schools, shop at neighborhood stores, and even tend their gardens. Today the South Bronx is everything it wasn't in 1980—a sustainable, low-income community. (Ubinas, 2010)

The Role of Youth in the South Bronx Action Space

In a scene from Charlie Ahearn's 1983 film *Wild Style*, a soldier returns to the South Bronx in order to encourage his younger brother to leave. Sounding like the president then occupying the White House, the soldier tells the brother, "There ain't nothing here for you." But the brother replies, "Oh, yes, there is." Pointing to a wall covered in graffiti, he says,

"This" (Ahearn, 1983; Gonzalez, 2008). The graffiti, then ubiquitous across the Bronx, was the first manifestation of what would become a major cultural phenomenon, one that would create multibillion-dollar industries. The phenomenon is hip-hop, arguably the most influential youth culture phenomenon of the late twentieth century, and it was created in the crucible of a devastated South Bronx. From a perception of urban blight, black and Latino youths created what Nelson George calls a "loud, scratchy, in-your-face aesthetic" (1998, p. xi).

Hip-hop includes not only graffiti—painted first on walls, later on designer clothes, museum canvases, and commercial advertising—but also a new music composed of bits or "breaks" of old music with spoken word overlays or "raps." This new music first appeared on Bronx playgrounds where neighborhood DJs with improvised equipment tapped electric current from streetlights (Cooper, 2004; George, 1998). Eventually it would be played in all the media outlets of the world. It has inspired both a fashion and a style of movement and speech that confronts fears of the urban other. It substitutes images of power for images of desolation and helplessness.

By the time of Ronald Reagan's visit to the South Bronx, hip-hop was already part of the area's swelling civic capacity, demanding that attention be paid to a part of the city that many had written off. The demand arrived every day in every New York neighborhood during this period in the form of spray-painted subway cars (Gonzalez, 2004). On the part of the senders, this was a message on some level about not taking youth for granted. It was a message brimming with attitude. The receivers of the message often took it as a sign that the city was coming undone— the whole city, not just the parts some had already discounted. The resulting alarm was useful in terms of justifying additional downtown investments in uptown. Martha Cooper's (2004) celebrated photos of the brightly painted trains speeding through the South Bronx—sometimes against a backdrop of Manhattan skyscrapers—seems to portray the "inner city" bursting out of its frame. At the same time, her work and that of other early documentarians portrays midnight vandalism turning into art, self-respect, and even influence.

Like many other cultural movements, hip-hop has its bad side. It has been associated with violence and misogyny, and also with crass commercialization. Still it has facets of what the authors of *Young, Gifted, and Black* call a "leveling culture" (Perry, Steele, & Hilliard, 2003, p. 107). This is a culture that fights disempowerment through achievement and respect, built on a strong sense of group membership and what we call without disparagement *attitude*. A number of CDCs connected with hip-hop on this basis. For example, The Point, which focuses on youth development and the cultural and economic revitalization of the Hunts Point neighborhood of the South Bronx, began in the earliest days of hip-hop not only to organize a local and self-respecting arts scene, but also to connect it to downtown professional arts expertise and money. Similarly, arts and culture organizations that sprang from hip-hop often took up community development goals and community peace—for example, the Universal Zulu Nation, founded by activist, hip-hop godfather, and former gang leader Afrika Bambaataa.

In her book about the South Bronx, Heidi Neumark (2003), longtime pastor of the Spanish-speaking Transfiguration Lutheran Church on East 156th Street, writes about battling futilely against graffiti on the church doors until she *invited* community youth to paint them. The resulting spray-painted mural depicts a young man opening a fire hydrant to spray water into a baptismal font; connects a hand giving communion to a meal of turkey, rice, and greens; and forecasts new building construction in what was, at the time it was painted, still a desolate neighborhood. Neumark and her church were founding members of the South Bronx Churches, a CDC she describes as a conspiracy against poverty. The conspirators include a cross-denominational partnership of local congregations; their deeper-pocketed coreligionists downtown; the Industrial Areas Foundation (IAF), founded by Saul Alinsky in 1940 to help poor neighborhoods generate civic capacity; other local civic action groups; a mix of downtown and uptown political leaders and a set of downtown financial backers, all drawn to the action; and a coterie of newly empowered uptown experts (both adults and youth) in areas like housing, the arts, and—eventually—schooling. The work of South Bronx Churches has resulted over the years in the creation of nearly a thousand new housing units in the South Bronx, as well as—and here we reach a bridge in our storytelling—several new high schools.

Jim Rooney's (1995) account of the work that South Bronx Churches accomplished in housing illustrates the struggle that attends the development of a powerful action space; professional, civic, and financial energies do not blend easily. Yet the CDC faced even tougher going when it took up school reform in the late 1980s. That effort started simply enough, in Rooney's account, with two questions: Why can't the failing Morris High School work as well as the borough's Catholic high schools do? Why can't it work as well as the small alternative high school that Deborah Meier (1995) had recently founded on the other side of the Harlem River? Morris was the oldest high school in the Bronx, founded in 1897—a Gothic edifice on a high hill. By the 1980s it was an ironic monument, however. Rooney cites the New York State Department of Education's 1989 listing of the state's most troubled schools, of which all but four were in New York City and nearly half in the South Bronx. The neighborhood's schools in those days ranked at or near the bottom of a citywide system that seemed colonial. A small number of mostly white schools were advantaged, while a much larger number serving students of color were allowed to sink into various depths of professional incompetence, where disregard for student need was rampant, and patronage and corruption abounded (Fruchter, 2009).

The situation at Morris was so dire that in 1990 South Bronx Churches had to beat a retreat from its earliest plans to remake the school. "It was not merely that an obstructionist principal prevented progress," Rooney explains. "In truth, having a clearly defined enemy is a plus in IAF-style organizing." It was more that South Bronx Churches could not at that moment find a match on the professional side for the civic capacity it was prepared to invest. It knew about Deborah Meier but not yet about the movement she was part of—one that in terms of the threads we've been following—scale, partnership, and attitude—had strong connections to the South Bronx. As Rooney realized later, "The answer was hidden in the open" (1995, p. 134).

This answer would soon become visible, however, as a massive effort to reform New York high schooling reached its climax. We tell this story next. Here we simply note that South Bronx Churches went on to found the Bronx Leadership Academy High School, as well as the Bronx Leadership Academy II High School. The latter was originally located on the campus of what is now the *former* Morris High School. Whereas Morris in 2001 had a four-year graduation rate of 25 percent, the Bronx Leadership Academy and Leadership Academy II High Schools had, in 2011, four-year graduation rates of 69.9 percent and 64.8 percent, respectively—not far from the citywide average of 71.9 percent. Moreover, the small high schools now sharing the Morris campus all had four-year graduation rates in 2011 more than double that of the building's original tenant ten years before. The High School for Violin and Dance came in at 71.4 percent; the Morris Academy for Collaborative Studies at 63.5 percent; the School for Excellence at 56.9 percent; and the Bronx International High School, one of a network of thirteen high schools serving recent immigrant youth, at 63.1 percent.[1]

Story Number 2: Small High Schools Emerge

This story is about the growth of small high schools in New York City and the extraordinary connections that undergirded this growth. By our count, three different action spaces over nearly a half century worked to create and sustain small high schools in the city. They were distinguished not only by different sources of funding but also by different civic backing, different generations of professional capacity, and very different political contexts. Although those associated with the later action spaces tended to draw on their predecessors' work, they rarely acknowledged the fact.

Heather Lewis and Norm Fruchter (2001) trace the origin of the small-schools movement in New York to the civil rights movement. In the 1960s, revisionist scholars and critics steeped in civil rights struggles challenged prevailing ideas about the fairness and effectiveness of American schooling, and teachers-turned-critics like Herb Kohl (1967) and Jonathan Kozol (1968) portrayed schools serving students of color as so big and indifferent as to be clueless about their impact on children and youth, and so broken by racism as to require reinvention (Lewis & Fruchter, 2001). The first small high schools were started by activists responding to these critiques—some of whom, like Irving Hamer and Ruth Messinger, would later become politically influential citywide. The schools they established were street academies and storefront schools in poor neighborhoods like Harlem and the Lower East Side in Manhattan and Bedford-Stuyvesant in Brooklyn. Supported by philanthropy and by federal antipoverty dollars, they originally operated independently of the district, though some were later incorporated into the district as alternative (or transfer) high schools. Indeed one of them, Lower East Side Prep, continues today (Phillips, 2000).

The schools were products of one of that era's encouraging beliefs—that empowerment could redress poverty, and that partners like the New York City Urban League could help reverse the effects of centuries of disempowerment. The assumption was that such partners were closer to poverty-impacted communities than city governments tend to be, and less co-optable by status quo forces (Lewis & Fruchter, 2001; Phillips,

2000). This was the same era of public policymaking that would later see the development of CDCs in the South Bronx.

In time, the small-schools movement in New York, which from the beginning involved elementary and middle schools as well as high schools, grew a certain kind of professional capacity. This was distinguished from ordinary professional capacity in the city by its insurgent quality. We associate this with what we call *attitude*, though with a shift in focus. In our first story, attitude meant a refusal on the part of economically disadvantaged people to accede to their political disempowerment, while in this story it means a refusal on the part of a mostly young and mission-driven group of educators to accede to bureaucratic constraints and other status quo enforcers.

When federal antipoverty dollars began to dry up, the street academies turned for survival to the district (Phillips, 2000). New York City schools chancellor Harvey Scribner, appointed in 1970, was a change-oriented outsider who thought he might usefully replicate these independently functioning, attitude-bearing schools. To do this, he drew on another federal funding source—a title in the still new Elementary and Secondary Education Act (the same law, several reauthorizations later, that would be called No Child Left Behind). Scribner first launched a design competition, which he insulated from the Division of High Schools. According to Phillips (2000), Scribner was eager to have more high schools that implicitly challenge core assumptions about what high schooling is. He was impressed in this regard by Philadelphia's Parkway Project, called a high school without walls (Bremer and von Moschzisker, 1971; McDonald, Klein, & Riordan, 2009). Scribner was gone before the schools could open, but the schools did open, and a few still survive, for example, City as School, modeled on the Parkway Project, and Satellite Academy and West Side High School, both modeled on the street academies (Lewis & Fruchter, 2001). Institutional survival in and of itself is not important to our story, though its power to build a reservoir of professional expertise is—in this case, expertise about how to run high schools on a different model and teach high school in a different way. And the effect of these experiences of difference on the cultivation of attitude is also important.

By the late 1970s, several newcomer schools had joined this first action space as options for direct rather than transfer admission. That is, they could accept students into the ninth grade. One was Middle College High School, located on the campus of LaGuardia Community College, the first in a series of college-partnered schools that are now pervasive in New York and, thanks to the Gates Foundation–funded early college initiative, elsewhere too. Association with a college seems the antithesis of association with the streets (as in "street academy"), but the connector is a sense of familiarity and belonging. A 1981 study by the Public Education Association pointed out that one of the academic strengths of the small high schools then operating in the city was their capacity to use dialogue and relationships to enrich the curriculum (Foley and McConnaughy, 1981). This was among the first articulations of an argument for small high schooling that, in its contemporary version, extols the power of what is called personalization (Toch, 2003).

When Anthony Alvarado became chancellor in 1983, he created a citywide subdistrict for the small high schools, as mentioned in chapter 3. Called the Alternative School District, it incorporated the surviving street academies, the small transfer high schools, and special high school programs serving populations like pregnant students and incarcerated students. It also absorbed the small, direct-admission high schools, including eventually the one that Deborah Meier created in East Harlem and that (in story number 1 above) caught the attention of the South Bronx Churches on the other side of the Harlem River. Alvarado believed in the small-high-school argument. He also believed that the effectiveness of the schools depended on their habits of creative non-compliance with ordinary system procedures and bureaucratic controls. According to Stephen Phillips, whom Alvarado appointed as superintendent of the new district, the chancellor thought that these schools should be kept "on the perimeter" (2000, p. 6). There they could demonstrate difference to those who might emulate difference, but be protected from the impulse of others in a big bureaucracy to stamp out difference. The schools were anomalous in another way too. Unlike the other high schools in the city that were operated by borough under a citywide Division of High Schools directly controlled by the chancellor, and the elementary and middle schools that were organized by community school districts, the alternative high schools were operated on a citywide basis, developed professional ties citywide, and traded students citywide—as necessary to meet the students' needs. For example, it was not uncommon for one principal within the Alternative School District to call another and ask if he or she would take a student who needed a change of peer group—in exchange for a student to be named later.

From Alternative to Mainstream

By the time Joseph Fernandez became chancellor in 1987, more than twenty thousand New York youth were attending the city's alternative high schools (Phillips, 2000). However, the schools themselves stayed mostly off the public radar, given the vastness of the city and the insulation of the Alternative School District. As our example at the end of the last section may suggest, the schools were mostly insulated too from the ordinary high school admissions process. Nevertheless, they did not elude Fernandez's notice. Formerly superintendent of schools in Dade County, Florida, he spent his initial months in New York poking around and finding unusual facets of his new district, including these schools. He also interacted with some of the schools' champions—including board members of the Fund for New York Public Education. When Superintendent Phillips approached the fund for support, board members told him that the city should expand aggressively the number of small high schools open for direct (as distinct from transfer) admission.

This was a period of great interest in high school reform—in the wake of major critiques of conventional high schooling like *A Nation at Risk* (National Commission on Excellence in Education, 1983), Ernest Boyer's Carnegie Foundation study (1983), and Theodore Sizer's Study of the American High School (Sizer, 1984; Powell, Cohen, & Farrar, 1985; Hampel, 1986). Sizer's Coalition of Essential Schools, a large-scale action project aimed at the deep reform of conventional high schooling, was then gaining many school members, including a large contingent from New York's small high schools. Among planners from the Fund for New York Public Education, the chancellor's office, and the Aaron Diamond Foundation, the idea of making New York the capital of unconventional high schooling gelled into a major solicitation of new school proposals and produced what we think of as a second action space for small high school development in New York.[2]

Plucking an argument out of the New York air—and straight from the South Bronx—the solicitation required that every new school have a partner, though the nature of the partner's capacity and the scope of its role were left undefined (and, we would add, untheorized). "It could be parents, it could be community groups," Phillips recalls, "[or] it could be Goldman Sachs as it turned out in one case" (2000, p. 7). Over 155 proposals responded to this solicitation, and nearly 60 new small schools

were created by 1993 (Phillips, 2000). Many of them were proposed, in-
cubated, and supported directly by the fund itself, which changed its
name to New Visions for Public Schools. In the process, it helped pio-
neer a new role with respect to school reform—that of intermediary. It
is important to note, however, that the rise of the intermediary in support of small schools did not necessarily preclude grassroots partners.
For example, when South Bronx Churches and ACORN entered this design competition, they entered as community partners for New Visions-
sponsored schools. On the other hand, grassroots partners were rare in
the competition—a pattern that would continue.

Stepping forward too as an intermediary was a group headed by Sy
Fliegel, Anthony Alvarado's deputy superintendent in District 4. He
had gone on to found a support network for schools with attitude called
the Center for Educational Innovation (CEI), originally based at the
Manhattan Institute, a politically conservative think tank. Later, Fliegel would prove instrumental in connecting the small regular public schools created in the 1990s with the small charter schools created
later. Still another intermediary was the Center for Collaborative Education (CCE), founded by Deborah Meier. CCE was the New York affiliate of Theodore Sizer's Coalition of Essential Schools, and it proposed a
project called the Coalition Campus Project. The goal was to phase out
three large high schools, one in each of the boroughs plagued by large
high schools with notoriously low graduation rates: Manhattan, Brooklyn, and the Bronx. The project also proposed to open multiple small
schools, which would be partnered with and mentored by some of the
city's already established small schools (Meier, 2003). In this initiative,
the big schools stayed open but took in no more ninth graders. Meanwhile, the project replaced the high school "seats" that were lost year by
year, though not necessarily by putting the new seats in the same buildings or neighborhoods. Meier argued that if the students attending the
failing high schools were simply reassigned to smaller ones in the same
buildings—or worse yet, if the teachers were—they would carry over
the old culture and reinforce "habits of defeat and resistance" (Meier,
2003, p. 162). In going the route it did, the project foreshadowed the
later development of a citywide office to manage the city's "portfolio"
of schools (including charter schools), and to decide on a continual basis
what schools are needed where and what schools should be closed. More
about this in story number 3.

The Coalition Campus Project never made it to Brooklyn, but it did close the Julia Richman High School on Manhattan's Upper East Side (which, despite its physical location, then mostly served students from central Harlem) and the James Monroe High School in the South Bronx. Both schools had enrollments in 1992 of about three thousand students each, with a four-year graduation rate at Richman of 36.9 percent, and at Monroe of 26.9 percent (Darling-Hammond, Ancess, & Ort, 2002). To replace the subtracted high school seat capacity, the project founded eleven new small high schools, but located only some of them (condolike) in the Richman and Monroe buildings. The others were located in various other sites—in an unused factory, for example, or on several floors of an otherwise commercial building. Both the condo pattern and the leasing pattern proved trailblazing for the many small high schools to come.

Although the Coalition Campus schools were intended to add schooling capacity generally, some ended up serving students who would likely have attended the closed schools. For example, a Monroe project school, Fannie Lou Hamer High School (named for the civil rights leader), is located in former factory space in the South Bronx not far from Monroe. On the other hand, another Monroe project school, Brooklyn International High School, is far away, as its name suggests. Yet its network and design partner, the Manhattan International High School, opened in the Richman complex, just as (much later) the Pan-American International High School opened in Monroe. They are all related through networking to International High School in Queens, a small high school founded by Eric Nadelstern, who as the city's chief schools officer would later champion networking for governance and support. By the end of Mayor Bloomberg's tenure, there were design-based and intermediary-supported networks of schools throughout New York, and networking had become the city's central mechanism for supporting all schools in the city.

Meanwhile, the Coalition Campus Project also worked with the United Federation of Teachers (UFT) to scale up a hiring mechanism first developed for Nadelstern's International High School. Teams of UFT-trained teachers interviewed and selected teachers for the new schools with attention to the fit of the teachers' qualifications to the unique mission and design of the schools. The UFT was so pleased by the results of what became known as the SBO (school-based option) that it introduced it into the next contract negotiations, and in time it came to be widely adopted in annual votes by school faculties (Darling-Hammond et al., 2002). Because one of its features protects a school's teachers in most

cases from "bumping" by senior teachers in other schools, the SBO became one of the policy pillars of small-school development and stability
in New York.

In 1995 this action space got a big financial boost with a $25 mil-
lion grant from the Annenberg Challenge (to be matched with $25 mil-
lion each from private and public sources). Deborah Meier was asked to
shepherd the effort in New York but was pressed by Vartan Gregorian,
who co-led the Challenge with Theodore Sizer, to assemble a coalition
of intermediaries with political breadth. Then president of Brown University and a longtime advisor to Walter Annenberg, Gregorian would
later become president of the Carnegie Corporation of New York. To
construct the coalition, Meier turned to Sy Fliegel of CEI and Beth Lief,
then president of New Visions. At the table too was the Industrial Areas Foundation, the national community organizing network of which
South Bronx Churches was a local affiliate. However, the IAF decided
not to play. Later, the partners added ACORN, also a national coalition
of community organizers. Together these politically diverse partners
created the New York Networks for School Renewal (NYNSR) (Pradl,
Donis-Keeler, Martinez, & Arroyo, 2001).

We note, by way of pulling our connective threads through this story,
that NYNSR's proposal to Annenberg emphasized *scale* (small school
size and personalization) and *partnership* (networks of small schools
supporting each other and holding themselves accountable). It also emphasized *attitude* in its insistence on autonomy with respect to the larger
systems of schooling in New York (Institute for Education and Social
Policy, 2001). A NYNSR proposal to the Charles Hayden Foundation
seeking matching funds begins as follows: "The best schools today tend
to be exceptions. They work despite, not because of the system." With
this in mind, the proposal continues, NYNSR will build a system of exceptions, an experimental "Learning Zone" in New York of about a hundred small schools to start, to be populated by the most effective and accountable existing small schools in the city (K–12), as well as new ones
the project would create (Annenberg Institute for School Reform, 2001;
Meier, 2003).

It makes sense now to think about this Learning Zone as more vision
or metaphor than blueprint for a policy entity. While all the partners
wanted autonomy, they meant different things by the word—a difference
deeply influenced by what was then a tumultuous larger political context
(Domanico, 2000). First, Chancellor Fernandez, who had been support-

ive of the small schools, had been fired by the board of education in the wake of a fierce outcry by some community groups over a curriculum he mandated. Among other points, it promoted tolerance toward gays and lesbians. Many of these same community groups also opposed a plan Fernandez had implemented citywide to combat AIDS and HIV among youth by providing free condoms in high schools (Fruchter, 2007). Next, a conservative mayor, Rudy Giuliani, was elected, committed to an education agenda that included mayoral control, charter schools, and vouchers for New Yorkers to attend private schools. Then, Fernandez's successor, Ramon Cortines, also a supporter of small schools and of NYNSR, was abruptly forced out by Giuliani. Next, his successor, Rudy Crew, in one of his first public references to NYNSR, voiced reservations about what he called "boutique" schools.[3] Finally, the rise of the standards movement—both nationally and in New York State, following the appointment of a new commissioner—seemed to some of the small-school leaders to undercut a premise of New York small-school development up to that point—namely the focus on difference, insurgency, autonomy, and creative noncompliance.

In the face of all this apparent threat, most of the NYNSR leaders decided it was best to steer clear of the complex politics and to make accommodations with Chancellor Crew as needed, including soft-pedaling the Learning Zone. In particular, Fliegel argued that the district was not likely to mess with success—as indeed proved to be the case—and that a formal Learning Zone, as opposed to a virtual one, was not necessary (Domanico, 2000). Only Meier strongly opposed this tack. Saying that she had become impatient with the district's foot dragging on the Learning Zone, and clearly more disturbed than her partners by the ascent of the standards argument, Meier pulled up stakes and moved to Boston to start a new small school there, one that joined a kind of learning zone already established (Pradl, Donis-Keeler, Martinez, & Arroyo, 2001; Meier, 2003).

NYNSR went on to develop sixty new schools. Consistent with the by then broader nature of the small-schools movement in the city, only 29 percent of these were high schools and only 76 percent were "small" as we have used the term in this story (that is, fewer than 550 students and independently led). In any case, these sixty, when assessed as an aggregate, achieved higher test score gains, higher attendance, and lower dropout rates than those of several sets of comparison schools that the NYNSR evaluators used. Importantly too, the schools did not do what

many skeptics thought they would do if they were to be successful—
namely "cream" students, accepting only those most likely to succeed,
the ones most advantaged by social and political capital. Across the
five-year existence of NYNSR, the schools it founded enrolled higher
percentages of poor students and students of color than did either the
comparison schools or the city's schools as a whole, albeit fewer English language learners and students with disabilities (Institute for Education and Social Policy, 2001; Fruchter, 2007). In the process, NYNSR effectively dispatched the boutique image and also managed to move the
small-schools "movement" beyond its starting point in the Alternative
School District and a few supportive community school districts in Manhattan and Brooklyn.

With respect to its other two goals, however (developing better support systems for the small schools and using the schools to leverage district-wide change), NYNSR's effectiveness becomes apparent only by
tracing connections—that is, looking retrospectively for elements that tie
it to later projects, which by and large give no credit to NYNSR. After
all, NYNSR was an organization of convenience—one that enabled the
partners that comprised it to do work on small-school development on
their own terms. Indeed, when it folded, two of the partners (New Visions and CEI) kept going on their own terms, both becoming key contributors to the Bloomberg-Klein action space.

Small High Schools under Bloomberg-Klein

While NYNSR was not just about high schools, several of its participating high schools proved highly influential as design models—none more
so than Deborah Meier's Central Park East Secondary School and Eric
Nadelstern's International High School. The latter school was influential
too in shaping the idea of a network of schools. And in this respect Nadelstern himself was influential. Indeed, while a focus on the prominent
Meier highlights discontinuity—her 2003 book emphasizes NYNSR's in-
effectiveness—a focus on the quieter Nadelstern reverses the impression.
A Bronx native and resident, he went on to lead the effort to transform
high schooling in that borough.

Other key figures in the leadership of this next phase of small high
school development in New York include Robert Hughes and Michelle
Cahill. Hughes succeeded Beth Lief as president of New Visions and re-
fined and expanded that organization's work as a school developer, in-

termediary, and, eventually, a charter school management organization. Cahill served first as senior program officer in education at the Carnegie Corporation of New York and later as senior counselor to Chancellor Joel Klein. Steeped in community development work and a close observer of the redevelopment of the South Bronx, she, like Hughes and Nadelstern in their own ways, was both supportive and critical of the city's earlier work in small high school development. She believed that small size and personalization, though key, merely set the stage, and that to make a real difference for students the new high schools would also need more internal accountability, greater innovation in instruction, and better supports at the district level (EducationNews.org, 2010; Herzenhorn, 2003). While still at Carnegie (to which she later returned as vice president), Cahill worked to assemble the financial capacity necessary to launch what we think of as a third action space for small high school development. It was funded by $30 million in grants from Carnegie, the Bill and Melinda Gates Foundation, and the Open Society Institute.

The first work of the new action space was to create some forty new small high schools, many of them under Eric Nadelstern's overall tutelage in the South Bronx. It also did several other important things. Under Bob Hughes's leadership, it articulated a set of design principles for the new small high schools that expanded the theory of action well beyond scale and personalization—including, for example, emphases on ambitious instruction, family support, collaborative leadership, teacher-learning communities, and student voice (New Visions for Public Schools, n.d.). It also undertook (with support from the Bill and Melinda Gates Foundation) an evaluation that went beyond measuring outcomes and provided useful feedback for action in progress (Hirota, 2005; Foley, Klinge, & Reisner, 2007; Hirota, Hughes, & Chaluison, 2008).

In 2003 Bill Gates, then still the chairman of the Microsoft Corporation, announced a grant of $51.2 million from the Gates Foundation to Mayor Bloomberg's announced project to create an additional two hundred small high schools in New York. Both Bloomberg and Gates spoke at the Morris High School campus in the South Bronx. The *New York Times* reported that "Mr. Gates awkwardly shared the stage with Schools Chancellor Joel I. Klein, a former Justice Department official who had led the government's aggressive antitrust prosecution of Microsoft. Asked about their previous dealings, Mr. Gates nodded and barely cracked a smile. 'I'm glad to be working on the same team,' he said. Behind him, Mr. Klein flashed a sheepish grin" (Herszenhorn, 2003).

New Visions served as intermediary for the largest number of these additional schools, but other intermediaries were also enlisted into the massive effort. Indeed, seventeen other intermediaries participated. Meanwhile, Eric Nadelstern moved to the Department of Education's headquarters at Tweed Courthouse, where he first oversaw what was called the Autonomy Zone (arguably the long-delayed Learning Zone that NYNSR had championed, and full of small high schools). Later he led the Empowerment Networks or scaled-up Autonomy Zone, and finally (in the role of chief schools officer) all of the city's schools. There is more detail in chapter 3 about these dimensions of New York's Children First reform. Here we note simply that the creation of these new small high schools was part of a much larger and quite complex reform. Although Nadelstern tended publicly to join other officials in describing the Bloomberg-Klein administration as *discontinuous* in its policymaking—that is, as an initiator of completely novel ideas—he operated privately as a connector (Green, 2008). Indeed, Klein's chief accountability officer, James Liebman, told a reporter that Nadelstern "has a vast historical perspective," one focused, he added, on insurgency. "He was long an insurgent voice for kids and for schools, saying, 'We really know how to move kids forward, just give us the responsibility and get out of the way and let us do that'" (Hawkins, 2010).

This third action space for small high school development in New York was closely and rigorously studied by the research firm MDRC with grants from the Gates Foundation. As a result, we know a great deal about its impact. First it closed more than twenty-three large high schools in New York with graduation rates under 45 percent. These included Morris High School and South Bronx High School. In their place, it created more than 200 new small high schools—including 123 academically nonselective ones (50 of them in the Bronx). In doing so, it drew on philanthropic contributions of $150 million, and deployed extraordinary professional and civic capacity—with each capacity leavened by expertise acquired in previous action space. In the process, the city decreased the overall number of its large nonselective high schools from seventy-one, serving 68.6 per cent of the city's overall high school enrollment, to sixty-two, serving only 51.8 percent. This was a huge reduction during a time when overall high school enrollment in the city increased by thirty-two thousand students. Meanwhile, New York also increased the number of small nonselective high schools from 58, serving 5.4 percent of the high school population, to 161, serving an astonishing 18.5 per cent.[4] In the process, the MDRC researchers claim, the city virtually eliminated its "big bad schools" (Quint, Smith, Unterman, & Moedano, 2010, p. 25). Thus, students entering the remaining nonselective large high schools in New York were by September 2007 no longer on average at exceptionally high risk of academic failure.

The students served by the 123 new small and academically nonselective high schools were mostly from the Bronx and Brooklyn, more than 90 percent black and Latino, and exceptionally disadvantaged on average in terms of a number of indicators: more than 80 percent low-income, more than 25 percent overage in grade eight, and more than 50 percent low scorers on eighth-grade tests in math and literacy. They were, in other words, the students whom the action space intended to benefit—youth living in neighborhoods with median household incomes under $40,000, who would otherwise have gone to schools like the ones the project closed.[5] As the MDRC study demonstrates in unusually definitive ways, the action space actually did benefit these students. MDRC measured the impact on students not just in terms of a single test score, but in terms of grade progression, high school graduation after four *and* five years (an important extension, though one typically ignored in accountability statistics), and attainment of New York's higher-tiered high school diploma, the Regents diploma. Because of the massive number of students involved in the study (roughly twenty-one thousand) and the fact that circumstances permitted a randomized trial, we know the impact with unusual precision, and across many subgroups of the population (Bloom, Thompson, & Unterman, 2010; Bloom & Unterman, 2012).[6]

In brief, the researchers found substantial positive benefit from assignment to the small high schools. Enrollees there were 10.8 percentage points more likely than students in the control group to earn ten or more credits in their first year; and 7.8 percent less likely to fail more than one core subject. This statistically significant beneficial difference was maintained across the study participants' years in high school, and it applied across all subgroups (categorized by race/ethnicity, gender, income, and eighth-grade academic proficiency). Meanwhile, after four years, 68.7 percent of the first cohort of students graduated, while only 61.9 percent of their control group counterparts did—a 6.8 percent difference in estimated effect, which is a big spread given the number of participants in the study. By the fifth year, 75.2 percent of the first cohort graduated, compared to 68.1 percent of the control group (Bloom et al.,

2010). Meanwhile, the second cohort of students maintained the four-year graduation edge. The addition of the second cohort also increased the sample size enough to estimate subgroup effects on graduation rate, and with respect to graduation rates, too, all subgroups benefited substantially and in a statistically significant way from assignment to one of the 105 new small schools in the study sample. Moreover, the difference in effect in both cohorts was associated with the receipt of the Regents diploma, rather than the less rigorous local diplomas. In an important subgroup analysis, the researchers also examined whether the 57 percent of small-school students who were "known" to the school prior to admission (because they had, for example, visited the school or participated in a recruitment event) fared differently in terms of assignment effects than the 43 percent who were not known. Participation in such activities is often taken as a proxy for social capital, since parents are often involved. The researchers found that the "known" group gained a 7.6 percent advantage over the control group in four-year graduation rates, while the "not-known" group gained a 10.1 percent advantage (a statistically insignificant difference but nonetheless a disconfirmation of the hypothesis that social capital might account for the small schools' success).

To put the overall statistics in perspective, the researchers point out that the small high schools in the study when at full capacity will serve over forty-five thousand students, roughly equivalent to the entire high school population of Houston, the seventh largest school district in the United States. Imagine, they write, "*a school district the size of Houston* increasing the percentage of ninth graders who are eligible for on-time promotion by 10.8 percentage points, the percentage of black males in ninth grade who are on track to graduate by 8.5 percentage points, or the percentage of high school graduates by 6.8 percentage points" (Bloom et al., 2010, p. ES-9; italics in original).

What are the key characteristics of the 105 schools in the MDRC study? Our answers (which dovetail for the most part with the researchers') will not surprise you in the context of this chapter. The first, of course, involves scale. The new small high schools had an average ninth-grade enrollment of 129, versus 635 in the control schools, though it should be noted that slightly more than 20 percent of the control group also attended schools as small as the target group (550 students or fewer) (Bloom et al., 2010). The latter are likely all products of one of the earlier small high school development efforts.

A second key characteristic of the 105 schools—as both the MDRC researchers and we conclude—involves partnership. All of the schools have partners. Indeed, most have two kinds. First are the intermediaries—eighteen of them, as we mentioned above.[7] They served as regrantors, parceling out the action space money to those qualified to fulfill its terms. But they also helped to develop proposals, coached implementation, and contributed in still other ways to capacity building. Peter Szanton (2003) traces today's widespread use of intermediaries by foundations to the Ford Foundation's establishment in 1979 of the Local Initiatives Support Corporation (LISC), whose first theater of operation was the South Bronx. There it helped the CDCs turn grassroots civic capacity into professional and financial capacity too.

All but two of the eighteen intermediaries in this action space are education organizations whose principal if not sole expertise is in professional capacity building.[8] Nevertheless, the Gates Foundation and its intermediaries sensibly encouraged the new schools to build civic capacity too, and the schools did this by taking on a second set of partners called community partners. These partners were not necessarily from the schools' immediate communities, however, and the civic capacity they brought to the school development effort was for the most part *not* grassroots civic capacity. They tended to be museums or theaters, employers who provided internships, after-school or other youth education providers, and organizations specializing in college-transition services (Foley, 2010). Such organizations may contribute very valuable civic capacity to high school development, though they are not likely to supply what grassroots organizations might contribute—for example, enhanced parental participation. Indeed, four of the intermediary leaders told researchers studying the partnerships that they were concerned about the absence of parents' and other community voices in the work (Foley, 2010).

A third key characteristic of the 105 schools is what we call *attitude*, incorporating several factors the MDRC researchers account for also. Attitude is a product, in this instance, of upstart culture, extra funding from the largest foundation in the world, a spotlight of expectation and extraordinarily personal support from Chancellor Klein and Mayor Bloomberg, and youthful and committed professional talent at the school level. It is also the product, we think, of a factor the MDRC researchers do not acknowledge. The new small high schools were founded for the most part by young, entrepreneurially minded principals, who were mentored and supported by people with direct experience of small high school development, teaching, and leadership in the earlier action spaces. Indeed, some members of this latter talent pool, whose careers had been steeped in creative noncompliance, had recently reached positions of considerable influence across the district (Hemphill et al., 2010). It is fair to say that this action space was founded on connection to past ones.

At the same time, however, this connection to past action space was far thicker on the professional side than on the civic side. In the story that concludes this chapter, we explore why this was so, and what the consequences were.

Story Number 3: Organizing for School Reform

We begin with an anecdote that foreshadows the tension at the heart of this story, and also connects it to the previous two stories in the chapter. This chapter is, after all, about connections. The anecdote features the voice of Fernando Carlo, a member of Sistas and Brothas United (SBU), a youth-led affiliate of the Northwest Bronx Community and Clergy Coalition, one of the oldest CDCs in the Bronx, founded in 1974 to fight arson. What Kids Can Do, a not-for-profit Web and print publisher that brings youth voices to policy debates, captured Carlo's voice in about 2002. WKCD's Kathleen Cushman interviewed him then because of his role in founding a new small high school in the Bronx. In the course of the interview, Carlo spoke also about the role he played in calling attention to bad conditions in the large Bronx high school he himself attended.

> We decided to go to the school and try to take pictures of all the things that was messed up—the doors, broken hanging lights, how easily the handrails to the escalators came off, the broken fire alarms, broken steps. There was this big community meeting, and we got a chance to speak to the Schools Chancellor. I was 15 years old and it was my first public meeting. So many people came that they had to stand on the tables to see, and the tables broke. I found a hard hat, a yellow construction hat, and I wore it through the whole day and to the meeting. And when I spoke, I said, "I shouldn't have to go to school wearing a hard hat, with things falling from the ceiling. The Chancellor's office was pissed off, but the news reporters started asking me for interviews.

And when they found out I was 15, it started bugging them out—most kids my age were chilling in the park. (What Kids Can Do, 2003, pp. 35-36)[9]

The attitude in Carlo's words is connected to that of the people who protested on Charlotte Street years before he was born. Like their voices, his voice had an impact. The school where he picked up the construction hat was one of the big Bronx high schools that eventually closed, and Leadership Institute, the small school that he and his Sistas and Brothas helped design, did eventually open, graduated its first senior class in 2009, and was one of the 105 schools in the MDRC study. However, as Carlo later told a team of writers for *Rethinking Schools*, the school's route from design to reality was an unusually tortuous one in comparison to other new school projects at the time. While attitude is crucial to achieving impact in situations where there is a major power imbalance, it also tends to spark resistance. Moreover, the idea of a high school with community organizing at the heart of its curriculum proved a difficult concept for the new school development experts at New Visions (the intermediary partner) and the city's Department of Education. It likely seemed to them out of phase with then prevailing arguments about school design—something out of the 1970s rather than the first decade of the 21st century. "We are trying to design a school," Carlo recalled, "where youth have an actual voice—besides sitting on a student council and figuring out what parties to throw—in figuring out what funds go to what programs and how teachers are hired, and in designing the curriculum. A lot of educators aren't used to hearing that type of thing from youth, and it scared them" (Carlo, Powell, Vasquez, Daniels, Smith, Mediratta, & Zimmer, 2005).

Pulling back from the perspective of this one anecdote—and making a claim relative to the rest of this story—we would add that professional leaders who are themselves crucial contributors to action space are often not used to thinking that grassroots contributors are equally crucial. This may be especially true when the latter are low-income students or their parents. These may be viewed variously as beneficiaries, customers, stakeholders, maybe clients, but rarely as partners. And the possibility of genuine partnership may be even less likely in circumstances where the students or parents or both are organized. This is because many professionals are averse to the kind of attitude associated with grassroots community organizing. They do not know how to deal with it forthrightly and respectfully; they do not understand its role as a leveler of otherwise unproductive power differences. Meanwhile, community members who have experienced years of disempowerment with respect to public institutions of all kinds may well be reluctant partners too (Cucchiara, 2013).

Today, Sistas and Brothas United campaigns against school "closings" and for school "fixings," and it does so in collaboration with many other grassroots civic organizing groups. In 2010, for example, a large number of students, parents, and other community members mobilized to block the closing of one of the last of the "big bad high schools" in the Bronx. As Sharon Otterman puts it, writing for the *New York Times*, "The boos cascaded over the auditorium as a city education official read out the case against the Christopher Columbus High School." The charges against the 3400-student school included a "long history of sustained academic failure, chronically poor performance [a 40 percent graduation rate], and low demand [a killer in the portfolio context]" (2010, p. A17). From the perspective of the MDRC statistics cited in the previous story, it seems irrational for stakeholders to mobilize on behalf of a failing school. However, Hemphill et al., help us understand the reaction; they describe what they call the "collateral damage" sustained by communities in previous school closings (2009, p. 35). As large failing high schools stopped admitting them, ninth graders (not admitted to the new schools) went to other schools, where they frequently contributed to increasingly severe overcrowding, often followed by declines in attendance, student and teacher morale, and graduation rates. Christopher Columbus High School was one of those schools. Others were small high schools created in a previous action space, and some of these ended up on closing lists too. Meanwhile, the new high school admissions system—a crucial element in developing New York's portfolio approach to school management—had unfortunate side effects for many students and families. Some parents were unable to spend the "hundreds of hours" that the director of the Office of Student Enrollment estimated were needed to navigate the admissions process (Hemphill et al., 2009, p. 55). Some eighth graders and their parents were unable to read critically the 584-page high school directory. Meanwhile, roughly seven thousand students arrived in the city each year too late to participate in the choice process and had to settle for the seats that were left over. Finally, some students (likely thousands in the massive district) ended up attending schools (even ones they listed as choices) that turned out to be poor matches for their interests and needs. Yet, in order to ward off postadmission gaming, the system precluded transfer for all but a small number of hardship cases (Hemphill et al., 2009). The collective annoyance with all this became associated over time with the very idea of "school closings," and implicitly with the argument about the role of portfolio management in school reform. It contributed to the community distrust that had been growing since the beginning of the Bloomberg-Klein action space—focused as it was on diminishing the role of communities in school governance overall.[10]

The Emergence of a Coalition

By the end of the first decade of the twenty-first century, protests and rallies related to school reform had become more frequent in New York. They typically opposed reforms put forward by the city's Department of Education—criticizing not only school closings, but the city's perceived emphasis on high schools over middle schools, its increasing emphasis on testing, and its pronounced de-emphasis on curriculum. The protestors have cited statistics related to the causes and evidence of school failure and recommended specific alternatives to closings as ways to address these—for example, organizing school-based committees of teachers, parents, students, school staff, and community-based organizations to find a better fix; adding 30 percent more time to the school day and year at low-performing schools; and turning schools into community centers, partnered with local organizations and providing services such as health care, recreation, cultural activities, youth development activities, and service learning. Clearly, some protesters have become well informed with respect to school reform arguments, and increasing numbers are also familiar with the New York Department of Education data systems. A key source of their capacity in this regard is an unusual coalition, years in the making. It includes neighborhood-based organizing groups across the city, the United Federation of Teachers and other unions, and the Community Organizing and Engagement Program (COE), now affiliated with the Annenberg Institute for School Reform. Note that the Annenberg Institute is one of the few direct (as opposed to indirect) descendants of the Annenberg Challenge, having been endowed by the ambassador's original gift.

COE began in 1995 as an effort to create parent-school partnerships with more attitude. Kavitha Mediratta and Norm Fruchter (2003) explain that official parent associations—particularly in neighborhoods of color—have traditionally been co-opted by principals and other school administrators. One result is that critical analysis of schooling failure is taboo within these associations. When parents without middle-class status challenge this taboo, Mediratta and Fruchter write, school and district leaders often respond by criticizing or dismissing them, "even treating them as threats to school safety" (p. 15). Thus COE looked for grassroots civic partners with less "co-optable" attitude. It began by identifying some fifty community-organizing groups operating in parts of the city plagued by bad schooling, and found some willing partners in the South Bronx and parts of Brooklyn. COE staff provided training in education policy, data analysis, and educational organizing for community organizers, parent leaders, and youth leaders affiliated with these groups (Fruchter, 2009; Mediratta & Karp, 2003; Zachary & Olatoye, 2001).

This phase of COE's work was intense, difficult, culturally complicated, and time-consuming. It resulted in some victories—for example, the replacement of some ineffective principals—but most of the groups instead found themselves locked in nonproductive struggles with school leaders. Rather than seeing community groups as potential allies in school improvement efforts, principals and district administrators often responded defensively. Over the course of several years, however, COE adjusted its theory of action to address these problems, and in ways that illuminate the connective threads we are exploring in this chapter. First, it owned up to the fact that organizing in education is more challenging than organizing in areas like housing. The fundamental reason is that effective learning depends on effective relationships at multiple levels—between teachers and students, among all the school's professionals, and between these professionals and parents (Bryk & Schneider, 2002; Bryk, Sebring, Allensworth, Luppescu, & Easton, 2010). Outside pressure alone—showing up with attitude, presenting data, and making arguments—cannot by itself accomplish a reordering of these relationships. COE and its partners realized they had to *scale down* their efforts in order to accomplish this reordering; they had to figure out how to get inside the schools targeted for reform and ensure that organizing affected ongoing relationships there (Fruchter, 2009). Paradoxically, they realized too that they had to *scale up* their partnering efforts, to seek partnerships in wider spheres—for example, with civic forces at the borough level and with the United Federation of Teachers (UFT) (Fruchter, 2009).[11]

To this end, COE staff and the leadership of New Settlement Apartments in the South Bronx convened a series of meetings in the winter of 2001 with five other South Bronx groups—all of them veterans of the

1980s redevelopment work. The result was the formation of a regional coalition to press for better schools in Community School District 9 (one of three community school districts in the South Bronx). The coalition was called CC9, or Community Collaborative for District 9. The Edward W. Hazen Foundation and the Donors' Education Collaborative helped fund the CC9 initiative, which raised about $400,000 in its first year (Grantmakers for Education, 2005).

Searching for common ground with teachers and school authorities, CC9 decided to focus its first campaign on reducing the high rates of teacher attrition in the South Bronx. It seized an argument for peer coaching then much in the New York air as a result of Richard Elmore's and Deanna Burney's (1997a, 1997b,1999) accounts of efforts in Anthony Alvarado's Community School District 2 (see chapter 3). Here, the argument was fashioned into a proposal for a Lead Teacher program. Lead teachers would teach half-time and spend the other half of their time coaching and mentoring new teachers in each CC9 school (Williams, 2004). They would earn an incentive bonus of $10,000 in salary and be recruited from across the city, thus lessening the isolation of South Bronx schools (Fruchter, 2009). After extensive discussion, the United Federation of Teachers endorsed the proposal and agreed to negotiate an addendum to its contract, first as a South Bronx trial and then as a citywide option.

The partnership that emerged over the next several years between the teachers' union and grassroots community groups helped heal a breach that had endured for nearly forty years—since the 1968 teachers' strike. What followed was an intensive effort by the partners to convince Chancellor Klein to accept, fund, and implement the Lead Teacher program. Discussions with key members of the chancellor's staff were punctuated by rallies, marches, demonstrations at Tweed and in the South Bronx, and by a petition drive that collected more than ten thousand signatures (Fabricant, 2010). From the perspective of COE, these were light-attitude events (Grantmakers for Education, 2005). From the perspective of the Department of Education, however, then fully engaged in adopting a corporate culture, they were uncomfortable and distasteful. With mayoral control in place, Mayor Bloomberg and Chancellor Klein were determined to "elevate" the long-standing ordinary politics of New York schooling to once-every-four-years electoral politics, and to pursue school reform between elections in largely technocratic rather than political ways—through data-based decision making, market mechanisms, and accountable and empowered management (Hemphill & Nauer, 2010). For their part, COE and an emerging citywide coalition of education organizers in New York were determined to reassert the role of democratic politics in school reform, though stripped of its previous associations with patronage and corruption.

Despite the underlying tensions, however, Klein indicated his support and financial backing for the Lead Teacher proposal in March 2004, and Ocynthia Williams marked the moment as historic. "In our communities," she wrote, "chancellors have almost never met with parent groups, let alone awarded them money for programs that they've developed" (2004, p. 37). Then in late April came another historic moment: UFT president Randi Weingarten invited the CC9 parent leadership to observe the negotiating session with the Department of Education that would seal the deal.[12] It would turn out to be an ironic moment, however. By this time, the Department of Education's effort to dismantle the community school districts—including District 9—was well under way.

At first, as we pointed out in chapter 3, the Department of Education replaced the community districts with ten mammoth cross-community regions and even bigger cross-regional support organizations. The arrangement separated instructional support from other support functions of particular interest to local communities and frequently targeted by local organizers—namely, special education, school safety, transportation, and school admissions. The communities lost opportunities to lobby and confront decision makers. Later, the department's pattern of frequent reorganization—again, as recounted in chapter 3—deepened the initial loss of voice, with parents and others left confused by a continual shuffling of responsibilities among entities called support organizations, service centers, and networks (Ravitch, 2010). And still other changes exacerbated the confusion, including some mentioned in our last story. These include new student assignment procedures that broke long-standing associations between schools and neighborhoods, networking schools in geographically noncontiguous ways, revamping the high school admissions process, closing big neighborhood high schools, and co-locating new independently operating small schools (including charter schools) within familiar buildings like Morris High School and South Bronx High School.

Yet, equity was a professed and legitimate purpose of all this destabilization and innovation: to break up the stubborn patterns in which New

York schooling advantages had long been distributed, and disadvantages locked in by zip code. Moreover, Children First (the formal name of the Bloomberg-Klein action space) established parent coordinators in every school, and incorporated yearly parent surveys in school-level account-ability data published online. However, the equity championed by Children First seemed to many parents and community groups insufficiently informed by their voices (Hemphill et al., 2010; Ravitch, 2010; Fabricant, 2010). In October 2009, for example, New York announced that it was adding forty operators prepared to handle parent calls about schooling to its popular 311 call system, which deals with citizen complaints about trash removal, loose manhole covers, and so on. The spokesman for the Department of Education who announced this innovation said that a trial run of the system had found that a majority of school-related questions could be answered in a single call lasting on average four and half minutes (Walz, 2009).

In 2005 Chancellor Klein announced the expansion of the CC9 Lead Teacher pilot program into a citywide initiative that would include at least a hundred schools. However, the program's structure was stripped of all its parent and community partnership components. The education organizers had by then grown substantially in collective strength, however, and this snub catalyzed still further growth. CC9 had been joined in a COE-led network by two education organizing collaboratives in Brooklyn and Queens. The Brooklyn group had initiated its own issue campaign with the Department of Education, a successful fight for science labs in poor neighborhoods. And they were joined in turn by a citywide youth organizing collaborative, including Sistas and Brothas United. Through networking at the regional and city level, local education organizers managed to achieve efficiencies in training, the learning power of a community of practice, growth in political leverage, and a sense of citywide mission plus common approaches to tackling it. In fairly short order, the partners had worked through a thicket of political concerns, funding and governance issues, and structural impediments, to form the New York City Coalition for Educational Justice. CEJ launched in the fall of 2006, and by 2012 it had become the city's preeminent parent organization working for better schools in African-American and Latino low-income and working-class neighborhoods. However, as Michael Fabricant (2010) points out in his book, *Organizing for Educational Justice*, CEJ still faces formidable challenges.

Connections Made and Not Made

Why did the Bloomberg-Klein administration, which had so evidently (if inconspicuously) connected its high school development work to past action space on the professional side, not do the same on the civic side—at least, the grassroots civic side? Indeed, why was it overall so clever in amassing elite civic capacity but so dismissive of grassroots civic capacity? We offer two answers, as follows.

Our first answer is the one we suggested at the beginning of this story, one that poses a design challenge for all leaders of school reform action space: that genuine professional-grassroots partnerships are very hard to initiate and manage. As Sarah Lawrence-Lightfoot (2003) points out, even teacher and parent conversations, though essential to teaching and learning, are difficult to initiate and manage. Going even deeper and broader is naturally even harder—though, we would argue, just as essential.

But our second answer is more particular to Bloomberg's and Klein's theory of action. This reform was more than the sum of the eclectic arguments it incorporated over time. At its core it was a Humpty Dumpty strategy: to break up the system so completely that it could never be put back together again. To do this, the reformers targeted the system's two most massive elements: its professional networks and its community roots. They then changed nearly everything again and again in order to make the networks dissipate and the roots give way. Indeed, over nearly twelve years, the professional networks that had previously bound the system in a complex, in-grown, and often dysfunctional pattern, did largely disappear—with the exception of the one tied to school-based entrepreneurship, as we discussed in story number 2. However, all the community roots stayed in place, and grew stronger from all the tugging at them. Thus it happens, ironically, that newly empowered parent and youth networks are among the many surviving elements of the action space Mayor Bloomberg built. They are connected, as we have argued, to forebears in the part of the city that nearly burned down more than thirty years before. And, of course, they are available for new connections to future action space.

CHAPTER 7

Implications for Practice

W e introduced four interrelated ideas in chapter 1 and have explored them throughout the book. They have to do with what we call *reframing, arguments, action space,* and *connections.* We think that these ideas—joined together in what we call a theory of action space— afford the many stakeholders of American school reform an opportunity to grasp reform's core dynamics. They especially include those upon whom all other stakeholders depend. We call them simply *the reformers,* and mean those who actually assemble action space and make it work. In this final chapter, we turn the four ideas into jobs for them.

Before we describe the reformers' jobs, however, we explain why even after decades of incessant American school reform, school reformers are still very much needed.

Two Big Things

On what we call our watch—beginning in the mid-1990s, and ending with the publication of this book—two big things happened in the United States that especially affected schools and that require our continued attention to school reform.

The first big thing involves changes in what we call the *constitution* of American schooling, using the term in a special sense. These changes originated as arguments but over the years have been wrestled to the ground in so many places that they have had a pronounced impact on how we think about school, school systems, teaching, and learning. One involves the development and proliferation of charter schools—publicly funded schools operated by private groups, which may be nonprofit or for-profit entities. New Orleans and Washington, DC now educate more than 60 percent of their students in charter schools; in Philadelphia—as we noted in chapter 4—the figure is 25 percent and climbing. Another change involves the growth of voucher programs that provide state-funded tuition benefits (typically partial) to attend private schools, including religious ones. Currently, seventeen states provide some version of vouchers (Santos & Rich, 2013).

A third change involves the development and proliferation of design-based networks of schools, both charter and not, operating within and also sometimes across communities—for example, Urban Assembly schools in New York, High Tech High schools in San Diego, Green Dot schools and Aspire schools in Los Angeles, and KIPP schools, Expeditionary Learning schools, and Big Picture schools in many places. These networks challenge the traditional conception of the school district as the key shaper of a school's mission, culture, instructional design, and curriculum. Some of these school design networks also challenge what was once a sharp distinction between in-school and out-of-school by means of their use of community settings and on-line formats for teaching and learning (McDonald, Klein, and Riordan, 2009; McDonald, Zydney, Dichter, and McDonald, 2012).

Finally, another "constitutional" change involves the use of standards in schooling, teaching, and learning. Beginning in the 1990s, teachers were urged to teach to specified learning targets—for the first time in American education—and to have zero tolerance for missing the targets. Then, increasingly over the next two decades, teachers became accountable for meeting these targets for all students. For their part, students were increasingly held accountable for reaching levels of intellectual achievement that earlier generations of Americans would have considered unreachable by most. In the process, standardized testing increased exponentially, with great consequences for curriculum, schools, teachers, and students. Today, a new set of "common core standards" have eclipsed the earlier ones in most states, and a new set of national examinations to measure students by these demanding new standards are being launched (Common Core Standards Initiative, 2010).

Although these constitutional changes have had a massive impact to date, this impact has not always conformed with reformers' intentions. Thus it tends to go in school reform: gaps develop among intentions, designs, and outcomes. And the real work of reform turns out to be different from what many reformers imagine as they set out to do it. It is not just about inventing good designs, installing them properly, and scaling up the installations. And it is not just about pressing ever harder for fidelity to original intention. It is instead about doing both of these things, *plus* working deliberately and continually to align intention, design, and outcomes within a context where misalignment can be expected and where it offers good cues for *revising* intentions and designs. All of this involves the application of what our colleague Donald Schön called a theory-of-action approach to reform, or what David Tyack and Larry Cuban call more simply *tinkering*.

The Second Big Thing

The second big thing that happened on our watch is the dramatic expansion of American educational inequality by income. This crisis is well documented in recent studies cosponsored by the Russell Sage and Spencer Foundations, and published in a weighty volume entitled *Whither Opportunity?* (Duncan & Murnane, 2011). Among other startling findings, the contributing researchers report that the role of education as an equalizer within American society has declined, and the long-term rise in educational attainment among Americans has halted. One contributor to the volume, Sean Reardon, reports that the "achievement gap between children from high- and low-income families [as measured in test scores] is roughly 30 to 40 percent larger among children born in 2001 than among those born 25 years earlier" (Reardon, 2011, p. 193). This gap grew much larger even as the historic achievement gap between white and black Americans narrowed.

Another contributor to the volume, Brian Rowan, reports that the proportion of high-poverty schools in the United States (defined as schools with more than three-quarters of the student body eligible for free or reduced-price lunch) jumped from 12 percent in the late 1990s to 17 percent a decade later. According to the National Center for Educational Statistics, 20 percent of American elementary children now attend such schools (Rowan, 2011). Through most of the twentieth century, economic growth raised the incomes and life prospects of rich and poor alike, but beginning in the 1980s the rich began benefiting disproportionately from continuing economic growth, and to a degree not characteristic of European and Asian nations experiencing similar growth in the same time frame (Duncan & Murnane, 2011).

This widening American income gap has exacerbated already existing educational inequality in myriad ways, as Reardon (2011) points out. These include increased segregation of schools by income—especially elementary schools. They also include very significant dimensions of educational inequality that affect children even before they reach school— but which school ends up addressing (unsuccessfully overall, as it turns out). For example, single parents (disproportionately clustered among the poor) have less time for parenting young children than do parents who live together. And parents working multiple jobs are similarly constrained (McLanahan, 2004). Meanwhile, parents with surplus income tend to invest heavily in what Annette Lareau (2011) calls "concerted cultivation," or the intensive organization of childhood around intellectual development. They are likely motivated by the perception that globalization has put every child in the world into competition with every other child. Concerted cultivation can go to absurd lengths—for example, showing babies DVDs on Shakespeare or engaging in aggressive academic redshirting (the practice of holding back age-eligible children from kindergarten in order to give them a competitive advantage over peers) (Katz, 2000). It can even involve intensive standardized test preparation for three- and four-year-olds. In 2012, for example, four years after requiring high standardized test scores for placements in gifted and talented kindergarten programs, New York City reported a surge in qualified children—double the number in 2008, and 22 percent higher than the previous year. Indeed in those parts of Manhattan most associated with surplus income, more children qualified for the gifted and talented slots than failed to qualify. A spokesperson for the New York City Department of Education said that the increase demonstrates a growth in parents' confidence in the public schools, but he acknowledged as well that test preparation might be a factor (Phillips, 2012).

Susan Neuman (2009), on the other hand, writes vividly of the impact on intellectual development of what might be called the opposite of concerted cultivation—when childhood is organized around deprivation. This happens, for example, when it is marked by maternal depression, violence, substance abuse, pervasive environmental toxicity, chronic and undertreated disease, and illiteracy. The markings of such deprivation might as well be announced on traffic signs, as Neuman and her colleague Donna Celano (2012) point out in their ten-year study of two Philadelphia neighborhoods just 6.6 miles apart, one of them poor, the other affluent.

In the face of the educationally, socially, and economically disturbing trends that Duncan and Murnane (2011) and fellow researchers describe, some scholars of schooling like Neuman and Celano (2012), Richard Rothstein (2004), Diane Ravitch (2010), and Anthony Bryk and his colleagues (2010) call for strategic enlargement of the typical American approach to school reform, particularly in schools serving neighborhoods with steep poverty. This involves reframing the role of schooling in the pursuit of social equality; school reform as generally conceived is an insufficient strategy. The continuing practice of urban school reform must take seriously the impact of poverty on schools. This need not be, and should not be, about excusing poor performance by students, teachers, schools, or districts. Nor should it be based on the faulty idea that poor children in general cannot learn at high levels. They can, and many do. But schools serving deeply disadvantaged neighborhoods, where social capital is low, are often distracted from efforts to build sufficiently strong academic systems by the poverty that accompanies a significant proportion of their children to school every day (Bryk, Sebring, Allensworth, Luppescu, & Easton, 2010). What reformers need to do, following the model of Geoffrey Canada, James Comer, and others, is to take this problem into account in their formulation of theories of action, and they also need to raise and deploy extra resources to deal with it. Meanwhile, all the rest of us need to support policies that help. This is a big reason to keep on pushing school reform, to keep on refining our theories of action, to keep on tinkering.

The Big Ideas Considered Together

So we have, on the one hand, significant disruption in conventional thinking about public schooling, and, on the other hand, a large expansion of educational need. The combination could be generative in terms of the creation of new action space, but only if we have reformers capable of sensing the opportunity and acting skillfully to exploit it.

Four Jobs for School Reformers

Like the ideas we laid out in chapter 1, the four jobs we describe below are interconnected, and this makes them easier to manage. With practice and the right perspective, a reformer can learn to handle and monitor all four at once.

To describe the four jobs, we use a rhetorical trick based on a famous line from a Marianne Moore poem. She called on poets to be "literalists of the imagination," capable of presenting a real toad in an imaginary garden (Moore, 1967). As it turns out, it is actually not a great stretch to associate school reformers with poets. Both have to offer expansive vision without compromising felt experience. We reverse Moore's image, however, making the toad imaginary and the garden real. In our analogy (without disparagement), the toad is the school reformer; and the garden is the set of contextual factors, capacity-raising opportunities, arguments, theories of action, and threats of collapse that school reformers encounter.[1]

Job 1: Reframing beliefs

School reformers expect to battle discouragement. They expect to encounter people whom they wish to mobilize but who resist mobilization. In urban contexts like most of the ones we studied, this resistance often stems from an ingrained association of cities with morbidity—with unhealthy density, uncontrollable violence, endemic poverty, bureaucratic stagnation, and so on. A similar association affects impoverished rural communities. Reformers who work in either context must search from the beginning for fresh perspectives.

Our imaginary reformer, for example, whose reform ambition is focused on urban communities, picks up Edward Glaeser's 2011 book, *The Triumph of the City.* Understandably, she expects a fresh perspective from a book whose subtitle is *How Our Greatest Invention Makes Us Richer, Smarter, Greener, Healthier, and Happier.* The density of cities, Glaeser writes, "creates miracles of human creativity" (p. 19). Innovations cluster in cities, he explains, "because ideas cross corridors and streets more easily than continents and seas" (p. 36). And here it possibly is—a phrase to spur reframing. Our imaginary reformer has already been thinking that early twenty-first-century schooling seems trapped in a twentieth-century frame too tied to buildings and classrooms, and too apt to see corridors and the streets outside as dangerous places beyond the reach of adult caring. What if she could associate them instead, as Glaeser does, with intellectual arteries? In such corridors and streets, couldn't youth join multiple adults in joint and highly energized creativity?

It helps at this point, as another of our basic ideas holds, for the reformer to make a connection. Has any previous school reformer reframed the default association of city schooling with dark corridors and dangerous streets? The answer is that multiple school reformers have—in a lineage that runs back through John Dewey to Socrates. There is the case, for example, of Lillian Weber, a school reformer working in 1970s Harlem who created the open corridor movement in New York City elementary schooling. Her idea was that teaching should spread beyond the confines of individual classrooms in order to provide young learners more opportunity for agency and movement, and in order to make teachers' work more transparent (Weber & Alberty, 1997). The Open Corridor movement was an important forerunner of workshop pedagogy and, by means of Weber's mentorship of Deborah Meier, of the small-schools movement, which has never been about smallness alone but about smallness as a catalyst for energized common purpose (Meier, 1995, 2004). Both workshop pedagogy and the small-schools strategy are now pervasive in New York and elsewhere, and it is important to note that they built on the pioneering work of the Harlem street academies, which in turn drew inspiration from the Mississippi freedom schools. The latter connection supports our contention that the dynamics we describe are not just urban. In all these historical instances, the reframing of a morbid image—whether of dangerous street or of "separate but equal" schools that were anything but equal—opened substantial opportunity for action space. Our imaginary reformer hopes to do the same.

However reframing *discouraging* beliefs is not enough. School reformers have to reframe *encouraging* ones too. In this respect, reframing is iconoclastic—though typically not *too* iconoclastic. Reformers need to work with the encouraging beliefs that have been handed them by the larger political economy—even if these beliefs, starkly put, seem overstated. Take, for example, the three encouraging beliefs we explored in chapter 2: that school reform can turn around the American economy, that it can redress American inequality, and that business can show the way to both of these outcomes. Yes, these beliefs are overstated, but a smart reformer like our imaginary one typically reframes rather than refutes them. She is mindful that school reform can indeed make contributions to economic development and to the reduction of inequality, and that business can indeed be the source of useful reform strategies. Thus she might use economic anxiety to claim a warrant for expanding creative opportunities for youth. This is an emphasis in Shanghai school reform today, she might point out (OECD, 2011). Shanghai was number one overall in the 2009 PISA results—the international benchmarking exam for fifteen-year-olds in reading, math, and science (OECD, 2010). And creative opportunities for youth are an emphasis in Finland too (number three in the same ranking) (Sahlberg, 2011).

Reframing often proceeds through juxtaposition. Thus our imaginary reformer does not claim that the United States should abandon its own inclinations about what school is for and how it should work. She merely lays US inclinations beside those of other places and raises questions about the differences, citing relevant data in the process. She might even add juxtaposition from another realm: Shanghai, Finland, and Mountain View, California. The latter is where Google is headquartered, and somewhere nearby, its secret playground, called Google X. There Google employees imagine and play with such things as driverless cars, lightbulbs that can be turned off by androids, and elevators that can travel to space. According to *New York Times* reporters Claire Cain Miller and Nick Bilton (2011), Google X aims to be this generation's Xerox PARC (which developed the personal computer in the 1970s and, as we pointed out in chapter 4, advanced the idea of a professional community of practice). Thus our imaginary reformer might conclude a pitch to some mayor and some potential funder of action space as follows: "If the three top-scoring PISA test sites [Hong Kong is number two], as well as one of America's most creative and successful companies are all investing in creative opportunities, then why not this city and this foundation?"

At the heart of this imaginary pitch is a real encouraging belief—namely, that business can show the way to successful school reform. Familiarity is important in such pitches. Resource providers—whether of money, civic capacity, or professional capacity—do not want to invest in projects that do not seem real, that are devoid of what they take to be common sense. On the other hand, they expect that common sense will be given a fresh spin. After all, investors crave innovation. As we see it, the craving invites reformers to reframe.

Meanwhile, it is important to note that reframing over time is subversive and eventually weakens the grip of particular encouraging beliefs to the point where outright refutation becomes effective. Indeed, this happened on our watch in the case of the long-standing belief associating democratic control of schooling by elected school boards with the role of education as a guarantor of democracy. In about 1990, reformers like Ted Kolderie and Joe Nathan, as well as theorists John Chubb and Terry Moe refuted this belief—to the initial shock of many. They called on states to withdraw what Kolderie (1990) called the exclusive franchise granted to school boards to open and manage public schools, and what Chubb and Moe (1990) rather exaggeratedly called the root problem of failure in American schooling. In 1991, connecting to previous reform work focused on school choice in New York, Chicago, Philadelphia, and the Twin Cities, Kolderie, Nathan, and others achieved passage in Minnesota of the nation's first charter school law (Nathan, 1996). Now, less than twenty-five years later, charter schools can be found nearly everywhere in the United States, and the idea that school choice and entrepreneurship are compatible with democracy is no longer shocking. Indeed, it is commonplace.

Job 2: Transforming arguments into a theory of action

Arguments tell reformers what to do in order to make effective school reform. Because they are derivatives of encouraging beliefs, they offer politically feasible direction for reform action. Reformers who have mastered the job of reframing encouraging beliefs can turn this *politically feasible* into *politically astute*. But this requires a lot of work. For one thing, reformers have to ensure that their action is not paralyzed by the sheer number of arguments they entertain and potential resource providers they court. They have to begin honing a theory of action early on, and use every contact to hone it further. They must also stay alert to the fact that somebody makes money on every school reform argument. The profit makers may be consultants, curriculum developers, professional development vendors, testing and textbook publishers, for-profit schools and school networks, and so on. This profit making is natural in the context of an encouraging belief that business entrepreneurship is essential to educational quality, and so long as it does not rise to the level of profiteering, it is not in itself objectionable. Snake-oil formulations abound, however, typically promising to "deliver" reform. But reform is not a commodity, and cannot be delivered. That said, most arguments make good raw material for the construction of a theory of action, and consultants and others can be useful partners in the construction.

A theory of action draws on arguments and contextual circumstances to lay out the espoused intentions, anticipated designs, and expected outcomes of reform. While revisable in all dimensions, the theory of action becomes the backbone of the action itself, and of the research plan to track the process and impact of the reform. To illustrate job 2, we invoke again our imaginary reformer, this time at a real symposium called "Students at the Center: Teaching and Learning in the Era of the Common Core."[2] Her still emerging project now has a tagline, "high schooling without borders." The project incorporates design scraps that range from Web-based gaming pedagogy and blended (online plus face-to-face) learning, to a system of "qualifications" roughly equivalent to merit badges in scouting. She picked up interest in the latter from a proliferation of digital badge activity on social media sites (Young, 2012). This led her to Eva Baker's provocative 2007 presidential address to the American Educational Research Association's annual meeting, calling for the creation of a secondary school assessment system in the United States based on qualifications, or concrete and validated accomplishments obtained inside or outside school.

The "Students at the Center" symposium has brought together expertise on a range of diverse topics that strike our reformer as relevant to her project: brain research, motivation research, Web 2.0 technology, and new conceptions of urban schooling. The symposium also yokes together an old argument with a new one, and our reformer finds this more stimulating than odd. Indeed, it is what first caught her attention—this plus the fact that a potential funder she has scouted is also attending, along with other philanthropists and reformers, including some adventurous district and union leaders and some education journalists she hopes to meet. The old argument embedded in the symposium's title and program—traceable to John Dewey and the progressive education movement of the 1920s and 1930s, but with many contemporary heirs— argues for student-centered approaches to teaching.[3] These include taking the student's personal and cultural experience as the starting point for teaching; providing opportunities for interest-driven projects and other individualized learning opportunities, including internships; working toward mastery with an emphasis on performance assessment; and rethinking the teacher's role to go beyond just curriculum-oriented small- and large-group instruction, to coaching, blended or technology-mediated teaching, and standards-oriented advising. The new argument—also embedded in the symposium's title and program—is that the

United States should have a set of "common core standards" in literacy and mathematics designed to prepare students for college and high-end work.[4]

Conversing with others at the symposium during breakouts and plenary session table talk, our reformer finds herself growing more concrete in her sense of what she wants to propose to whom, and what kinds of resources she needs. In a session that discusses a paper by Barbara Cervone and Kathleen Cushman (2012) on the characteristics of a range of high-performing and "student-centered" schools, she meets the principal of one of the schools. She asks if she can visit the school soon and makes arrangements. At the coffee break following the session, she bumps into the prospective funder and asks if he might like to join her on this visit.

All this is just enough for our imaginary reformer to leave the symposium with a sharper intention than before, and intentionality is the keystone of a theory of action. The reformer leaves also with a school to visit, a follow-up appointment with the funder, some papers to read more closely and intentionally, and a handful of business cards of people to call upon later as needed. Of course, such developing intentionality will be tested by these and other prospective action-space partners, and properly so. Moreover, intentionality is hardly enough. Concrete designing and budgeting will be crucial too, as will the development of a research plan to track the ways in which the intentions, designs, and actions match up or not, and if not why not. One way that our reformer can keep her stable of reformers focused at once on the power and the limitations of the arguments they eventually settle on is to engage them in dialogue based on examinations of evidence that everyone has helped to generate. These may be questions that even a tenth grader can ask, as well as a foundation officer or a network leader: What do we want to do? Why do we think that doing it will improve learning? What are we actually doing now? How well are we meeting our goals? What adjustments should we make?

Job 3: Taking action

School reform requires two paradoxical kinds of action, and school reformers need to know this and tolerate whatever discomfort they may feel as a result. On the one hand, a reformer must confront low expectations, short-circuit existing systems, subvert prevailing cultures, and change long-standing patterns of behavior. These are all disruptive actions. On the other hand, the reformer must engage in constructive actions, like offering stakeholders the vision of a different kind of schooling, raising resources for action space, and fashioning a coherent and useful theory of action. To understand the paradox at the heart of job 2, it helps to think of the Hindu god Shiva, often depicted as a dancer whose continuous dancing within a ring of fire simultaneously burns down the world and recreates it from the ashes. Like images from other religions— for example, the crucifixion of Christ—the image is meant to point beyond apparent reality and to generate hope in the face of despair. On what is obviously a more mundane level, urban school reformers do the same. Thus our imaginary reformer is as much interested in destroying what she considers the confinements of twentieth-century schooling as in creating a twenty-first-century alternative.

Yet it's not easy for human beings to play Shiva. For one thing, it is hard to apportion constructive and disruptive action effectively. Sometimes the critic within the reformer grows too dominant, and a sense of urgency proves counterproductive. For example, a reformer may rush to action without all the resources necessary to support it. He or she may think that good leadership, or good leadership plus money, or these plus elite civic support, will provide enough support. This is a particularly inviting trap for people with the most access to these kinds of resources— namely, philanthropists, political leaders, and educational leaders. But successful school reform needs other resources too, beyond what philanthropy, politics, and certain levels of professional expertise can supply— for example, teacher voice, student voice, faith-based activism, community roots, parent trust, and sweat equity.

Of course, no one can assemble this many resources at the same time. For her part, our imaginary reformer says she is after "three things right now: money, smart people, and cutting-edge ideas," and she is willing to go anywhere and talk to anyone who seems a likely provider. This includes foundations, private philanthropists, venture capitalists, academics, adventurous teachers and parents, activist students, visionary district leaders, and authors from any era. She says that her motto is "Connect, connect. Every connection is a potential resource gain."[5]

Although her strategy makes sense for her at this moment of development, it is also possible to acquire an incongruous coalition of supporters. And, indeed, sometimes it is the coalition builder rather than the critic who grows too dominant within the reformer. This imbalance may sacrifice the potency of disruptive action. A reformer might become too careful in choosing a course of action for fear of losing the teachers, the parents, the students—or the network leader, the mayor, the foundation, the business community. To avoid this fate, some reformers invite stark imbalance from the start. For example, Washington, DC, schools chancellor Michelle Rhee—to cite a real reformer—took too little account of the sensibilities of educators and parents. She even fired the popular principal of her own children's school, arousing opposition within her home, as she admitted to Amanda Ripley (2008) for a *Time* magazine story. For that story, she famously agreed to be photographed wielding a broom—an image that made it onto the magazine's cover and infuriated educators within the city and beyond. But Rhee told Ripley that a ruthless image is useful for a school reformer. "There's real danger in acting in a way that makes adults feel better," she added, "because where does that stop?"

In a similar vein, Rhee's mentor, New York's schools chancellor Joel Klein, called "collaboration"—in his usage, a code word for dealing with grassroots civic forces and his city's United Federation of Teachers—"the elixir of the status quo" (Klein, 2011). Indeed, as Rhee and Klein suggest, disruptive action cannot be limited to status quo operations, as some reformers hope. It also inevitably involves relations among the humans participating in the operations. After all, action space requires that discouraging and encouraging beliefs be confronted and reframed, that arguments be altered and combined in order to suit them to coalitions and to context. Practically speaking, this means that peoples' interests have to be threatened and compromised—often severely—and that even willing partners in reform action have to be forced to some extent to make adjustments. Reformers must have the stomach for all of this. If they are working in big-city contexts, as Charles Payne (2010) points out, they must have a good grasp of the sheer toxicity of some big-city school systems, and of the power of these systems to turn both students and educators irrationally against their own best interests.

Still, disruptively dominant reformers like Rhee and Klein must consider in advance what will be left of their innovations after their action space collapses. Will the disruption and the necessarily frayed relationships have strengthened or weakened others' capacity and inclination to connect with these innovations and thereby sustain them? As we put it in chapter 1, there is something that does not love an action space, and wants to tear it down. Although built to accommodate conflict, action space is nevertheless provisional—part of an implicit game of two steps forward and one step back. Reformers have to have the stomach for this too, and in the actions they take, they must not only overtly plan the initial two steps forward but also covertly anticipate the step backward—as well as the desirable *next* two steps forward.

Job 4: Connecting action space

Jobs 1, 2, and 3 make school reform happen. They tip the balance, move the status quo—whether at the level of a school, network of schools, or school district. But they cannot sustain the impact of what they bring about. Every action space is ephemeral. It is bound to collapse. There is irony in the fact that something so hard to build and so resilient at first is ultimately fragile. But it is the perception of fragility that keeps us hopeful over time. If we did not at one level expect collapse—in the same way that someone who first tries to ride a bicycle expects to fall—then we would not be prepared to try again and again. Yet trying again and again is crucial—indeed, much more so in reform than in bicycling. This is because reform requires more than individual effort. As Seymour Sarason puts it in his seminal work *The Culture of the School and the Problem of Change* (1996), none of us should expect that our individual efforts at innovation will be anything more than an approximation of what needs to be done.

Job 4 for the reformer is about amassing approximations—not only within action space but across action space over time. We call this connecting, though for us it is not exclusively a way to gain resources—financial, human, and intellectual. It is also a way to ensure that reform stays hopeful in the face of the inescapable entropy of action space. It confronts amnesia, or the reluctance among reformers to associate themselves with their predecessors' or competitors' efforts. So it involves retrospective connections. Although connecting with other action space can be challenging, politically, conceptually, even viscerally, doing it makes for better and even more durable action space in at least two ways. It sharpens the strategic insight of reformers, and it inclines them toward keeping richer records of their action. Meanwhile, connecting is also prospective. It accepts the sad fact that real change accrues in increments that often exceed the reach of any individual action space. Thus the reformer must not only build on past work but anticipate emerging work. Our imaginary reformer, for example, initially inspired by what turned out to be an old argument—the one about corridors and streets as intellectual arteries—became fascinated too by the symposium's effort to tie an old thread to a new one. Indeed, her current plan combines the use of Web 2.0 tools with common core standards as the basis for an international network of urban schools with a curriculum, as she puts it in her prospectus, "of world-class intellectual coaching, globally connected student projects, and immersion in local issues of consequence." She is currently involved in design-focused conversations with school reform counterparts in India, Turkey, and South Africa. Eva Baker's (2007) idea about qualifications remains crucial to her and her colleagues' theory of action, as does Baker's admonition to build a research-based system for validating the qualifications.

Implicitly—though she would likely not say this—our imaginary reformer imagines herself as using and contributing to a collective memory of action, a great feedback loop that has the power to shift invisible beliefs and, by degrees, make innovative practice commonplace. Tyack and Cuban (1995) call this "tinkering toward utopia"—a physical metaphor. We tend to think of it, however, in verbal terms, and associate it with storytelling. Of course, school reform leaders begin their work by telling stories—ones they hope will help them gain resources for action space. They try to fashion compelling stories of what they aim to accomplish within the space and how they intend to do it—ones aligned with a sense of their audience regarding what is needed and what is possible. The reformers try to appeal to these stakeholders' sense of adventure, though if they are smart, they ground their stories in evidence too—indirect evidence at first, drawn from other action space and applied to the emerging one by means of what Schön and Rein (1994) call reflective transfer. Because the action space is indeed emerging, the story that reformers tell has to be elastic—able to grow more complex and supple as the reform experience progresses. It has to explain *all* the mounting experience associated with the rise and activation of action space, including stumbles and corrections in action, and it has to do this with fidelity. Otherwise it will lose the loyalty of its listeners. This means accounting for such vicissitudes as strains in the coalition, changes in context, alterations of the theory of practice, and so on. But it has to frame all of these within a hopeful arc in order to satisfy stakeholders that the vision is intact (even if revised), and that progress is under way. Finally, of course, the story has to be constructed to survive the predictable collapse of the action space. Like most stories, it has to foreshadow subtly how it will end.

To address all of these dimensions, the storytelling requires two things. The first is a storytelling partner who pays close attention to what the storyline implicitly predicts, and how over a period of time it jibes or not with what the action produces, and who also systematically feeds back what he or she finds as grist for the continuing story. In effect, the partner helps the storytelling stay true. This is one conception of the school reform researcher or evaluator. Our imaginary school reformer has searched for just this kind of partner, though she has had a hard time finding one. She has found no shortage of potential partners who hire out their research skills but define those skills largely in terms of measuring and comparing baselines and outcomes. Our reformer wants more. She is looking for a research partner who will raise funds with her to support a kind of dialogical storytelling. She would like the kind of research partner that Donald Schön once told us—the authors of this book—that he hoped we would strive to be. The image he offered was of a dialogue between reformer and researcher as both run furiously downhill (we would say *downhill* in two senses of the word: with an emphasis on acceleration, and with an expectation of collapse). He warned us that we researchers could never actually catch up to the reformers in the Annenberg Challenge, whom we had just begun to study, but that we could fashion rich, evidence-based pictures of the places on the hill that they had just passed. And we could learn together how to put these pictures before the reformers' eyes, distracting them for a moment from their necessary focus on the path. Imagine a long rod from which a picture dangles. As the researcher chases the reformer down the hill, he or she also manages to position the picture just in the front of the reformer's face, then yells breathlessly over the din of all the running, "Is *this* what you mean to do?"

The second thing that good storytelling needs in order to meet all the demands of job 4 is a fresh genre. As our imaginary storyteller put it in grilling one potential evaluator, "I do not want research reports that no one but my funders will ever read. I want ones that will startle me with their presence as well as their feedback, and be multidimensional too— not just 'this works or not, and the test scores and focus group data tell us so.'" We extend her sensible call beyond evaluation reports to urban school reform reporting generally. Although it has its place, there is currently too much dry academic reporting. There is also too much reliance on heroic epic (good forces struggling against evil forces) and on tragedy (whereby the collapse of action space is taken to be more blameworthy and disheartening than we think it really is in most cases). We prefer a genre more akin to high-end contemporary nonfiction, wherein complications of intention and behavior exceed the embrace of a simple narrative. This is the kind of genre where different voices can carry different perspectives that are neither fully right nor wrong, and where narrators are avowedly limited in their perspective and reliability. For her part, our imaginary reformer hopes for reports on her work someday that are at once accessible and empirical, and that are both thought-provoking and realistic without also implying that reform is futile. She adds that she doesn't care if her project falls short, so long as the likes of a Larry Cuban or Charles Payne, or the beneficent ghosts of Seymour Sarason and Ted Sizer, admire the effort in it.

Notes

Chapter One

1. For a spirited discussion of the impact and influence of the Annenberg Challenge, see Gregorian, Katzir, Kirby, Milken, Solomon, and Hess (2007).

Chapter Two

1. Note that the data on which the report is based were collected prior to the 2010 austerity measures undertaken by many OECD countries—for example, Ireland, which ranked well above the United States, and the United Kingdom and Greece, which ranked just above. Similarly, they may not reflect the full impact of the recession that began in the United States in 2008.

Chapter Three

1. These three organizations helped spearhead an effort among left-leaning activists—political, philanthropic, and educational—to create a school reform agenda distinct from that of the two national teacher unions. See Brill (2011) for an account of the rise of "new reformers."

2. The 2012 CCSR study just cited demonstrates the value of having permanent local research capacity in place. It takes account of data from as long ago as 1997, when the turnaround reform strategy was first tried in Chicago, and thus includes data from schools "turned around" more than once.

3. New York City also had a second Annenberg Challenge project, which funded the development of arts education in the city.

4. For arguments on either side of the comparability question, see Weiner (2003) and Resnick (2003).

5. The bureaucratic infamy of the first address (See Rogers, 1968) was thereby exchanged for the historical irony of the second. The courthouse had been informally named after Boss Tweed, the corrupt nineteenth-century political leader, because of the enormous sums of money he extorted during its construction. Today, however, the name Tweed is actually etched in the base of the building's grand entrance and is widely used as a synonym for the Department of Education.

6. See Wilson (1996). See also Fruchter (2007); Harvey (2004).

Chapter Four

1. Riessman (2008) points out that social science researchers who use stories must deal with the fact that stories, like all other accounts of experience, do not wholly account for the complexity of lived experience. Thus they must be constructed deliberately to include some things and exclude others.

2. Cucchiara (2013) provides a fascinating, intimate, and critical account of civic capacity building in Vallas' Philadelphia from the perspective of one Center City school "marketed" to its white affluent neighborhood.

3. There were actually three studies and three reports. The second, by the independent Accountability Review Council (2007), established under the state takeover policies, agreed substantially with the Rand/Research for Action report. The third, by Peterson and Chingos (2007), was partly funded by Edison Schools. It incorporated results from multiple tests (rather than merely the state achievement tests) and found statistically significant greater gains by the for-profit EMOs in math, though none in reading, as compared with all the other schools.

4. This two-step analysis mitigates the selection bias effect associated with the fact that the EMO schools were, by all accounts, the lowest-performing schools on the baseline.

5. Initially, the district tried to shield the Promise Academies from the cuts, but the Philadelphia Federation of Teachers threatened a lawsuit, and the district agreed to spread the layoffs across the whole district.

6. The US Census Bureau's American Community Survey treats the Bay Area as two separate metropolitan regions (San Francisco–Oakland–Fremont and nearby communities, and San Jose–Sunnyvale–Santa Clara and nearby communities). Our statistics here are composite ones.

7. As in most externally funded reform projects, BASRC was responsive to its funders as well as its founders in the shaping of its theory of action. The Hewlett Foundation was supportive of what we are calling here BASRC's social networking aspect, while the Annenberg Challenge especially encouraged its emphasis

on school networking. Overall, the Challenge was eclectic in its policy preferences, but the eclecticism masked the different preferences of its co-designers, Vartan Gregorian and Ted Sizer. Gregorian especially prized the Challenge's capacity to catalyze civic-district partnerships for school reform—for example, in Philadelphia, Los Angeles, and Chattanooga/Hamilton County; while Sizer especially prized its capacity to support school networking—for example, in New York and the Bay Area. In some projects, the partners managed to do both, investing in Boston in both a civic/district partnership (the Boston Plan for Excellence or BPE) and also a network of quasi-charter schools or pilot schools. Later, Gregorian claimed that a great strength of the Challenge was its resulting diversity (Gregorian, Katzir, Kirby, Milken, Solomon, and Hess, 2005).

8. The practice is further elaborated in Brown and Duguid (2000). The term *community of practice* originated with Lave and Wenger (1991), who used it to describe the complex social environments that envelop apprenticeships and result in *situated learning*. The latter term (and underlying concept) became influential in the development of contemporary learning theory, and through this route it too has had an impact on school reform (National Research Council, 2000; McLaughlin & Talbert, 2001, 2006).

9. For practical explorations of the complex professional capacity that BASRC aimed to build at the school level on too short a timeline, see Allen, Ort, Constantini, Reist, & Schmidt, 2008; Boudett, City, & Murnane, 2005; Breidenstein, Fahey, Glickman, & Hensley, 2012; and McDonald, Mohr, Dichter, and McDonald, 2013. For explorations at the district level, see Burch & Spillane, 2004; and City, Elmore, Fiarman, & Teitel, 2009.

Chapter Five

1. The theory is one that is widely called *constructivism*, originally a theory of learning which holds that learners construct understanding based on an interaction between what they already know and what they discover in encounters with new materials, ideas, and activities (see National Research Council, 2000). But the theory has also been applied to teaching whereby the teacher is urged to be a guide and facilitator to educational encounters rather than a dispenser of ready-made knowledge (Richardson, 1997).

2. The initiative was the Philadelphia Schools Collaborative, funded by Pew Charitable Trusts, and co-led by Michelle Fine, then of the University of Pennsylvania, and Janis Somerville. See Fine (1994).

3. The words that appear within quotation marks in these scenes are drawn from the following sources: McDonald, 1997 (scene 3); Aarons, 2008b (scenes 7 and 116); Sconzert, Shipps, & Smylie, 1998 (scenes 15 and 18); Smylie & Wen-

zel, 2003 (scene 35); Aarons, 2008a (scene 109). The political ad (scene 117) was approved by Senator John McCain (see http://americanpowerblog.blogspot.mx/2008/10/new-mccain-ad-hammers-obamas-ayers.html).

4. As had been the case in Philadelphia, the test used for these high-stakes purposes was not constructed on the basis of the city's curriculum. Nor did retro-fitting the curriculum to the test repair the psychometric flaw (Shipps, 2003).

Chapter Six

1. The source for these and the statistics reported below are the 2011–2012 school progress reports (http://schools.nyc.gov/Accountability/tools/report/FindAProgressReport/default.htm). For the first time in 2012, New York City high schools were also evaluated on a college- and career-readiness index that adjusts the four-year graduation rate by incorporating other academic measures necessary to avoid placement in remedial coursework at the City University of New York. Researchers at the Annenberg Institute found significant variance on this indicator by neighborhood. They report, for example, that "only 8 per-cent of students from Mott Haven [a South Bronx neighborhood] graduate ready for college, while nearly 80 percent of students from Tribeca [a lower Manhat-tan neighborhood] do" (Fruchter, Hester, Mokhtar, & Shahn, 2012). It is there-fore important to take these index scores into account also in evaluating the out-comes of the schools we report on here. Ratings on this indicator in 2012 for Leadership Academy II (7.6 percent), Morris Academy for Collaborative Studies (9.6 percent), and Bronx International (7.1 percent) were substantially below the citywide average of 21.7 percent. Leadership Academy High School, at 16.7 per-cent, was closer to the citywide average, and the High School for Violin and Dance, at 63.3 percent, nearly tripled the citywide score.

2. Distinguishing between one action space and the next can be difficult, as readers of this book will have noticed by now. We apply a pragmatic standard that considers changes in sources, volume, and qualities of funding, professional capacity, and civic capacity; shifts or stability in leadership; and the emphasis put by leadership on either continuity or discontinuity. Although we explore the value to school reform of connections and memory in this chapter, we do not deny the value at times of emphasizing discontinuity.

3. Victoria Van Cleef, special assistant to Chancellor Crew, told the NYNSR evaluators that NYNSR itself—perhaps conditioned by the history of small schools staying on the "perimeter"—was partly responsible for Crew's hesitant embrace. "NYNSR didn't do a good job of communicating how large they were. It wasn't until mid-way through 1998 that somebody actually pointed it out to the Chancellor that there were something like 300 small schools in the system. They may not have all been NYNSR schools, but if you looked at schools that

had 400 students and less, it was nearly a third of the system. That's huge! It's not a novel new reform tool anymore, it's here" (Institute for Education and Social Policy, 2001, p. 16). In the end, Crew opened the first Office of New School Development, regularized the appointment of principals of small schools (previously most had been considered merely "directors"), and in other ways as well proved supportive of the action space.

4. This count of small high schools does not include transfer high schools that admit only older students or small secondary schools that serve students in grades 6–12. With these included, the percentages swell.

5. The new schools were not, however, one-to-one replacements for the closed schools. In this respect, New York connected with previous action spaces that defined the change from large to small high schools in terms of overall high school seat capacity added and subtracted rather than schools reconstituted or redesigned In this same period, however, many other cities—also with funding from the Gates Foundation—took the latter approach with poor results (Evan et al., 2006). Although New York initially permitted the new small high schools to exclude special education students and English language learners, a lawsuit stopped this practice after two years, and by the 2007–2008 school year, the new small schools were serving such students at rates comparable to the citywide averages (Bloom & Unterman, 2012; Hemphill, et al., 2009; Quint, Smith, Unterman, & Moedano, 2010).

6. Many of the new small high schools were oversubscribed, and admission was determined by lottery. Thus, the researchers were able to compare outcomes of students randomly assigned to these schools—a sample of 105—with those of students randomly assigned to about 200 older and mostly bigger high schools. The randomization made the two groups of students indistinguishable except for school assignment, enabling the researchers to estimate the effect of that assignment.

7. Most of the intermediary partners in this case had two to eight schools each; the National Academy Foundation had only one. New Visions for Public Schools had eighty-three (including what we called above the first-phase schools); the Institute for Student Achievement, twenty-four; the Urban Assembly, eighteen; and the College Board, twelve (Foley, 2010).

8. The exceptions are Good Shepherd Services, a youth development and family services organization with roots in Brooklyn and Catholic charity, and National Council of La Raza, the largest Hispanic civil rights and advocacy organization in the United States.

9. What Kids Can Do was cofounded by Barbara Cervone, national coordinator of the Annenberg Challenge, and Kathleen Cushman, a journalist who edited the *Challenge Journal*. See http://whatkidscando.org.

10. By 2013, opposition to school closings as a major school reform strategy had increased substantially. Several of the major candidates vying to replace

Mayor Bloomberg had pledged to halt or dramatically scale back closings, and state education commissioner John King had expressed concern about the strategy's impact on high-needs students. Meanwhile, the Urban Youth Collaborative and the Coalition for Educational Justice had filed a civil rights complaint with the U.S Justice Department arguing that the strategy disproportionately affects students of color and students with disabilities (Cramer, 2013).

11. For a theory of how *scaling up* and *scaling down* work together in school reform, see McDonald, Buchanan, & Sterling (2004); McDonald, Klein, & Riordan (2009). McDonald credits Heather Lewis, the codirector of NYNSR, for the phrase as a descriptor of small-school reform in New York.

12. An evaluation of the implementation of the Lead Teacher pilot program conducted by the Academy for Educational Development (2006) found a beneficial impact of the program on the new teacher attrition rate. See also Grantmakers for Education (2005); Fabricant (2010). In 2010 the Lead Teacher program became one of the elements proposed for scale-up in New York State's successful application for Race to the Top federal funding.

Chapter Seven

1. Our research reporting model here is Ted Sizer, who represented the research findings of the early 1980s Study of the American High School that he directed by means of an imaginary teacher he called Horace Smith. See his 1984 book, *Horace's Compromise*.

2. The symposium was held in Boston on April 25 and 26, 2012, hosted by Jobs for the Future, and funded by the Nellie Mae Education Foundation. See conference papers and other details at http://www.studentsatthecenter.org.

3. See, for example, Dewey, 1938; Sizer, 1984; Ladson-Billings, 2009; Berger, 2003; Littky & Grabelle, 2004; & Chen, 2010.

4. See http://www.corestandards.org/

5. The quotations are from McDonald, Klein, and Riordan and their study of scaling up Big Picture Learning (2009, pp. 121 and 122).

References

Aarons, D. I. (2008a, October 9). Chicago Annenberg Challenge in spotlight. *Education Week*. Retrieved from http://www.edweek.org/ew/articles/2008/10/09/08annenberg.h28.html?print=1

Aarons, D. I. (2008b, October 15). Backers say Chicago project not "radical." *Education Week*. Retrieved from http://www.edweek.org/ew/articles/2008/10/09/08annenberg_ep.h28.html?print=1

Academy for Educational Development. (2006). Lead teacher project second year report. New York, NY: Author.

Accountability Review Council. (2007, February). Report to the School Reform Commission: The status of 2005–2006 academic performance in the School District of Philadelphia. Retrieved from http://webgui.phila.k12.pa.us/uploads/4t/oz/4tozbxxIo-pZ0Pl93eplpA/ARC-Report-_Feb-7-07.pdf

Ahearn, C. (Director). (1983). *Wild side* [Motion picture]. First Run Features, Rhino Home Video.

Ahmed-Ullah, N., & Mack, K. (2012, August 31). CPS chief Brizard on his way out? Mayor dissatisfied with handpicked leader, sources say. *Chicago Tribune*. Retrieved from http://articles.chicagotribune.com/2012-08-31/news/ct-met-emanuel-brizard-20120831_1_cps-chief-brizard-president-david-vitale-emanuel-spokeswoman-sarah-hamilton

Allen, D., Ort, S. W., Constantini, A., Reist, J., & Schmidt, J. (2008). *Coaching whole school change: Lessons in practice from a small high school*. New York, NY: Teachers College Press.

American Community Survey. (2008). American Factfinder: ACS 3-year estimates. US Census Bureau.

American Community Survey. (2010). American Factfinder: ACS 3-year estimates. US Census Bureau. Retrieved from http://factfinder2.census.gov/faces/nav/jsf/pages/index.xhtml

American Institutes for Research. (2006). *Effects of the implementation of Proposition 227 on the education of English learners, K–12: Findings from a five-year evaluation*. Retrieved from http://www.wested.org/online_pubs/ 227Reportb.pdf

Annenberg Foundation. (n.d.). *The Annenberg Challenge: Lessons and reflections on public school reform*. St. David's, PA: Author.

Annenberg Institute for School Reform. (2001). The Annenberg Challenge: New York Networks for School Renewal. Retrieved from http://www.aisr.brown .edu/challenge/newyork.html

Archer, J. (2004, March 24). Mayor's firm hand over N.Y.C. schools sparks new debate. *Education Week*.

Argyris, C., & Schön, D. A. (1996). *Organizational learning II: Theory, method, and practice*. Reading, MA: Addison-Wesley.

Baden, M., & Roach, M. (2001). *Dead reckoning: The new science of catching killers*. New York, NY: Simon & Schuster.

Baker, E. L. (2007). The end(s) of testing: Presidential address to the American Educational Research Association Annual Meeting. *Educational Researcher, 36*(6), 309–317.

Ball, D. L., & Forzani, F. M. (2007). 2007 Wallace Foundation distinguished lecture: What makes education research "educational"? *Educational Researcher, 36*(9), 529–40.

Ballou, D., Sanders, W., & Wright, P. (2004). Controlling for student background in value-added assessment of teachers. *Journal of Educational and Behavioral Statistics, 29*(1), 37–65.

Barbaro, M. (2011, April 9). Ex-Chancellor acknowledges being poorly prepared for post. *New York Times*, p. A18.

Barbaro, M., & Chen, D. W. (2009, November 4). Mayor mends fences after slim victory. *New York Times*. Retrieved from http://www.nytimes .com/2009/11/05/nyregion/05bloomberg.html

Bay Area Economic Forum. (2006). The innovation economy: Protecting the talent advantage. Retrieved from http://www.bayareaeconomy.org/media/ files/pdf/BAEP_February06web.pdf

Berger, R. (2003). *An ethic of excellence: Building a culture of craftsmanship with students*. Portsmouth, NH: Heinemann.

Berman, P., & McLaughlin, M. W. (1978). *Federal programs supporting educational change: Vol. 8. Implementing and sustaining innovations*. Santa Monica, CA: Rand.

Berthoff, A. E. (1999). *The mysterious barricade: Language and its limits*. Toronto, Ontario, Canada: University of Toronto Press.

Bloom, H. S., Thompson, S. L., & Unterman, R. (2010). Transforming the high school experience: How New York City's new small schools are boosting student achievement and graduation rates. New York, NY: MDRC. Retrieved from http://www.mdrc.org/publications/560/full.pdf

Bloom, H. S., & Unterman, R. (2012). Sustained positive effects on graduation rates produced by New York City's small public high schools of choice. New York, NY: MDRC. Retrieved from http://www.mdrc.org/publications/614/overview.html

Bolman, L. G., & Deal, T. E. (1997). *Reframing organizations: Artistry, choice, and leadership* (2nd ed.). San Francisco, CA: Jossey Bass.

Boston Consulting Group. (2012). Transforming Philadelphia's public schools: Key findings and recommendations. Retrieved from http://www.philasd.org/announcements/BCG-Summary-Findings-and-Recommendations_August_2012.pdf

Boudett, K. P., City, E. A., & Murnane, R. J. (2005). *Data wise.* Cambridge, MA: Harvard Education Press.

Bowers, M. J., Wilson, R. E., & Hyde, R. L. (2011). Special investigation into CRCT cheating at APS. Atlanta, GA: Office of the Governor, Special Investigations. Retrieved from http://www.ajc.com/news/volume-1-of-special-1000798.html

Boyd, W. L., & Christman, J. B. (2003). A tall order for Philadelphia's new approach to school governance: Heal the political rifts, close the budget gap, *and* improve the schools. In L. Cuban & M. Usdan (Eds.), *Powerful reforms with shallow roots* (pp. 96–124). New York, NY: Teachers College Press.

Boyer, E. L. (1983). *High school: A report of the Carnegie Foundation for the Advancement of Teaching.* New York, NY: Harper and Row.

Breidenstein, A., Fahey, K., Glickman, C., & Hensley, F. (2012). *Leading for powerful learning: A guide for instructional leaders.* New York, NY: Teachers College Press.

Bremer, J., & von Moschzisker, M. (1971). *The school without walls: Philadelphia's Parkway Program.* New York, NY: Holt, Rinehart, and Winston.

Brill, S. (2011). *Class warfare: Inside the fight to fix America's schools.* New York, NY: Simon & Schuster.

Brown, J. S., & Duguid, P. (2000). *The social life of information.* Boston, MA: Harvard Business School Press.

Brown, J. S., & Gray, E. S. (1995, November). The people are the company: How to build your company around your people. *Fast Company.* Retrieved from http://www.fastcompany.com/magazine/01/people.html

Bryk, A. S., & Schneider, B. L. (2002). *Trust in Schools: A core resource for improvement.* New York, NY: Russell Sage Foundation.

Bryk, A. S., Sebring, P. B., Allensworth, E., Luppescu, S., & Easton, J. Q. (2010). *Organizing schools for improvement: Lessons from Chicago.* Chicago, IL: University of Chicago Press.

Burch, P., & Spillane, J. P. (2004). *Leading from the middle: Mid-level district staff and instructional improvement.* Chicago, IL: Cross-City Campaign for Urban School Reform. Retrieved from http://eric.ed.gov/PDFS/ED509005.pdf

Burke, W. W. (2008). *Organization change: Theory and practice* (2nd ed.). Los Angeles: Sage.

Byrne, J., & Dardick, H. (2012, October 12). Challenges abound for new CPS chief. *Chicago Tribune.* Retrieved from http://articles.chicagotribune.com/2012-10-12/news/ct-met-cps-ceo-replaced-1013-20121013_1_school-closings-jean-claude-brizard-education-president-david-vitale

California Department of Education. (2006). History of school district organization in California. *District organization handbook*, chap. 2. Retrieved from http://www.cde.ca.gov/re/lr/do/documents/dochap2.doc

Carlo, F., Powell, A., Vasquez, L., Daniels, S., & Smith, C., with Mediratta, K., & Zimmer, A. (2005, Summer). Youth take the lead on high school reform issues. *Rethinking Schools, 19*(4). Retrieved from http://www.rethinkingschools.org/archive/19 04/you194.shtml

Caro, R. A. (1975). *The power broker: Robert Moses and the fall of New York.* New York, NY: Vintage.

Center on Reinventing Public Education. (2012, June). The 7 components of a portfolio strategy. Seattle, WA: Author, University of Washington. Retrieved from http://www.crpe.org/portfolio/components

Cervone, B., & Cushman, K. (2012). Teachers at work: Six exemplars of everyday practice. Paper presented at Students at the Center Symposium, March 25–26. Boston, MA: Jobs for the Future.

Chen, D. W., & Barbaro, M. (2009, November 4). Bloomberg wins 3rd term as mayor in unexpectedly close race. *New York Times.* Retrieved from http://www.nytimes.com/2009/11/04/nyregion/04mayor.html?_r=1&sq=november%204,%202009,%20Bloomberg%20elected&st=cse&scp=1&pagewanted=print2009

Chen, M. (2010). *Education nation.* San Francisco, CA: Jossey-Bass.

Chenoweth, K. (2007). *"It's being done": Academic success in unexpected schools.* Cambridge, MA: Harvard Education Press.

Chetty, R., Hendren, N., Kline, P., & Saez, E. (July 2013). The economic impacts of tax expenditures: Evidence from spatial variation across the U.S. Harvard University and the University of California/Berkeley. Retrieved from http://obs.rc.fas.harvard.edu/chetty/tax_expenditure_soi_whitepaper.pdf

Chicago Public Schools. (2012). Stats and facts. Retrieved from http://www.cps.edu/About_CPS/At-a-glance/Pages/Stats_and_facts.aspx

Chicago Tribune. (2012, October 30). Why some CPS schools must close [Editorial]. Retrieved from http://articles.chicagotribune.com/2012-10-30/news/ct-edit-closings-20121030_1_cps-schools-cps-students-new-schools

Chilcott, L. (Producer), & Guggenheim, D. (Director). (2010). *Waiting for superman* [Motion picture]. Available from http://www.waitingforsuperman.com

Christman, J. B., Gold, E., & Herold, B. (2006). Privatization "Philly style":

What can be learned from Philadelphia's diverse provider model of school management. Philadelphia, PA: Research for Action. Updated June 2006.

Chubb, J. E., & Moe, T. M. (1990). *Politics, markets, and America's schools.* Washington, DC: Brookings Institution.

City, E. A., Elmore, R. F., Fiarman, S. E., & Teitel, L. (2009). *Instructional rounds in education: A network approach to improving teaching and learning.* Cambridge, MA: Harvard Education Press.

Cohen, D. K. (1990). A revolution in one classroom: The case of Mrs. Oublier. *Educational Evaluation and Policy Analysis,* 12(3), 311–29.

Cohen, D. K. (2011). *Teaching and its predicaments.* Cambridge, MA: Harvard University Press.

Cohen, D. K., & Moffitt, S. L. (2009). *The ordeal of equality: Did federal regulation fix the schools?* Cambridge, MA: Harvard University Press

Comer, J. P. (2009). *What I learned in school: Reflections on race, child development, and school reform.* San Francisco, CA: Jossey-Bass.

Common Core Standards Initiative. (2010). Common core standards in English language arts and mathematics. Retrieved from http://www.corestandards .org

Cooper, M. (2004). *Hip hop files: Photographs 1979–1984.* Berlin, Germany: From Here to Fame Publishing.

Corcoran, T., & Christman, J. B. (2002). The limits and contradictions of systemic reform: The Philadelphia story. Philadelphia: University of Pennsylvania, Consortium for Policy Research in Education.

Corcoran, T., & Foley, E. (2003). The promise and challenge of evaluating systemic reform in an urban district. In Annenberg Institute for School Reform (Ed.), *Research perspectives on school reform: Lessons from the Annenberg Challenge* (pp. 97–116). Providence, RI: Annenberg Institute for School Reform, Brown University.

Counts, G. S. (1928). *School and society in Chicago.* New York, NY: Harcourt, Brace, and Company.

Cramer, P. (2010). Teaching division to disappear in latest DOE reshuffling. *Gotham Schools.* Retrieved from http://gothamschools.org/2010/04/26/ teaching-division-to-disappear-in-latest-doe-reshuffling/

Cramer, P. (2013). Against mounting criticism, city targets 17 schools for closure. *Gotham Schools.* Retrieved from http://gothamschools.org/2013/01/07/ against-mounting-criticism-city-targets-17-schools-for-closure/

CSR Research Consortium. (2002, August). Class size reduction in California: The 1998–99 evaluation findings. Retrieved from http://www.classize.org/ summary/98-99/summary-00.pdf

Cuban, L., & Usdan, M. D. (2003). *Powerful reforms with shallow roots: Improving America's urban schools.* New York, NY: Teachers College Press.

168 REFERENCES

Cucchiara, M. B. (2013). *Marketing schools, marketing cities.* Chicago: University of Chicago Press.

Darling-Hammond, L., Ancess, J., & Ort, S. W. (2002). Reinventing high school: Outcomes of the coalition campus schools project. *American Educational Research Journal, 30*(3), 639–73.

Darling-Hammond, L., Hightower, A., Husbands, J. L., LaFors, J. R., Young, V. M., & Christopher, C. (2005). *Instructional leadership for systemic change: The story of San Diego's reform.* Lanham, MD: Scarecrow Education.

Datnow, A., Hubbard, L., & Mehan, H. (2002). Extending educational reform: From one school to many. London, UK: Routledge Falmer.

Davey, M. (2012, September 7). School year just begun, teachers strike looms in Chicago. *New York Times.* Retrieved from http://www.nytimes.com/2012/09/08/us/teachers-union-strike-looms-in-chicago.html

David, J. L., & Shields, P. M. (2001). *When theory hits reality: Standards-based reform in urban districts: Final narrative report.* Philadelphia, PA: Pew Charitable Trusts.

de la Torre, M., Allensworth, E., Jagesic, S., Sebastian, J., Salmonowicz, M., Meyers, C., & Gerdeman, R. D. (2013). Turning around low-performing schools in Chicago: Full report. Chicago, IL: Consortium on Chicago School Research, University of Chicago. Retrieved from http://ccsr.uchicago.edu/sites/default/files/publications/Turnaround%20Report%20-%20Long%20Version%20FINAL.pdf

de la Torre, M., & Gwynne, J. (2009). *When schools close: Effects on displaced students in Chicago Public Schools.* Chicago, IL: Consortium on Chicago School Research, University of Chicago. Retrieved from http://ccsr.uchicago.edu/sites/default/files/publications/12CCSRTurnAround-3.pdf

Dembart, L. (1977, October 6). Carter takes "sobering" trip to South Bronx. *New York Times.* Retrieved from http://select.nytimes.com/gst/abstract.html?res=F30D12F83E59157493C4A9178BD95F438785F9

Dewey, J. (1938). *Experience and education.* New York, NY: Touchstone.

Domanico, R. (2000). A small footprint on the nation's largest school system. In C. E. Finn, C. Innerst, M. Kanstoroom, & A. Russo (Eds.), *Can philanthropy fix our schools? Appraising Walter Annenberg's $500 million gift to public education.* Washington, DC: Thomas B. Fordham Institute. Retrieved from http://208.106.213.194/detail/news.cfm?news_id=41&pubsubid=617#617

Duncan, G. J., & Murnane, R. J. (Eds.). (2011). *Whither opportunity? Rising inequality, schools, and children's life chances.* New York, NY: Russell Sage Foundation; Chicago, IL: Spencer Foundation.

EdSource. (2009. January). The basics of California's school finance system. Retrieved from http://www.edsource.org/pub_QA_FinanceSyst06.html

EducationNews.org. (2010, June 23). Carnegie Corporation comments on

MDRC report "Transforming the high school experience." Retrieved from http://www.educationnews.org/pr_releases/93318.html

Ehrenhalt, A. (2012). *The great inversion and the future of the American city.* New York, NY: Alfred A. Knopf.

Elmore, R. F. (1996). Getting to scale with good educational practice. *Harvard Educational Review, 66*(1), 1–26.

Elmore, R. F. (2000). *Building a New Structure for School Leadership.* Washington, DC: Albert Shanker Institute.

Elmore, R. F., & Burney, D. (1997a). *School variation and systemic instructional improvement in Community School District #2, New York City.* Pittsburgh, PA: Institute for Learning, Learning Research and Development Center, University of Pittsburgh.

Elmore, R. F., & Burney, D. (1997b). *Investing in teacher learning: Staff development and instructional improvement in Community School District #2, New York City.* New York, NY: National Commission on Teaching and America's Future/Consortium for Policy Research in Education.

Elmore, R. F., & Burney, D. (1999). Investing in teacher learning: Staff development and instructional improvement. In L. Darling-Hammond & G. Sykes (Eds.), *Teaching as the learning profession: Handbook of policy and practice* (pp. 263–91). San Francisco, CA: Jossey-Bass.

Elmore, R., & McLaughlin, M. W. (1998). *Steady work: Policy, practice, and the reform of American education.* Santa Monica, CA: Rand.

Evan, A., Shkolnik, J, Huberman, M., Smerdon, B., Means, B., Song, M., . . . & Uekawa, K. (2006). Evaluation of the Bill and Melinda Gates Foundation's High School Grants Initiative. Washington, DC: American Institutes for Research.

Fabricant, M. B. (2010). *Organizing for educational justice: The campaign for public school reform in the South Bronx.* Minneapolis: University of Minnesota Press.

Fernandez, M. (2006, October 29). A study links trucks' exhaust to Bronx schoolchildren's asthma. *New York Times.* Retrieved from http://www.nytimes.com/2006/10/29/nyregion/29asthma.html?scp=1&sq=A+study+links+trucks%92+exhaust+to+Bronx+schoolchildren%92s+asthma&st=nyt

Fernandez, M. (2007a, October 5). In the Bronx, blight gave way to renewal. *New York Times.* Retrieved from http://www.nytimes.com/2007/10/05/nyregion/05charlotte.html?_r=1&adxnnl=1&adxnnlx=1339611819-JhSYHZl0Bhnltlh+1s5dnA

Fernandez, M. (2007b, October 5). When presidents visited the South Bronx. *New York Times.* Retrieved from http://cityroom.blogs.nytimes.com/2007/10/05/when-presidents-visited-the-south-bronx/

Fine, M. (Ed.). (1994). *Chartering urban school reform: Reflections on public high schools in the midst of change.* New York, NY: Teachers College Press.

Fischer, F. (2003). *Reframing public policy: Discursive politics and deliberative practices.* New York, NY: Oxford University Press.

Fliegel, S., & MacGuire, J. (1993). *Miracle in East Harlem: The fight for choice in public education.* New York, NY: Crown.

Flyvbjerg, B. (2001). *Making social science matter: Why social inquiry fails and how it can succeed again.* S. Sampson (Trans.). Cambridge, UK: Cambridge University Press.

Foley, E. (1998). *Restructuring student services: Redefining the role of the school district.* Philadelphia, PA: Children Achieving Challenge. Consortium on Policy Research in Education. Retrieved from http://www.cpre.org/images/stories/cpre_pdfs/careport01.pdf

Foley, E. (2001). *Contradictions and control in systemic reform: The ascendancy of the central office in Philadelphia schools.* Consortium for Policy Research in Education. Retrieved from http://www.cpre.org/sites/default/files/researchreport/799_children03.pdf

Foley, E. (2010). *Approaches of Bill & Melinda Gates Foundation–funded intermediary organizations to structuring and supporting small high schools in New York City.* Washington, DC: Policy Studies Associates.

Foley, E., & McConnaughy, S. B. (1981). *Towards school improvement: Lessons from alternative high schools.* New York, NY: Public Education Association.

Foley, E. M., Klinge, A., & Reisner, E. R. (2007, October). Evaluation of New Century High Schools: Profile of an initiative to create and sustain small successful high schools, revised May 30, 2008. http://www.bing.com/search?q=Policy%20studies%20institute%2C%20New%20Visions%20for%20public%20Schools%2C%202006&pc=conduit&ptag=A51450462C75B48FCA2F&form=CONBNT&conlogo=CT3210127&ShowAppsUI=1

Freeman, J. B. (2000). *Working-class New York: Life and labor since World War II.* New York, NY: New Press.

Fruchter, N. (2007). *Urban schools: Public will.* New York, NY: Teachers College Press.

Fruchter, N. (2009). Bottom-up efforts to improve New York City's schooling: The new localism as neighborhood-based education organizing. *Yearbook of the National Society for the Study of Education, 108*(1), 86–110.

Fruchter, N., Hester, M., Mokhtar, C., & Shahn, Z. (2012). *Is demography still destiny? Neighborhood demographics and public high school students' readiness for college in New York City.* Providence, RI: Annenberg Institute for School Reform, Brown University.

Fullan, M. (2001). *The new meaning of educational change* (3rd ed.). New York, NY: Teachers College Press.

Fullan, M. G., & Miles, M. B. (1992, June). Getting reform right: What works and what doesn't. *Phi Delta Kappan, 73*(10), 744–52.

George, N. (1998). *Hip-hop America.* New York, NY: Penguin.

Gewertz, C. (2001, December 5). Phila. takeover deadline marked by protests. *Education Week*. Retrieved from http://www.edweek.org/ew/articles/
2001/12/05/14philly.h21.html

Gewertz, C. (2004, July 14). Chicago to "start over" with 100 small schools. *Education Week*.

Gewertz, C., & Associated Press. (2009, February 3). Transit chief to run Chicago schools. *Education Week*. Retrieved from http://www.edweek.org/ew/
articles/2009/02/04/20brief-b2.h28.html?qs=Jesse+Jackson

Gill, B., Zimmer, R, Christman, J., & Blanc, S. (2007). State takeover, school restructuring, private management, and student achievement in Philadelphia.
Santa Monica, CA: Rand.

Glaeser, E. (2011). *The triumph of the city: How our greatest invention makes us
richer, smarter, greener, healthier, and happier.* New York, NY: Penguin.

Goffman, E. (1974). *Frame analysis: An essay on the organization of experience.*
Cambridge, MA: Harvard University Press.

Gold, E. (2006, Fall). What is the "diverse provider model"? How did we get it? Is
it here for good? *The Philadelphia Public School Notebook, 14*(1). Retrieved
from http://www.thenotebook.org/content/what-diverse-provider-model

Gold, E., Norton, M. H., Good, D., & Levin, S. (2012, February). *Philadelphia's
Renaissance Schools Initiative: 18 month interim report.* Philadelphia, PA:
Research for Action. Retrieved from http://www.researchforaction.org/wp
-content/uploads/2012/02/RFA-Renaissance-Schools-18-Month-Report.pdf

Gold, E., Simon, E., Cucchiara, M., Mitchell, C., & Riffer, M. A. (2007). *A Philadelphia story: Building civic capacity for school reform in a privatizing system.* Philadelphia, PA: Research for Action.

Gonzalez, D. (2004, November 16). Remembering and defending subway graffiti. *New York Times*. Retrieved from http://www.nytimes.com/2004/11/16/
nyregion/16wide.html?scp=7&sq=+Bronx&st=nyt

Gonzalez, D. (2008, November 12). "Wild Style" at 25: A film that envisioned the
future of hip-hop culture. *New York Times*, p. A26.

Gootman, E. (2004, April 13). School's almost out, and "balanced literacy" curriculum is still misunderstood, aide says. *New York Times*. Retrieved from
http://www.nytimes.com/2004/04/13/nyregion/school-s-almost-balanced
-literacy-curriculum-still-misunderstood-aide-says.html?ref=elissagootman

Gootman, E., & Herszenhorn, D. M. (2004, January 5). Broad overhaul of city
schools causing strains. *New York Times*. Retrieved from http://www.nytimes
.com/2004/01/05/nyregion/broad-overhaul-of-city-schools-causing-strains
.html?ref=elissagootman

Grantmakers for Education. (2005). A true "Bronx Tale": Parents and teachers
joined forces to improve teacher quality. Case study presented at "Philanthropy's role in fostering partnerships: Collaborating with unions, school districts and communities," New York City, February 10. Retrieved from http://

elan.wallacefoundation.org/SiteCollectionDocuments/WF/ELAN/2007%20 Second%20Half/A%20True%20Bronx%20Tale.pdf

Green, E. (2008, February 11). Old-guard educator finds empowerment at Tweed. *The New York Sun.*

Gregorian, V., Katzir, D., Kirby, E., Milken, L., Solomon, L. C., and Hess, F. (2005, March/April). Four major funders respond to Frederick Hess's critique of the new education philanthropy. *Philanthropy Magazine.* Retrieved from http:// www.philanthropyroundtable.org/site/print/rethinking_americas_schools

Grogan, P. S., & Proscio, T. (2001). *Comeback cities: A blueprint for urban neighborhood revival.* Boulder, CO: Westview Press.

Hampel, R. L. (1986). *The last little citadel: American high schools since 1940.* Boston, MA: Houghton-Mifflin.

Hangley, B. (2012, October). Learning from Chicago. *The Philadelphia Public Schools Notebook, 20*(2). Retrieved from http://thenotebook.org/october-2012/125184/learning-chicago

Harris, R. (2010a, February 3). Helping principals, teachers: The next wave of performance management. *Catalyst Notebook.* Retrieved from http://www .catalyst-chicago.org/notebook/index.php/entry/533

Harris, R. (2010b, February 5). Huberman to Chicago principals: Do performance management, school improvement will follow. *Catalyst Notebook.* Retrieved from http://www.catalyst-chicago.org/notebook/index.php/ entry/539/

Hart, H. M., Sporte, S. E., Ponisciak, S. M., Stevens, W. D., & Cambronne, A. (2008). *Teacher and principal leadership in Chicago: Ongoing analyses of preparation programs.* Chicago, IL: Consortium on Chicago School Research, University of Chicago.

Harvey, J. (2004). A school inspectorate. In P. T. Hill & J. Harvey (Eds.), *Making school reform work: New partnerships for real change* (pp. 98–114). Washington, DC: Brookings Institution Press.

Hawkins, A. J. (2010, June 4). Amid more bureaucratic shuffling at DOE, a deputy's star rises. *City Hall News.* Retrieved from http://www.cityhallnews.com/ newyork/article-1307-amid-more-bureaucratic-shuffling-at-doe-a-deputys -star-rises.html

Hemphill, C., & Nauer, K. (2010). *Managing by the numbers: Empowerment and accountability in New York City's schools.* Center for New York City Affairs, The New School. Retrieved from http://www.newschool.edu/ milano/nycaffairs/documents/ManagingByTheNumbers_Empowermentand AccountabilityinNYCSchools.pdf

Hemphill, C., Nauer, K., Zelon, H., & Jacobs, T. (2009). *The new marketplace: How small school reforms and school choice have reshaped New York City's high schools.* New York, NY: Center for New York City Affairs, New School.

Retrieved from http://www.newschool.edu/milano/nycaffairs/documents/ TheNewMarketplace_Report.pdf

Hemphill, C., Nauer, K., Zelon, H., Jacobs, T., Raimondi, A., McCloskey, S., & Yerneni, R. (2010). *Managing by the numbers: Empowerment and account- ability in New York City's schools.* New York, NY: Center for New York City Affairs, New School. Retrieved from http://www.newschool.edu/milano/ nycaffairs/publications_schools.aspx

Hendrie, C. (1999, May 5). After four years, Chicago ponders Vallas' future. *Education Week.*

Hendrie, C. (2007, May 9). New leadership vows to make New Orleans schools a model. *Education Week.*

Henig, J. R., Hula, R. C., Orr, M., & Pedescleaux, D. S. (1999). *The color of school reform: Race, politics, and the challenge of urban education.* Prince- ton, NJ: Princeton University Press.

Henig. J. R., & Rich, W. C. (Eds.). (2003). *Mayors in the middle: Politics, race, and mayoral control of urban schools.* Princeton, NJ: Princeton University Press.

Herold, B. (2010a, November 4). Provider responses in; innovation model out. *The Philadelphia Public School Notebook.* Retrieved from http://www .thenotebook.org/blog/103023/provider-proposals-innovation-model-out

Herold, B. (2010b, December). Renaissance redux. *The Philadelphia Public School Notebook, 18*(3), 6–7. Retrieved from http://www.thenotebook.org/ sites/default/files/editionpdfs/dec-10-web.pdf

Herold, B. (2012, November 7). SRC approves $300 million bond sale to plug deficit. *The Philadelphia Public School Notebook.* Retrieved from http:// thenotebook.org/blog/125314/school-reform-commission-approves-300m -bond-sale-plug-deficit

Herold, B. (2013, February). Playing with fire. *The Philadelphia Public Schools Notebook, 20* (4). Retrieved from http://thenotebook.org/february-2013/ 135570/playing-fire

Herszenhorn, D. (2003, September 18). Gates gives money to New York City to start 67 schools. *New York Times.* Retrieved from http://www.nytimes .com/2003/09/18/education/18SCHO.html

Herszenhorn, D. (2004, March 25). Not so long out of school, yet running the system. *New York Times.* Retrieved from http://www.nytimes.com/ 2004/03/25/nyregion/not-so-long-out-of-school-yet-running-the-system.html? scp=1&sq=Not%20so%20long%20out%20of%20school%20but%20running %20the%20system&st=cse

Herszenhorn, D. (2006, April 9). New York rethinks its remaking of the schools. *New York Times.* Retrieved from http://www.nytimes.com/2006/04/09/ nyregion/09Klein.html?pagewanted=all&_r=0

Hess, F. M. (2004, September/October). New funders with new strategies seek success where others have failed. *Philanthropy Magazine.* Retrieved from http://www.philanthropyroundtable.org/topic/excellence_in_philanthropy/re-tooling_k-12_giving

Hess, F. M. (2005a). *Common sense school reform.* NY: Palgrave Macmillan.

Hess, F. M. (2005b). *Urban school reform: Lessons from San Diego.* Cambridge, MA: Harvard Education Press.

Hess, G. A. (1991). *School restructuring, Chicago style.* Newbury Park, CA: Corwin.

Hightower, A. M. (2008, December 31). Quality counts 2009. *Education Week.* Retrieved from http://www.edweek.org/ew/articles/2009/01/08/17sos.h28.html?intc=ml

Hill, P. T. (2006). *Put learning first: A portfolio approach to public schools.* Progressive Policy Institute. Retrieved from http://www.eric.ed.gov/ERICWebPortal/search/detailmini.jsp?_nfpb=true&_&ERICExtSearch_SearchValue_0=ED491223&ERICExtSearch_SearchType_0=no&accno=ED491223

Hill, P. T., Campbell, C., & Harvey, J. (2000). *It takes a city: Getting serious about urban school reform.* Washington, DC: Brookings Institution Press.

Hill, P. T., & Celio, M. B. (1998). *Fixing urban schools.* Washington, DC: Brookings Institution Press.

Hill, P. T., & Harvey, J. (Eds.). (2004). *Making school reform work: New partnerships for real change.* Washington, DC: Brookings Institution Press.

Hill, H. C., Kapitula, L., & Umland, K. (2010). A validity argument approach to evaluating teacher value-added scores. *American Educational Research Journal, 48*(3), 794–831.

Hill, P. T., Pierce, L. C., & Guthrie, J. W. (1997). *Reinventing public education: How contracting can transform America's schools.* Chicago, IL: University of Chicago Press.

Hing, J. (2012, May 14). The remaking of Philadelphia public schools: Privatization or bust. *Colorlines.com.* Retrieved from http://www.alternet.org/story/155416/the_remaking_of_philadelphia_public_schools%3A_privatization_or_bust

Hirota, J. M. (2005). *Reframing education: A report to Carnegie Corporation of New York.* Retrieved from http://www.newvisions.org/sites/default/files/publications/hirotalores.pdf

Hirota, J. M., Hughes, R. L., & Chaluison, R. (2008, Fall). Partnering for success: The creation of urban schools that work better. *VUE,* Annenberg Institute for School Reform, Brown University, 36–48.

Hornbeck, D. W., with Conner, K. (2009). *Choosing excellence in public schools: Where there's a will, there's a way.* Lanham, MD: Rowman and Littlefield Education.

Hubbard, L., Mehan, H., & Stein, M. K. (2006). *Reform as learning: School re-*

form, organizational culture, and community politics in San Diego. New York, NY: Routledge.

Hurdle, J. (2013, March 7). Philadelphia officials vote to close 23 schools. *New York Times.* Retrieved from http://www.nytimes.com/2013/03/08/education/ philadelphia-officials-vote-to-close-23-schools.html

Institute for Education and Social Policy. (2001). *Final report of the evaluation of New York Networks for School Renewal: An Annenberg Foundation Challenge for New York City, 1996–2001.* New York, NY: New York University. [ERIC: ED464 164]

Jaquith, A., & McLaughlin, M. W. (2009). A temporary, intermediary organization at the helm of regional education reform: Lessons from the Bay Area School Reform Collaborative. *Second international handbook of educational change, 23(1),* 85–103.

Jargowsky, P. (1996). *Poverty and place: Ghettos, barrios, and the American city.* New York, NY: Russell Sage Foundation.

Johnston, R. C. (1996, October 9). Calif. scurries to find space for students. *Education Week.* Retrieved from http://www.edweek.org/ew/articles/1996/10/09/ 06facil.h16.html?qs=class-size+cuts+set+off+hiring+spree

Johnston, R. C. (2001, June 13). Chicago schools' chief will step down. *Education Week.* Retrieved from http://www.edweek.org/ew/articles/2001/06/13/40 chicago.h20.html?qs=Chicago+schools'+chief+will+step+down

Jonnes, J. (1986). *We're still here: The rise, fall, and resurrection of the South Bronx.* Boston, MA: Atlantic Monthly Press.

Jonnes, J. (2002). *South Bronx rising: The rise, fall, and resurrection of an American city.* New York, NY: Fordham University Press.

Kahne, J. E., Sporte, S. E., & de la Torre, M., with Easton, J. Q. (2006). *Small schools on a larger scale: The first three years of the Chicago High School Redesign Initiative.* Chicago, IL: Consortium on Chicago School Research, University of Chicago.

Katz, L. G. (2000). Academic redshirting and young children. *ERIC Digest.* Retrieved from http://ecap.crc.illinois.edu/eecearchive/digests/2000/katzred00 .pdf

Kelleher, M. (2004, October). Rocky start for Renaissance. *Catalyst Chicago.* Retrieved from http://www.catalyst-chicago.org/news/index.php?item=1323 &cat=23

Klein, J. (2007). Chancellor Klein's prepared remarks to the Partnership for New York City on the next phase of the Children First school reforms. Retrieved from http://schools.nyc.gov

Klein, J. (2011, June). The failure of American schools. *The Atlantic Monthly.* Retrieved from http://www.theatlantic.com/magazine/archive/2011/06/the -failure-of-american-schools/8497/4/

Kohl, H. (1967). *36 children.* New York, NY: Penguin.

Kolderie, T. (1990, July). *The states will have to withdraw the exclusive franchise.* St. Paul, MN: Center for Policy Studies.

Kozol, J. (1968). *Death at an early age.* New York, NY: New American Library.

Kozol, J. (2005). *The shame of the nation.* New York, NY: Random House.

Labaree, D. F. (1997). Public goods, private goods: The American struggle over educational goals. *American Educational Research Journal, 34*(1), 39–81.

Ladson-Billings, G. (2009). *The dreamkeepers: Successful teaching for African-American students* (2nd ed.). San Francisco, CA: Jossey-Bass.

Lakoff, G. (2002). *Moral politics: How liberals and conservatives think* (2nd ed.). Chicago, IL: University of Chicago Press.

Lakoff, G. (2004). *Don't think of an elephant! Know your values and frame the debate.* White River Junction, VT: Chelsea Green Publishing.

Lareau, A. (2011). *Unequal childhoods: Class, race, and family life,* 2nd edition. Berkeley, CA: University of California Press.

Lave, J., & Wenger, E. (1991). *Situated learning: Legitimate peripheral participation.* New York, NY: Cambridge University Press.

Lawrence-Lightfoot, S. (2003). *The essential conversation: What parents and teachers can learn from each other.* New York, NY: Random House.

Learning Matters. (2008). First to worst: California schools: America's future. *The Merrow Report.* Learning Matters, PBS [DVD].

Levine, L. W. (1996). The *opening of the American mind: Canons, culture, and history.* Boston, MA: Beacon Press.

Lewin, K. (1947). Group decision and social change. In T. M. Newcomb & E. L. Hartley (Eds.), *Readings in social psychology* (pp. 330–44). New York, NY. Henry Holt.

Lewis, H. (2006). Protest, place and pedagogy: New York City's community control movement and its aftermath, 1966–1996. PhD thesis. New York, NY: New York University.

Lewis, H., & Fruchter, N. (2001). The evolution of high schools for dropouts in New York City. Unpublished paper. February 14.

Lipman, P. (2004). *High stakes education: Inequality, globalization, and urban school reform.* New York, NY: Routledge Falmer.

Lipman, P. (2005, Summer). "We're not blind: Just follow the dollar sign." *Rethinking Schools, 19* (4).

Littky, D., with Grabelle, S. (2004). *The big picture: Education is everybody's business.* Alexandria, VA: Association of Supervisors and Curriculum Developers.

Little, J. W. (1999). Teachers' professional development in the context of high school reform: Findings from a three-year study of restructuring schools. N.p. [ERIC].

Little, J. W., & Dorph, R. (1998). *Lessons about comprehensive school reform: California's School Restructuring Demonstration Program: Final report to the Stuart Foundation and Hewlett Foundation*. Berkeley: Graduate School of Education, University of California, Berkeley.

Loeb, S., Bryk, A., & Hanushek, E. (2007). *Getting down to facts: School finance and governance in California*. Palo Alto, CA: Stanford University. Retrieved from http://irepp.stanford.edu/documents/GDF/GDF-Overview-Paper.pdf

Mahler, J. (2005). *The Bronx is burning: 1977, baseball, politics, and the battle for the soul of a city*. New York, NY: Macmillan.

Maxwell, L. A. (2009, June 10). California crisis slams K–12 hard. *Education Week*. Retrieved from http://www.edweek.org/ew/articles/2009/06/10/33california.h28.html?qs=California+recession+24+California

McDonald, J. P. (1992). *Teaching: Making sense of an uncertain craft*. New York, NY: Teachers College Press.

McDonald, J. P. (1997). Unpublished fieldnotes from a visit to the Chicago Annenberg Challenge, October 4.

McDonald, J. P., Buchanan, J., & Sterling, R. (2004). The National Writing Project: Scaling up *and* scaling down. In T. Glennan S. Bodilly, J. Galegher, & K. Kerr (Eds.), *Expanding the reach of education reforms* (pp. 81–105). Santa Monica, CA: Rand.

McDonald, J. P, Klein, E., & Riordan, M. (2009). *Going to scale with new school designs: Reinventing high school*. New York, NY: Teachers College Press.

McDonald, J. P., McLaughlin, M. W., & Corcoran, T. (2000). Agents of reform: The role and function of intermediary organizations in the Annenberg challenge. Paper presented at the Annual Meeting of the American Educational Research Association, New Orleans.

McDonald, J. P., Mohr, N., Dichter, A., & McDonald, E. C. (2013). *The power of protocols: An educator's guide to better practice* (3rd ed.). New York, NY: Teachers College Press.

McDonald, J. P., Zydney, J. M., Dichter, A., & McDonald, E. C. (2012). *Going online with protocols: New tools for teaching and learning*. New York, NY: Teachers College Press.

McHugh, M. (2008, Summer). Coalition: Rendell funding plan is formula for success. *The Philadelphia Public School Notebook*, *15*. Retrieved from http://thenotebook.org/summer-2008/08232/coalition-rendell-funding-plan-formula-success

McLanahan, S. (2004). Diverging destinies: How children are faring under the second demographic transition. *Demography, 41*(4), 607-627.

McLaughlin, M. W. (1998). Listening and learning from the field: Tales of policy implementation and situated practice. In A. Hargreaves, A. Lieberman, M. Fullan, & D. Hopkins (Eds.), *The international handbook of educational change* (pp. 70–84). London: Kluwer Academic.

McLaughlin, M. W., & Talbert, J. E. (2001). *Professional communities and the work of high school teaching*. Chicago, IL: University of Chicago Press.

McLaughlin, M. W., & Talbert, J. E. (2002). *Bay Area School Reform Collaborative: Phase one (1995–2001) evaluation*. Center for Research on the Context of Teaching. Stanford, CA: Stanford University.

McLaughlin, M. W., & Talbert, J. E. (2003). *Reforming districts: How districts support school reform*. Seattle, WA: University of Washington, Center for the Study of Teaching and Policy.

McLaughlin, M. W., & Talbert, J. E. (2006). *Building school-based teacher learning communities*. New York, NY: Teachers College Press.

McNeil, M. (2009, November 13). Rules set for $4 billion "race to top" contest, *Education Week*. Retrieved from http://www.edweek.org/ew/articles/2009/11/11/12stim-race.h29.html?tkn=[TNFY0nUi7%2FBozokdJnafn0bwN1vl9Y v6dby

Medina, J. (2011, March 26). Political odd couple, united by crisis in California budget. *New York Times*. Retrieved from http://www.nytimes.com/2011/03/27/us/27director.html?scp=1&sq=political+odd+couple%2C+united+by+crisis+in+California+budget&st=nyt

Mediratta, K., & Fruchter, N. (2003). *From governance to accountability: Building relationships that make schools work*. New York, NY: Drum Major Institute for Public Policy.

Mediratta, K., & Karp, J. (2003). *Parent power and urban school reform: The story of Mothers on the Move*. New York, NY: New York University, Institute for Education and Social Policy, New York University.

Meier, D. (1995). *The power of their ideas: Lessons for America from a small school in Harlem*. Boston, MA: Beacon Press.

Meier, D. (2003). *In schools we trust*. Boston, MA: Beacon Press.

Meier, D. (2004, Summer). Smallness, autonomy, and choice: Scaling up. *Educational Horizons*, pp. 290–99.

Meyer, J. W., & Scott, W. R. (1983). *Organizational environments: Ritual and rationality*. Los Angeles, CA: Sage.

Mezzacappa, D. (2012, May 31). Q+A with William Penn's Jeremy Nowak on transformation plan. *The Philadelphia Public School Notebook*. Retrieved from http://thenotebook.org/blog/124902/q-and-william-penns-jeremy-nowak-transformation-plan

Mezzacappa, D., & Venkataramanan R. (2012, October). Rendell: Education investments "moved the ball forward." *The Philadelphia Public School Notebook, 18*(2), 20–21. Retrieved from http://thenotebook.org/october-2010/102883/rendell-education-investments-moved-ball-forward

Miller, C. C., & Bilton, N. (2011, November 14). Google's lab of wildest dreams. *New York Times*, p. 1.

Moore, M. (1967). *The complete poems*. New York, NY: Viking.

Myers, J. (2008, November/December). The challenges of choice. *Catalyst Chicago*.

Myers, J. (2009, November 4). Fewer new schools planned next year under Chicago's Renaissance 2010. *Catalyst Chicago*. Retrieved from http://www .catalystchicago.org/notebook/index.php/entry/435/Fewer_new_schools_ planned_next_year_under_Chicago%2592s_Renaissance_2010?tr=y&auid= 5556187

Nathan, J. (1996). *Charter schools: Creating hope and opportunity for American education*. San Francisco, CA: Jossey-Bass.

National Center for Education Statistics. (2011). *National Assessment of Educational Progress (NAEP)*. Washington, DC: Institute for Education Sciences. Retrieved from http://nces.ed.gov/nationsreportcard/subjectareas.asp

National Commission on Excellence in Education. (1983). *A nation at risk*. Washington, DC: US Government Printing Office.

National Research Council. (2000). *How people learn: Brain, mind, experience, and school* (expanded ed.). Washington, DC: National Academy Press.

Neuman, S. B. (2009). *Changing the odds for children at risk: Seven essential principles of educational programs that break the cycle of poverty*. New York, NY: Teachers College Press.

Neuman, S. B., & Celano, D. C. (2012). *Giving our children a fighting chance: Poverty, literacy, and the development of information capital*. New York, NY: Teachers College Press.

Neumark, H. B. (2003). *Breathing space: A spiritual journey in the South Bronx*. Boston, MA: Beacon Press.

New Visions for Public Schools. (n.d.). *Ten principles of effective school design*. Retrieved from http://www.newvisions.org/sites/default/files/publications/10 principleslong.pdf

New York City Department of Education. (2006). *Empowerment schools reference guide*. New York, NY: New York City Department of Education.

New York Times (1980, August 6). Reagan, in South Bronx, says Carter broke vow. Retrieved from http://query.nytimes.com/mem/archive/pdf?res=F2061F F73B5F12728DDDAF0894D0405B8084F1D3

New Zealand Ministry of Education. (1996). *Reading for life: The learner as a reader*. Wellington, New Zealand: Learning Media Limited.

Nonaka, I. (1991, November–December). The knowledge-creating company. *Harvard Business Review*, 96–104. Retrieved from http://www3.uma.pt/filipe jmsousa/ge/Nonaka,%201991.pdf

OAAI. (2007). *Draft OAAI report: Findings and recommendation on EMOs*. Philadelphia, PA: School District of Philadelphia, Office of Accountability, Assessment, and Intervention. Retrieved from www.philasd.org/announcements/ Sheffield_Report_EMOs.pdf

Oakes, J., Quartz, K. H., Ryan, S., & Lipton, M. (1999). *Becoming good American schools: The struggle for civic virtue in educational reform*. San Francisco, CA: Jossey Bass.

O'Day, J. A., Bitter C. S., & Gomez, L. M. (Eds.). (2011). *Education reform in New York City: Ambitious change in the nation's most complex school system*. Cambridge, MA: Harvard Education Press.

OECD. (2010). *PISA 2009 results: What students know and can do—student performance in reading, mathematics, and science* (Vol. 1). OECD Publishing. Retrieved from http://dx.doi.org/10.1787/9789264091450-en

OECD. (2011). *Lessons from PISA for the United States, strong performers and successful reformers in education*. OECD Publishing. Retrieved from http://dx.doi.org/10.1787/9789264096660-en

Olson, D. R. (1994). *The world on paper: The conceptual and cognitive implications of writing and reading*. New York, NY: Cambridge University Press.

Olson, D. R. (2003). *Psychological theory and educational reform*. New York, NY: Cambridge University Press.

Onishi, N. (1995, February 18). Neighborhood report: Mapping the lower Bronx. It's south, but south of what? *New York Times*. Retrieved from http://www.nytimes.com/1995/02/19/nyregion/neighborhood-report-south-bronx-mapping-lower-bronx-it-s-south-but-south-what.html

Otterman, S. (2010, January 26). Big schools fall hard in city plan. *New York Times*, A. 17. Retrieved from http://ezproxy.library.nyu.edu:2148/nytimes/docview/434260158/13AA38FD53A27524604/10?accountid=12768

Paulson, A. (2008, February 15). Chicago looks to "turnarounds" to lift failing schools. *The Christian Science Monitor*. Retrieved from http://www.csmonitor.com/2008/0215/p01s03-usgn.html

Payne, C. M. (2010). *So much reform. So little change*. Cambridge, MA: Harvard Education Press.

Penn GSE. (2012). A blueprint for transforming Philadelphia's public schools: Safe, high-quality schools, fiscal sustainability: A discussion facilitated by Penn GSE's James H. Lytle and Vivian Gadsden. Retrieved from http://www.youtube.com/watch?v=x1DcGBFfCdo&feature=plcp

Perry, T., Steele, C., & Hilliard, A. G. (2003). *Young, gifted, and black: Promoting high academic achievement among African-American students*. Boston, MA: Beacon Press.

Peters, J. W., Barbaro, M., & Hernandez, J. C. (2011, July 23). Ex-schools chief emerges as unlikely Murdoch ally. *New York Times*. Retrieved from http://www.nytimes.com/2011/07/24/business/media/joel-klein-ex-schools-chief-leads-internal-news-corp-inquiry.html?pagewanted=all

Peterson, P. E., & Chingos, M. M. (2007). *Impact of for-profit and non-profit management on student achievement: The Philadelphia experiment*. Cambridge, MA: Program on Education Policy and Governance, Kennedy School of Government, Harvard University.

Phenix, D., Siegel, D., Zaltsman, A., & Fruchter, N. (2004). *Virtual district, real im-*

provement: A retrospective evaluation of the Chancellor's District, 1996–2003. New York, NY: Institute for Education and Social Policy, New York University.

Phillips, A. (2012, April 13). After number of gifted soars, a fight for kindergarten slots. *New York Times.* Retrieved from http://www.nytimes.com/2012/04/14/nyregion/as-ranks-of-gifted-soar-in-ny-fight-brews-for-kindergarten-slots.html?pagewanted=1&_r=1&ref=education

Phillips, S. (2000). The Alternative School District in New York City. Unpublished paper. Seminar on the future of the American high school, New York University, May 12.

Phillips, V. C. (2009). Speech to the Council of Great City Schools. Retrieved from http://www.gatesfoundation.org/speeches-commentary/pages/vicki-phillips-council-great-city-schools.aspx

Polaneczky, R. (2002, August 13). This Vallas is my kind of guy. *Philadelphia Daily News,* p.10.

Porter, K. E., & Snipes, J. C. (2006). *The challenge of supporting change: Elementary student achievement and the Bay Area School Reform Collaborative's focal strategy: Final report.* New York, NY: MDRC.

Powell, A. G., Cohen, D. K., & Farrar, E. (1985). *The shopping-mall high school: Winners and losers in the educational marketplace.* Boston, MA: Houghton-Mifflin.

Pradl, G., Donis-Keeler, C., Martinez, M., & Arroyo, C. (2001). *NYNSR implementation study: A brief organizational history.* New York, NY: Institute for Education and Social Policy, New York University.

Putnam, R. D. (2000). *Bowling alone: Collapse and revival of American community.* New York, NY: Simon & Schuster.

Quint, J. C., Smith, J. K., Unterman, R., & Moedano, A. (2010). *New York City's changing high school landscape.* New York, NY: MDRC. Retrieved from http://www.mdrc.org/publications/543/full.pdf

Raines, H. (1980, October 19). Reagan, in speeches, doesn't let the facts spoil a good anecdote or effective symbol. *New York Times.* Retrieved from http://query.nytimes.com/mem/archive/pdf?res=F60916FE3C5D12718DDDA00994D8415B8084F1D3

Ravitch, D. (1974). *The great school wars, New York City, 1805–1973.* New York, NY: Basic Books.

Ravitch, D. (2010). *The death and life of the great American school system.* New York, NY: Basic Books.

Reardon, S. F. (2011). The widening academic achievement gap between the rich and the poor: New evidence and possible explanations. In G. J. Duncan & R. J. Murnane (Eds.), *Whither opportunity? Rising inequality, schools, and children's life chances* (pp. 91–116). New York, NY: Russell Sage Foundation; Chicago, IL: Spencer Foundation.

Reissman, C. K. (2008). *Narrative methods for the human sciences.* Thousand Oaks, CA: Sage.

Resnick, L. B. (2003). Reforms, research, and variability: A reply to Lois Weiner. *Education Policy Analysis Archives 11*(28). Retrieved from http://epaa.asu.edu/epaa/v11n28/

Rich, M., & Hurdle, J. (2013, March 8). Rational decisions and heartbreak on school closings. *New York Times.* Retrieved from http://www.nytimes.com/2013/03/09/education/rational-decisions-and-heartbreak-on-school-closings.html?ref=motokorich

Richards, M. (Producer), & Petrie, D. (Director). (1981). *Fort Apache, the Bronx* [Motion picture]. United States: Twentieth Century-Fox Film Corporation.

Richardson, V. (1997). Constructivist teaching and teacher education: Theory and practice. In V. Richardson (Ed.), *Constructivist Teacher Education: Building New Understandings* (pp. 3–14). Washington, DC: Falmer Press.

Riessman, C. K. (2008). *Narrative methods for the human sciences.* Los Angeles, CA: Sage.

Ripley, A. (2008, December 8). Rhee tackles classroom challenge. *Time.* Retrieved from http://www.time.com/time/magazine/article/0,9171,1862444,00.html

Rogers, D. (1968). *110 Livingston St.: Politics and bureaucracy in the New York City schools.* New York, NY: Random House.

Rooney, J. (1995). *Organizing the South Bronx.* Albany, NY: State University of New York Press.

Rossi, R. & Fitzpatrick, L. (2012, October 11). Next schools CEO Barbara Byrd-Bennet has done it all from teacher to superintendent. *Chicago Sun-Times.* Retrieved from http://www.suntimes.com/news/education/15699903-418/next-schools-ceo-barbara-byrd-bennett-has-done-it-all-from-teacher-to-superintendent.html

Rothstein, R. (2004). *Class and schools : Using social, economic, and educational reform to close the black-white achievement gap.* Washington, DC: Economic Policy Institute, Teachers College, Columbia University.

Rowan, B. (2011). Intervening to improve the educational outcomes of students in poverty: Lessons from recent work in high-poverty schools. In G. J. Duncan & R. J. Murnane (Eds.), *Whither opportunity? Rising inequality, schools, and children's life chances* (pp. 523-538). New York, NY: Russell Sage Foundation; Chicago, IL: Spencer Foundation.

Russ, V. (2007, August 11). Nevels to quit school-reform post. *Philadelphia Daily News.*

Sahlberg, P. (2011). *Finnish lessons: What can the world learn from educational change in Finland?* New York, NY: Teachers College Press.

Samuels, C. (2012, April 16). *Philadelphia Inquirer* wins Pulitzer for school violence reporting. *Education Week*. Retrieved from http://blogs.edweek.org/edweek/District_Dossier/2012/04/philadelphia_inquirer_wins_pul.html

Santos, F., & Rich, M. (2013, March 27). With vouchers, states shift aid for schools to families. *New York Times*. Retrieved from http://www.nytimes.com/2013/03/28/education/states-shifting-aid-for-schools-to-the-families.html?pagewanted=all

Sarason, S. B. (1990). *The predictable failure of educational reform*. San Francisco, CA: Jossey Bass.

Sarason, S. B. (1996). *Revisiting "The culture of the school and the problem of change."* New York, NY: Teachers College Press.

Sawchuk, S. (2012, September 17). Teachers' strike continues amid wrangling in Chicago. *Education Week*. Retrieved from http://www.edweek.org/ew/articles/2012/09/17/05strike-update.h32.html?qs=Teacher+strike+in+chicago,+2012

Schön, D. A. (1983). *The reflective practitioner: How professionals think in action*. New York, NY: Basic Books.

Schön, D. A., & McDonald, J. P. (1998). *Doing what you mean to do in school reform: Lessons from the Annenberg Challenge*. Providence, RI: Annenberg Institute for School Reform, Brown University.

Schön, D. A., & Rein, M. (1994). *Frame reflection: Toward the resolution of intractable policy controversies*. New York, NY: Basic Books.

School District of Philadelphia. (1995). *Children Achieving action design*. Philadelphia, PA: Author.

School District of Philadelphia. (2012). *A blueprint for transforming Philadelphia's public schools*. Retrieved from http://thenotebook.org/sites/default/files/BlueprintPublicPresentation_4_22_12.pdf

Sconzert, K., Shipps, D., & Smylie, M. (1998). The case of the Chicago Annenberg Challenge. Unpublished paper. University of Chicago, IL: Consortium on Chicago School Reform, University of Chicago.

Sconzert, K., Smylie, M. A., & Wenzel, S. A. (2004). *Working for school improvement: Reflections of Chicago Annenberg external partners*. Chicago, IL: Consortium on Chicago School Research, University of Chicago.

Sebring, P. B., Hallman, S., & Smylie, M. A. (2003). When distributed leadership is called back. Paper presented at the Annual Meeting of the American Educational Research Association, Chicago.

Shaw, K. (2012, August 3). The past should inform school district reform. *Philadelphia Daily News*. Retrieved from http://articles.philly.com/2012-08-03/news/33001830_1_high-quality-schools-school-district-enrollment-and-school-choice

Shipps, D. (2003). The businessman's educator: Mayoral takeover and nontraditional leadership in Chicago. In L. Cuban & M. Usdan (Eds.), *Powerful reforms with shallow roots* (pp. 16–37). New York, NY: Teachers College Press.

Shipps, D. (2006). *School reform, corporate style: Chicago, 1880–2000.* Lawrence: University Press of Kansas.

Shipps, D., Kahne, J., & Smylie, M. (1999). The politics of urban school reform: Legitimacy, city growth, and school improvement in Chicago. *Education Policy, 13*(4), 518–45.

Simmons, W. (2009). *Smart education systems: Community-centered school reform.* Providence, RI: Annenberg Institute for School Reform, Brown University. Retrieved from http://annenberginstitute.org/about/smart-education -systems

Sizer, T. R. (1984). *Horace's compromise.* Boston, MA: Houghton-Mifflin.

Smylie, M. A., & Wenzel, S. A. (2003). *The Chicago Annenberg Challenge: Successes, failures, and lessons for the future: Final technical report of the Chicago Annenberg Research Project.* Chicago, IL: Consortium on Chicago School Research, University of Chicago.

Sparks, S. D. (2012, September 19). Scholars and educators team up for the long haul. *Education Week*, p. 9.

Spillane, J. P. (2004). *Standards deviation: How schools misunderstand education policy.* Cambridge, MA: Harvard University Press.

Spiri, M. H. (2001). *School leadership and reform: Case studies of Philadelphia principals.* Philadelphia, PA: Consortium for Policy Research in Education, University of Pennsylvania.

Stein, M. K., D'Amico, L., & Resnick, L. (2001). *High performance learning communities project: Final report.* Submitted to the Office of Educational Research and Improvement, Department of Education, Washington, DC.

Steinhauer, J. (2009a, July 28). California Budget Trimmed Further. *New York Times.* Retrieved from http://www.nytimes.com/2009/07/29/us/29calif.html

Steinhauer, J. (2009b, June 21). California's solution to the $24 billion budget gap is going to bring some pain. *New York Times.* Retrieved from http://www .nytimes.com/2009/06/22/us/22calif.html

Stevens, W. D., with Kahne, J. (2006). *Professional communities and instructional improvement practices: A study of small high schools in Chicago.* Chicago, IL: Consortium on Chicago School Research, University of Chicago.

Stolberg, S. G. (2005, January 5). In Congress, raising hands before rolling up sleeves, *New York Times.*

Stone, C. N., Henig, J. R., Jones, B. D., & Pierannunzi, C. (2001). *Building civic capacity: The politics of reforming urban schools.* Lawrence: University Press of Kansas.

Szanton, Peter (2003). Toward more effective use of intermediaries. In P. Patrizi, K. Sherwood, & A. Spector (Eds.), *Practice matters: The improving philanthropy project.* New York, NY: Foundation Center.

Talbert, J. E. (2011). Collaborative inquiry to expand student success in New York City schools. In J. A. O'Day, C. S. Bitter & L. M. Gomez (Eds.), *Education reform in New York City: Ambitious change in the nation's most complex school system* (pp. 131–56). Cambridge, MA: Harvard Education Press.

Talbert, J. E., Wood, A., & Lin, W. (2007). *Evaluation of BASRC Phase II: Evidence-based reform: Outcomes, challenges, promising practices.* Stanford, CA: Center for Research on the Context of Teaching.

Tavernise, S., & Gebeloff, R. (2010, December 15). Immigrants make paths to suburbia, not cities. *New York Times,* p. A15.

Tichy, N. M., & Sherman, S. (1993). *Control your destiny or someone else will: How Jack Welch is making General Electric the world's most competitive corporation.* New York, NY: Doubleday.

Toch, T. (2003). *High schools on a human scale: How small schools can transform American education.* Boston, MA: Beacon Press.

Tyack, D. B., & Cuban, L. (1995). *Tinkering toward utopia: A century of public school reform.* Cambridge, MA: Harvard University Press.

Ubinas, L. A. (2010). Ubinas gives opening remarks at Washington, D.C. summit on auto communities and the next economy. Retrieved from http://www.fordfoundation.org/issues/metropolitan-opportunity/connecting-people-to-opportunity/news?id=376

UNICEF. (2010, November). *The children left behind: A league table of inequality in child well-being in the world's rich countries.* Florence, Italy: UNICEF Innocenti Research Centre. Retrieved from http://www.unicef-irc.org/publications/pdf/rc9_eng.pdf

US Census Bureau. (2011, March). Population distribution and change: 2000–2010. *2010 Census Briefs.* Retrieved from http://www.census.gov/prod/cen2010/briefs/c2010br-01.pdf

US Census Bureau. (2012, April). Census estimates show new patterns of growth nationwide. Retrieved from http://www.census.gov/newsroom/releases/archives/population/cb12-55.html

US Department of Education. (2009). Race to the Top points system. *Education Week.* Retrieved from http://www.edweek.org/media/racetoppointssystem.pdf

Useem, E., Christman, J. B., & Boyd, W. L. (2006). *The role of district leadership in radical reform: Philadelphia's experience under the state takeover, 2001–2006.* Philadelphia, PA: Research for Action.

Vargo, M. (2004). Choices and consequences in the Bay Area School Reform Collaborative: Building the capacity to scale up whole-school improvement. In T. Glennan, S. Bodilly, J. Galegher, & K. Kerr (Eds.), *Expanding the reach of education reforms* (pp. 565–601). Santa Monica, CA: Rand.

Venkataramanan, R., & Mezzacappa, D. (2010, October). How state funding has changed since the costing-out study. *The Philadephia Public School Note-*

book, 18(2). Retrieved from http://thenotebook.org/october-2010/102893/how-state-funding-has-changed-costing-out-study

Walz, M. (2009, October 21). City adds new corps of "education experts" to 311 call service. *GothamSchools*. Retrieved from http://gothamschools.org/2009/10/21/city-adds-new-corps-of-education-experts-to-311-call-service/

Weber, L., & Alberty, B. (1997). *Looking back and thinking forward: Reexaminations of teaching and schooling*. New York, NY: Teachers College Press.

Weiner, L. (2003, August 7). Research or "cheerleading"? Scholarship on Community School District 2, New York City. *Education Policy Analysis Archives*, 11(27). Retrieved from http://epaa.asu.edu/epaa/v11n27/

Weiss, C. H. (1998). *Evaluation* (2nd ed.). Upper Saddle Brook, NJ: Prentice Hall.

Welch, J. (2005). *Winning*. New York, NY: Harper Collins.

Wenger, E., McDermott, R., & Snyder, W. M. (2002). *Cultivating communities of practice: A guide to managing knowledge*. Boston, MA: Harvard Business School Press.

What Kids Can Do. (2003). *The schools we need: Creating small high schools that work for us*. Retrieved from http://www.whatkidscando.org/publications/pdfs/bronxbooklet.PDF

Williams, D., & Forte, L. (2008, December 15, 18, & 19). Duncan's track record (parts 1, 2, & 3). *Catalyst Chicago*.

Williams, O. (2004, Fall). A community-led reform: Improving schools in the South Bronx. *VUE, 5*, 33–40.

Wilson, T. A. (1996). *Reaching for a better standard: English school inspection and the dilemma of accountability for American schools*. New York, NY: Teachers College Press.

Winerip, M. (2013, March 30). 35 indicted in test scandal at Atlanta Schools. *New York Times*, p. 1.

Worth, R. (1999). Guess who saved the South Bronx? Big government. *The Washington Monthly, 31*(4), 26-33.

Yardley, J. (1997, December 11). Clinton praises Bronx renewal as U.S. model. *New York Times*. Retrieved from http://www.nytimes.com/1997/12/11/nyregion/clinton-praises-bronx-renewal-as-us-model.html

Young, J. R. (2012, January 8). "Badges" earned online pose challenge to traditional college diplomas. *The Chronicle of Higher Education*. Retrieved from http://chronicle.com/article/Badges-Earned-Online-Pose/130241/

Zachary, E., & Olatoye, S. (2001). *Community organizing for school improvement in the South Bronx*. New York, NY: Institute for Education and Social Policy, New York University.

Index